CRIME

WITHOUT

FRONTIERS

CRIME

WITHOUT

FRONTIERS

The worldwide expansion of
organised crime and the
Pax Mafiosa

CLAIRE STERLING

A *Little, Brown* Book

First published in Great Britain in 1994
by Little, Brown and Company

Copyright © Claire Sterling, 1994

The moral right of the author has been asserted

A CIP catalogue record for this book is
available from the British Library.

ISBN 0 316 91121 6

Typeset by M Rules
Printed and bound in Great Britain by
Clays Ltd, St Ives plc

Little, Brown and Company (UK) Limited
Brettenham House
Lancaster Place
London WC2E 7EN

For My Dearest Vida
and Victor

Contents

Part 4   The Great Ruble Scam

Part 5   The Problem of the Solution

Acknowledgements

I am grateful as always to Dr Alessandro Pansa of the Servizio Centrale Operativo, one of Italy's most gifted policemen.

I am indebted once again to Maria Antonietta Calabrò of the *Corriere della Sera*, for her meticulous accuracy, knowledge and judgement.

My warm thanks to Joe Serio, who started me on my way in Russia; to Gianna in Moscow; to Rita Wallace in Bonn; to Dan Starer in New York.

A special word of thanks to Jurgen Maurer of the Bundeskriminalamt in Wiesbaden: to Chuck Saphos of the US Justice Department, who was ahead of me from first to last; to Jim Moody of the FBI for his patience and generous assistance.

I have no adequate words for my gratitude to Judith Crist, my old and dear friend.

Author's Note

As this book was going to press, the US State Department confirmed the part readers may find hardest to believe: the birth of a worldwide Mafia International, the first in history.

The collapse of the Soviet empire, 'opening new markets of vast potential', has brought the big crime groups of East and West together, said a spokesman for the State Department's Office of Diplomatic Security.

The Sicilian and American mafias in particular are now 'working with their counterparts in Eastern Europe and the former Soviet Union', operating across and beyond Europe and the United States, he declared.

Their leaders have met at the summit three times in as many years, he reported: in Warsaw in 1991, in Prague in 1992, in Berlin in 1993. There, 'they agreed to apply strategic planning and market development policies for the new emerging free markets, to programme legitimate investments much as corporations do, and to develop and expand extremely illegal activities besides.' These last mostly involve trafficking in narcotics, conventional arms and weapons of mass destruction, he said.[1]

So, long overlooked or underrated, the threat of international organized crime is coming to be seen in all its enormity. For the head of the FBI, Louis Freeh, it is indeed 'the gravest menace to civil society' in our time.

Prologue

When I finished writing *Crime Without Frontiers* in the autumn of 1993, a few words from a high authority in Washington provided the epilogue. 'We think they've given the US to Yaponchik,' he told me.[1]

'They' were the men guiding the Russian mafia in Moscow. Yaponchik is one of their three most powerful leaders.

The idea that a so-called Russian mafia could 'give' the US to a certain Yaponchik would have been laughable only a couple of years ago. Nobody in the West had heard of Yaponchik; not many had heard of a Russian mafia, for that matter.

The rise of both within that couple of years – their ability to stake out whole blocks of the planet, half a continent here, another there – conveys all the menace of an international crime community in a phase of stunning expansion, threatening the integrity and even the survival of democratic governments in America, Europe, everywhere.

I had watched it happening from the time I began working on this book in 1990. The book was supposed to have been about a predictable surge of organized crime in Western Europe as its inner borders went down. But such simple notions were soon swept aside by the uncontrollable forces set loose in the course of that momentous year.

Organized crime was transformed when the Soviet Empire crashed, and with it a world order that had kept mankind more or less in line for the previous half a century. As the old geopolitical frontiers fell away, the big crime syndicates drew together, put an end to wars over turf and declared a *pax mafiosa*. The world has never seen a planet-wide criminal consortium like the one that came into being with the end of the communist era.

Perhaps something like it would have come anyway sooner or later. Most of the big syndicates had worked with one or more of the others for years, the Sicilian Mafia with all of them. But the opportunities opening up for them in 1990 were immense – fabulous – and they responded accordingly.

International organized crime, an imaginary menace for many in 1990, was a worldwide emergency by 1993. The big syndicates of East and West were pooling services and personnel, rapidly colonizing Western Europe and the United States, running the drug traffic up to half a trillion dollars a year, laundering and re-investing an estimated quarter of a trillion dollars a year in legitimate enterprise.

Much of their phenomenal growth derived from the fact that they had the free run of a territory covering half the continent of Europe and a good part of Asia – a sixth of the earth's land mass, essentially ungoverned and unpoliced.

The whole international underworld had moved in on post-communist Russia and the rest of the ex-Soviet bloc: raced in, from the day the Berlin Wall fell. Where Western governments tended to see Russia itself as a basket case, the big syndicates saw it as a privileged sanctuary and bottomless source of instant wealth.

Russia had a runaway black market, a huge potential for producing and moving drugs, an enormous military arsenal, the world's richest natural resources, and an insatiable hunger for dollars of whatever provenance. Furthermore, it had a rampant mafia of its own, in need of Western partners to make the most of these prospects.

Even before the Soviet Union disintegrated altogether, the Sicilian, American, Colombian and Asian mafias were hooking up with the Russian one, forming a borderless criminal underground that went right around the globe.

All have been growing prodigiously rich since then, by swapping their dirty money for Russia's real estate, factories, shops, and above all weapons and raw materials, bought on the cheap and sold for up to a thousand times more abroad.

Twenty billion dollars' worth of raw materials alone were exported illegally from Russia in 1992: petroleum, timber, titanium, cesium, strontium, uranium, plutonium. Thousands of crooks and swindlers were involved, native and otherwise, many of them loners. But the big players were the Russian mafia and its foreign partners.

Though these last were making and laundering ten times as much as the rest of the world, this was the easiest, safest and most miraculously lucrative way ever invented. Colombia's cocaine cartels are *paying* twenty cents and more on the dollar to bring their drug money home clean today. The Sicilian Mafia makes more by laundering it for them in Russia than by dealing the cocaine itself.[2]

And this is undetectable investment capital when it comes out of Russia, filtering into money markets, stock and commodity markets, business, industry and commerce, largely in the West, helping to underwrite the most massive and insidious criminal assault in history.

Western authorities are staggered by the strength of the attacking forces and the speed of their advance, driven home by the Russian mafia's startling performance.

It took just two years for Yaponchik to move from a prison camp in Siberia to the Russian mafia's top command in New York. Russia's chief Big Crimes Investigator had warned me of something like this. 'You people in the West don't know our mafia yet: you will, you will,' he had said. He did not say how soon, however.

Yaponchik (Vyacheslav Ivankov in real life) was barely out of prison when I first went to Russia in the autumn of 1991. Sentenced to fifteen years for robbery, he had done eleven.

He had left Siberia in a private chartered plane, and been welcomed home with a grand champagne party at Moscow's posh Metropol Hotel.[3]

For Yaponchik was no ordinary Russian crook. He was one of the chosen of Russia's ancient Thieves' World, an aristocrat of his profession and keeper of its code: a thief-within-the-law.

By the time I came across his name that autumn, he had already moved on to Berlin, where his mafia colleagues had landed in force after the fall of the Wall. A few months later, he was back in Moscow draped in gold chains and driving around in a Mercedes. Then he took off for America.

He arrived exactly a year after leaving Siberia, in March 1992, on a regular business visa. Getting in was ridiculously easy. The American embassy in Moscow issued 139,000 business visas to Russian citizens that year. Applicants were not checked for possible criminal records, lest that might 'slow the international business process', a Washington spokesman explains.[4]

On paper, Yaponchik is in the film business in America; in fact, says the FBI, he is the supreme thief-within-the-law for the United States.

His fellow of that rank assigned to Berlin, Alizam Tochtachunov, recently applied for a business visa to join him.

Much as Lucky Luciano did with the American mafia sixty-odd years ago, Yaponchik is turning an assortment of unruly and loosely-articulated Russian gangs on American soil into a modern, nationwide crime corporation. Doubtless as Luciano would also have done in these changing times, he is 'slowly building a chain from Moscow to the US and back', declares the FBI's organized crime chief, Jim Moody.[5]

The Russian mafia can hardly be compared for size and clout to others tormenting America: the American mafia itself, the Sicilian one, the Chinese Triads, the Japanese Yakuza, the Colombians. There as in Europe, however, the Russians stand out among their peers because they are talented enough, and frightening enough, to have achieved in two or three years what the others have achieved in twenty or a hundred.

Nevertheless, they could not have done it before 1990. Their astonishing spurt came only when the old world order collapsed and frontiers everywhere began to fall, and the deep but ordered corruption of the old Nomenklatura in Russia gave way to the terrible cancerous growth consuming the country now.

Inevitably, the Russian side of my story grew as I saw the drama playing out – the Russian mafia gaining an oppressive hold over the country, its lengthening reach abroad, the arrival of world-class syndicates to share in the plunder at home.

This was how international organized crime could take a huge country captive by 1993, buying up its governing class, looting it systematically, crippling its economic capacity and suffocating its political will.

It is not just as an object lesson that I have described these facts at length. The more urgent reason is that liberated Russia is becoming an active danger to its Western friends, as the underworld's new country of choice.

There is no way for Western law enforcement agencies to investigate, still less pursue, their own criminals drifting East: they have no lawful right to do it and, until very recently, did not much care. Their Eastern counterparts have practically no suitable laws of their own, no money, pitiful equipment, and hardly any properly trained personnel. There are no provisions for extradition on either side, and next to none for exchanging police and intelligence information.

In effect, then, the big syndicates have come upon a safehouse the size of Western Europe and America combined, where they can dodge the cops, meet, plan strategy, work out new drug routes, manage their money, settle territorial disputes and carve up the planet undisturbed, all of which they appear to be doing.

The shift has come so swiftly that Western investigators can hardly take it in. Because the Sicilian Mafia still towers over the underworld, as always, many still believe that the centre of worldwide criminal power is Italy, as always. In the autumn of 1993, however, the head of Italy's parliamentary Anti-Mafia Commission made it plain that the venue had changed. 'The world capital of organized crime is Russia,' he said.[6]

The thieves' world I have tried to describe here is that one.

Part I

The New Underworld Order

1

Happy Families on Treasure Island

The world's first independent mafia state emerged in 1993. The sovereign Caribbean island of Aruba, sixty-nine square miles of emerald hills and golden sand, proved to belong to the Sicilian Mafia in fact if not in name.

Small islands are not so hard to acquire. From this one, however, the story leads to the making of a mafia state in Russia, a hundred thousand times bigger and incomparably more crucial to our peace of mind.

Aruba was bought and paid for by the most powerful Mafia family abroad: the Cuntrera brothers of Siculiana, Sicily, and Caracas, Venezuela, who had amassed a billion dollars of their own in their twenty-five years as kingpins of the Mafia's North American heroin trade.

The drugging of America had provided the wherewithal for their purchase of Aruba, starting in the late 1980s. From the Venezuelan mainland just fifteen miles away, they had drawn on their seventy-odd bank accounts to buy up everything of importance on the island: hotels, casinos, tourism, building land, construction, banks, police, customs, the justice minister, the prime minister, the governing and opposition parties.[1]

The new order has brought exceptional prosperity to the 65,000 inhabitants of this former Dutch colony, which calls itself 'One Happy Island'. Tourists flock to its twenty-four new high-rise hotels and seven casinos, shop at its Cartier and Gucci boutiques, drift in and out of its throbbing banks with suitcases full of dollar bills. Nobody pays taxes.

Not many care to ask questions, therefore, still less answer any.

The Cuntreras are gone now. The Venezuelan government had always protected them from harm, more particularly from international arrest warrants going back nearly a decade. In September 1992, however, it yielded to Italian and American pressure and deported them to Italy. The US Drug Enforcement Administration had threatened to kidnap them otherwise, as it was entitled to do under a US Supreme Court ruling.[2]

Their work was done, however. Aruba today is just what it was meant to be when the Cuntreras' plan got under way: the headquarters of the first international joint venture in organized crime.

It was on the island of Aruba that the Sicilian Mafia and Colombia's Medellín cartel decided to join forces, in October 1987. Things have moved so fast since then that the pact they sealed seems old-fashioned now. But for the late Judge Giovanni Falcone, who knew the Mafia best, it was 'a shattering and terrifying portent'.[3]

Judge Falcone, world-famous for his valiant and resolute war on the Sicilian Mafia, did not live to see how far this pact would lead; the Mafia murdered him in Palermo in the spring of 1992. Few had understood the sweep of its imperial designs as he did, however.

The two giants of the underworld made a hair-raising pair. Colombia's drug traffickers are among the most vicious on earth; Sicily's, only a shade less so, are the most sophisticated and best connected.

Each has a huge international army of helpers, the financial resources of a fair-sized country, and the power of a state within a state. The global turnover for the merchandise the two dealt in ran to around $300 billion a year when they came together.[4]

What frightened Judge Falcone was not so much the pact they made as his growing conviction, by the start of the 1990s, that all the great crime syndicates were coming together: the Sicilian and American mafias, the Turkish arms-drugs mafia, the Russian mafia, the Chinese Triads, the Japanese Yakuza.[5]

Separated by thousands of miles and centuries of history, these massive criminal organizations were tending to coordinate the use of their money, men and markets in 'a kind of operational welding', Falcone said.[6]

The big syndicates had already 'stipulated a sort of non-aggression pact, dividing up the world,' he warned. The whole international underworld appeared to be moving towards a broader *pax mafiosa* – an agreement to avoid conflict, devise common strategy, and work the planet peaceably together.

If that happened, the lawful world would be exposed to an unimaginably malignant criminal force, and desperately unready to resist it.

In the space of four or five years after the 1987 Aruba summit, that did happen.

Secret conclaves like the one in Aruba rarely come to light. This one did because a backsliding Sicilian trafficker named Joe Cuffaro was there. Picked up two years later on a drug charge in Miami, he took a plea and gave his interrogators an earful.[7]

As Cuffaro told it, the meeting came about when the most formidable boss in Palermo, Francesco 'Ciccio' Madonia, sent a trusted aide named John Galatolo to set it up. 'My godfather instructed me, but this venture is actually controlled by the four most powerful families in the Sicilian Mafia,' he informed Cuffaro: Ciccio Madonia's family in Palermo, Giuseppe Madonia's in Gela, Nitto Santapaola's in Catania and the Corleonesi, rulers of the Mafia realm.

Upon leaving Palermo, Galatolo went first to the Sicilians' enclave on 18th Avenue in Brooklyn, command centre of their heroin network in America for a quarter of a century.

The network was an inseparable part of the triangle – from Palermo to Caracas to New York – that had created and fed what was now a heroin addict population of half a million in the United States. The men running it out of their Brooklyn headquarters were ranking members of the Mafia's inner circle in Palermo. Their advice and consent were indispensable to the deal Galatolo was about to propose.

When four or five of their top traffickers in New York agreed to come in on it, Galatolo went down to Aruba, taking Joe Cuffaro with him.[8]

The Medellín cartel sent one Waldo Aponte Romero, who flew in with his party from Colombia in a private Lear jet.

Photographs show Galatolo and Aponte, bronzed and smiling in shorts and flowered shirts, posing with a splendid marlin. As they sailed, fished, drank strawberry daiquiris and sunned, they talked over a stupendous proposition.

The cocaine market was saturated in America, where consumption had shot up from thirty-one to seventy-two tons, forcing the price down by more than two-thirds in two years. At the time of the Aruba meet, it was selling wholesale there for $11,000 a kilo.[9]

On the other hand, the rage for cocaine was just beginning to devour Europe. From 'virtually nothing' in 1985, the quantity reaching the old continent was approaching forty tons in 1987, and selling for nearly five times the going price in America: $50,000 a kilo.[10]

Meanwhile, heroin was still the drug of preference in America, selling for around $200,000 a kilo. In Europe, where it was easier to procure and transport, the price was four times lower: $50,000.

Therefore, the Sicilians proposed to swap heroin from Europe for cocaine from Colombia. That would give the Medellín cartel a chance to branch out into America's lucrative heroin market. In exchange, the Mafia wanted an exclusive franchise for the wholesale cocaine market in Europe. If not, said John Galatolo, any Colombians trying to deliver to Europe would be killed.[11]

Here was the answer to those who thought the Mafia was as good as finished.

The days of its corner on the American heroin market were over. The Pizza Connection case had knocked out one of its major rings and two dozen of its best men in New York halfway through the 1980s. Judge Falcone's anti-Mafia pool had closed down its refineries in Sicily during the same years, and hauled the entire Mafia hierarchy into court.

Chinese Triads were taking over the American supply line. Nigerians and hundreds of smaller ethnic groups were crowding into the field. Many wondered what there was left for the Sicilian Mafia to do. Cornering Europe's cocaine market appeared to be the answer.

The Colombians, who did not like being pushed around, would have preferred to let the Mafia simply broker for them as always. It was moving 'huge amounts' of their cocaine to Europe already, according to the DEA. The Cuntrera brothers alone handled nearly two-thirds of all their shipments in transit through Venezuela; and four-fifths of all the cocaine leaving Colombia passed through Venezuela.[12]

But Europe was home for the Sicilians, their prime marketplace for decades. Here they could do what the Medellín cartel could not do. 'We expect the Sicilian Mafia to take over cocaine distribution in Europe. They have the network; the Colombians don't,' predicted the lead prosecutor in the Pizza Connection case, Louis Freeh, now head of the FBI.[13]

So the deal was on. The Medellín cartel would ship straight to Sicily by way of Aruba, 'four, five, six, seven hundred kilos at a time,' explained Cuffaro. 'This is one of the biggest adventures ever attempted by the Sicilian Mafia,' Galatolo told him, as indeed it was.

Europe would soon overtake and surpass America as the cocaine explosion took its devastating course. The forty tons reaching the continent by 1987 would quintuple to 200 tons in the next five years.[14] The Sicilian Mafia, given up for dead in some quarters, would make an enormous leap in money and criminal power.

In the space of those five years, that first deal in Aruba would lead to a second of much greater importance, elevating the Colombian-Sicilian partnership to new heights, carrying the Sicilian Mafia to rarified levels of international finance, providing a clear view of the underworld's exponentially rising interest in Russia – the *pax mafiosa* emerging.

On January 7, 1988, the *Big John* sailed from Aruba under a devil-may-care Chilean skipper, carrying over half a ton of cocaine (569 kilos). Joe Cuffaro was waiting in Palermo when it offloaded near a fishing village on Sicily's western coast. 'Your shipment came in successful,' he informed Waldo Aponte, waiting at a public phone in Spain.

Before the *Big John* turned around for home, Cuffaro informed the Chilean skipper that 'the Sicilian Mafia was interested to send back heroin in the same boat, send back to the United States.' The skipper replied that he would be 'more than glad to'.

The next trip was going to be 'a two-to three-thousand kilo cocaine trip . . . So they were thinking to distribute that cocaine to other parts of Europe, Germany, France,' Cuffaro told Judge Falcone, who went to New York to question him. But a hitch had set in over money.

Aside from the heroin, the four Mafia families had agreed to pay for half of the first consignment in dollars, $12 million in all. A million-dollar down payment in cash had been sent up to Milan's wholesale produce market in a truckload of lemons, and then gone astray.

Cuffaro had flown to Milan with John Galatolo to look for it, and they had found it. The Colombians' Milanese money-washer had simply sent the laundered money to the wrong place – Los Angeles instead of Aruba – a minor error, which he corrected.

But Cuffaro had met him. He knew the man only as 'Giuseppe', a Milanese who talked incessantly of horses. Italian police, hunting for a rich Milanese who dealt in currency and loved horses, found their prey three years later.

Giuseppe Lottusi, a casually elegant financier with a magnificent racing stable, was arrested in October 1991. He had been the Colombians' chief money-washer for years. After the *Big John* affair, he had become the Sicilian Mafia's as well.

Lottusi was 'a perfect launderer', said the head of the Italian

Criminalpol's Economic Crime section, meaning that he was a master at bleaching the last criminal stains out of a narcodollar: through bank-to-bank transfers, loanbacks, currency swaps, stocks and bonds, real estate buys – including $100 million worth in Los Angeles – and shell companies billing other shell companies for non-existent goods.

But Lottusi's laundry was not the only one servicing the Colombian-Sicilian joint venture. Even before it was dismantled, American and Italian police were hunting for others.

Discovering the Aruba deal had underlined the urgency of finding and seizing the money. Here was the first hard evidence of a strategic merger in the international underworld, moving towards a more rationalized and cost-effective drug trade, greatly increasing its impact on Europe and America.

Every effort to contain the trade on either continent had failed. Taking away the money – the sole reason for the drug cartels' existence and source of their strength – was the only thing that might work, before it was too late.

Some thought it was too late already. 'Colombia is *gone* – the Cali cartel owns it. We've let them get too much money down there,' says the DEA's Greg Passic. Nevertheless, the DEA was still going after it.

The biggest police money-hunt on record ended in the biggest intercontinental crime bust ever made, in September 1992. An eight-country operation coordinated by the DEA, it was known as Operation Green Ice – Freeze the Green.[15]

In the course of this operation, investigators came upon the second Colombian-Sicilian summit, tracked the high-powered delegations attending it, and caught them in the act.

The DEA had set out to break the Colombians' money-washing circuit. Forty-five DEA undercovers had passed as crooks, laundered Colombian narcodollars through a 'Trans-Americas Ventures Associates' in San Diego, tapped phones, bugged hotel rooms, trailed contacts up and down the western hemisphere and across the Atlantic.

Italian undercover agents, running a similar laundry for the Colombians in Rome, were doing much the same.

When investigators were ready to move that September, they had penetrated five major Colombian cocaine cartels, nailed seven of their top financial managers, uncovered a superlative mole within the Colombian government, and learned almost everything there was to know about the second Colombian-Sicilian summit, underway in Rome.[16]

A hundred and sixty-seven people were rounded up on a single day in September 1992, in San Diego, Los Angeles, Chicago, Miami, New York, Canada, Costa Rica, the Cayman Islands, Britain, Spain, Italy and Colombia itself.

A sting operation right out of the movies – an offer to invest twenty million dirty dollars – had lured the Cali cartel's financial *consigliere* to San Diego. He was Carlos Rodriguez Polonia-Camargo, Inspector-General of Colombia's Central Bank, special agent of Colombia's secret anti-narcotics squad (DAS), and the Colombian government's representative to every kind of international anti-narcotics conference.

In Rome, an extravagantly brilliantined gentleman dressed in dazzling white was picked up as he sipped a martini in Piazza Navona. His passport said he was Jose Guillermo Duran of Venezuela, but he was actually Orlando Cediel Ospina-Vargas of Colombia – the man behind Pablo Escobar's escape from a gilded Colombian prison.

'Tony' Duran headed the Colombian delegation meeting with the Mafia in Italy. This time, however, he was not merely speaking for the Medellín cartel, nor was he dealing merely with the Mafia's four most powerful families. He was in Italy on behalf of all the cocaine cartels in Colombia. He had brought along their top distributor for Europe, Pedro Villaquiran, aka 'Grajalas'. He was negotiating not just with the Mafia, but with all three of its Italian subalterns also – the Camorra of Naples, the 'Ndrangheta of Calabria, the younger Sacra Corona Unita of Puglia.[17]

And he was dealing directly with the chairman of the board: Salvatore 'Totò' Riina, chief of Sicily's regnant Corleonesi clan, the Mafia's grand *capo di tutti i capi*. 'Duran was going for a pact with the Cupola of Cosa Nostra,' Italy's Criminalpol declared.

Italian undercover agents knew all about the Colombians' proposition because they had microphones and video cameras inside Tony Duran's Rome bureau. A nest of five money-washing offices in a modest apartment building in middle-class Prati, it called itself the European Institute for the Protection of Animals.

There, Duran had settled down to negotiate with a personal emissary of Totò Riina's, while animal protectors from all over Italy kept dropping in with cartons full of cash for the laundry.

What they agreed to, five years after Aruba, was in effect a full treaty, committing all of Italy's organized crime groups and Colombia's cocaine cartels to the kind of 'operational welding' that Judge Falcone had feared. Henceforth, the two titans of the underworld would take the Western half of the European continent under joint management. Evidently it was time to consolidate and restructure what had become a gigantic enterprise.

Europe was drowning in cocaine by 1992. The 200-odd tons coming in that year, up five times since the Aruba summit in 1987, was worth $10 billion on the street.[18]

But this was not nextdoor America, where the Colombians could easily run in supplies by air, land and sea, even by submarine, with a huge army of helpers melting into the background. Europe, four thousand miles away, was much costlier to supply and harder to oversee.

Despite their solemn covenant in Aruba, the Colombians had not given the Mafia an altogether exclusive franchise for Europe. The partnership was close, but Colombian traffickers were doing a lot of networking on their own. Many of their throwaway helpers were inexperienced, rash, slipshod or stupid, and it showed.

By 1992, the Colombians were suffering intolerable reverses on the continent. A careless error had very nearly cost them half a ton of cocaine bound for Sicily that June. The frozen fish it was hidden in proved to be loaded with mercury. (A Mafia military commando was on the verge of mounting an attack to grab the shipment, but decided to have a bogus government inspector liberate it instead.)

Earlier, in Holland, two tons of cocaine were lost. Impatient to extract the packets from cans of orange juice, helpers with room temperature IQs had dumped the juice into Amsterdam's canals. When the water turned orange, the police arrived.

The Colombians sent Tony Duran to Italy because they'd had enough. 'Tony came here to set up a point-to-point system for the most powerful cocaine and laundering network in the world,' said Criminalpol's Alessandro Pansa. 'The Colombians wanted stable ties with the Sicilian Mafia; they wanted efficiency, dependability, professionalism; they wanted legality,' he explained.[19]

Transporting the cocaine to Europe was costing them twelve times more than actually producing it ($12,000 to $1,000 a kilo).[20] They wanted the Sicilian Mafia to cut out the middlemen and cut down the risks.

Under the terms of their 1992 Rome treaty, Sicilians would be stationed in Colombia to help supervise shipments to Europe. The cocaine would go directly to reliable Sicilian agents posted at strategic entry points – Amsterdam, Rotterdam, Spain, Portugal, Germany – for the new routes passing by way of Eastern Europe. Italy itself would be 'the cocaine warehouse for the continent'.[21]

Communications between Palermo and Colombian cocaine depots would be strictly by radio; even cellular telephones were out.

The cover for shipping the coke to Europe would have to be genuine. The product used for camouflage would have to be good, the company receiving it legitimate and credible. If cans of orange juice were used, they would have to be imported by a firm in the business of importing and selling orange juice. If the proceeds were laundered through an insurance company, it would have to be a straight-up company selling a lot of insurance.

'Find me a company that really buys frozen fish, and we'll send them frozen fish. Open a shop that sells dried flowers, and we'll send dried flowers,' the Colombians' Tony Duran told his Italian associates.

In exchange, the Sicilian Mafia and its subalterns would become part of a financial conglomerate altogether new to the underworld and still more menacing to the lawful one.[22]

The Mafia had already risen above the primitive drug trafficking of the 1970s and 80s. Moving the drugs was for its lower classes, still the best in the business. By 1992, its managerial class was engaging more and more in straight (or slightly bent) capitalist ventures. Half of all the Sicilian Mafia's laundered capital – *half* –was re-invested in legitimate enterprises all over the world, according to Italy's Ministry of Justice.[23]

Obviously it could provide legitimate companies to camouflage the cocaine trade, as well as the skilled professional labour to direct it in Europe. More importantly, however, it was ideally placed to manage the most troublesome and crucial part of the operation: the money.

Colossal sums of Colombian narcodollars were backing up around the world. Getting them home clean from America alone was exhausting and endlessly complex. Therefore, the Colombians asked the Mafia to take a good part of the laundry service for Europe off their hands.

In short, the Sicilians were going to launder the proceeds of the European cocaine traffic for the Colombians as well as themselves. 'Corleone can wash and move any amount of money,' announced Salvatore Riina's emissary proudly to Tony Duran, marking the Mafia's passage to the highest spheres of international finance.[24]

Far from the commonplace affair it may seem, laundering crime money can be an intoxicating power game. A global turnover of half a trillion narcodollars a year produces colossal amounts of converted, expendable capital that can go anywhere, overnight.

A launderer converting it by re-reinvesting it can move faster than any company accountable to stockholders, or state agency, or international body. 'The Mafia can get a billion dollars into Russia whenever it likes; look how long it takes the G-7, or the US government,' observes Greg Passic.

Furthermore, a good launderer today does not merely manipulate the capital of others; a healthy share becomes his.

Five hundred billion dollars of drug money means an endless torrent of cash, in small bills. The ordeal of counting it is such that it is often weighed by the bale or measured by the cubic yard. (British customs found twenty cubic yards of various currencies stacked to the roof of a London safehouse in Operation Green Ice.)

The Colombian cartels pay a fortune to turn this into useable money. They were offering up to 15% on the dollar when Tony Duran sat down with the Sicilians in Rome. The rate leaped to 25% after they were hit by Operation Green Ice, the DEA says.

By late 1992, that is, they were paying twenty-five cents on the dollar: giving away a fourth of their take, one billion dollars in every four.[25]

Operation Green Ice had caught them short by identifying and destroying seven of their major money-washing circuits. Investigators had never cracked more than one at a time before.

Nevertheless the DEA thought there were at least another hundred, and this only in the West. It could not begin to estimate what was going on among the ruins of the formerly communist East, where the trail led now.

In the communist East, in 1992, the Mafia could turn a billion dollars into four, five, even ten billion dollars, washed and re-invested. It could do that for its own cut of the Colombians' drug money, and for the Colombians' share, without the smallest risk of detection.

The former Soviet republics had the world's largest petroleum reserves (80 billion barrels), a quarter of the world's gold and timber reserves (twice the Amazon's), a fifth of the world's diamond reserves, and the world's second largest deposits of copper, iron ore, coal, nickel and zinc. They abounded besides in uranium, plutonium, manganese, cobalt, bauxite, chromium, lead, molybdenum, carbon, titanium, platinum, silver, tin and a range of rare earth metals.

Furthermore, they had inherited what was once the world's largest standing army, with its requisite weapons, tanks, missiles, planes, nuclear warheads and materials.

All this was up for grabs in a prostrate and chaotic land, boiling with corruption and flat broke.

All the ex-communist states were a bargain, but the Russian Republic was unique. Not only was everything for sale there at incredibly low prices, but payment could be made in local currency by a foreigner with the right connections, and the wit, to buy a seemingly worthless currency on the black market.

A well-connected foreigner could buy a ton of crude petroleum in Russia for the equivalent of $5 in rubles in 1990, and sell it for $140 in Western Europe. This was more or less the case for all of the country's natural wealth and manmade resources.

To be well-connected, a foreign crook had only to hook up with a fellow crook in the Russian mafia, or a corrupt Russian politician, both readily available. With their help, the crook could obtain a Russian bank account and a licence to export, buy rubles for his dirty dollars at a huge discount, pay in rubles for his raw material exports, and so not only launder his money but come out 400% or 500% ahead. Some were coming out 1,000% ahead.[26]

By the time the Colombians asked the mafia to help launder their European profits, therefore, the entire ex-Soviet bloc had become an enormous washing-machine for dirty money, rapidly replacing familiar ones elsewhere, arguably the largest, safest and most profitable ever invented.

Naturally the Colombians were in there also. The Cali cartel in particular had hired an authentic Harvard professor named Frank Jurado in 1990 to explore the terrain. Presentable, relaxed, and urbane, Prof. Jurado had been working the whole continent when the DEA picked him up in Luxembourg with a ticket to Moscow in his pocket.

Apart from $32 million on deposit in a Luxembourg bank, and $55 million in a Monte Carlo bank, he had another 115 bank accounts in sixteen other countries, including a $2 million account in Budapest, Hungary.[27]

All the big syndicates and any number of other crooks were homing in on Moscow by then. But the Sicilian Mafia had got there first, forming a privileged partnership with the Russian mafia just as it did with the Colombians.

The very Sicilian bosses who thought up the Aruba plan in 1987 were already starting to buy hundreds of millions of Russian rubles in 1989 – the Cuntrera brothers, Ciccio Madonia, Nitto Santapaola.

The Cuntrera brothers bought only $28 million worth of rubles that year, to acquire cut-rate Soviet building materials for their new high-rise hotels in Aruba.[28] But a close fellow boss of Nitto Santapaola's bought half a billion rubles the same year. A year later, the Sicilian and American mafias were both part of a consortium negotiating for eight billion dollars' worth of rubles.[29]

Western authorities could not imagine why a Sicilian Mafia boss, or any sane person, would want to buy eight billion dollars' worth of rubles at the time. Certainly they did not realize that these crooks meant to buy up all the rubles in Russia, the better to sack it, and in good part succeeded.

The story of that monumental scam is told here for the first time. The hundreds of documents confirming it are disturbing evidence of the planetary criminal collusion that Judge Falcone feared. The 'shattering and terrifying' consequences are before our eyes.

Russia is where the big crime syndicates discovered how useful they could be to one another, to capture and ransack a vast and prostrate country.

Of the five thousand organized crime gangs emerging there and in the rest of the ex-Soviet Union, a thousand were working with some foreign criminal group by early 1993. This was President Boris Yeltsin's own estimate at a conference of several hundred politicians, civil servants, judges and police chiefs summoned to discuss the spreading scourge.

'Organized crime is destroying the economy, interfering with politics, undermining public morale, threatening individual citizens and the entire Russian nation . . . Our country is already considered a great mafia power!' he exclaimed.[30]

It was true, though no Western government appeared to notice it.

2

After the Wall

To an expectant commission of the Italian parliament, gathered in a secret location towards the end of 1992, a Sicilian Man of Honour with impressive credentials and exalted connections told an amazing story:

'One night I was in Pietraperzia, in the province of Enna, and there were lots of pairs of shoes. "Is this a party?" I asked. "No," they told me. "You should be happy because your boss was elected yesterday to be the underboss of all the criminal organizations in the world." So they gave us all presents of expensive shoes . . .'[1]

Leonardo Messina, descendant of a family whose Men of Honour went back seven generations, had been second-in-command to the boss who ranked second in power only to Salvatore 'Totò' Riina: the most fearsome *capo di tutti i capi* to rule Sicily's Cosa Nostra for the better part of a century.[2]

In months of interrogation, Messina had provided enough credible testimony to generate 200 arrests up and down the Italian peninsula. Much of what he said was corroborated by other mafiosi, 275 of whom had collaborated with the law that year. But he alone spoke of an elected government presiding over the international underworld.

He had known since 1980 that Cosa Nostra 'belonged to a world-wide structure,' he declared. 'There's a summit, a meeting place for everybody. We sit around a table with other organizations for consultations, but also to make important decisions.'

Others had been in charge until November 1991, he went on. Then, at a meeting somewhere on the planet, they gave us the *rappresentanza* for all the organizations.' Totò Riina had succeeded to the top, with Messina's boss at his side.

An enduring cult of disbelief where the Mafia is concerned made it particularly hard to believe this story. Even believers had trouble with the details – the table, the secret meeting place, the formal elections.

The *capo di tutti i capi* supposedly elected to the supreme command seemed still more improbable, when the public finally got a look at him. Captured early in 1993 after twenty-three years in hiding of a sort (he was in the Sicilian capital of Palermo all along), Totò Riina proved to be no movie godfather. Pudgy and flabby, shoulders slumped and small eyes peering out from folds of flesh, he looked and acted the part of a humble, obsequious, forelock-tugging peasant.

He was nothing of the sort; his questioners found him to be astute, imperious and indescribably frightening – which did not necessarily mean that he ruled a worldwide criminal government. Perhaps he didn't. There is no hard proof that the elite of the international underworld, Sicilian, American, Colombian, Turkish, Russian, Chinese, Japanese, all meet at once and vote leaders in or out of office. But they have certainly arrived at some kind of *pax mafiosa*.

For all the killing on the turf of each, there are no killings where their paths cross. Though more or less in the same lines of business, increasingly in the same countries, where competition is supposedly fierce for stakes in the billions of dollars, they may work jointly or concurrently, or withdraw from the field, but they don't fight.

'If there was competition among them, we would be turning up a lot of dead bodies. But the evidence so far is that they are looking for ways to work together,' says one of Sicily's leading judicial authorities, Giuseppe Ayala.[3]

According to Judge Falcone, close on their heels when the mafia killed him in 1992, they have in fact 'stipulated a sort of non-aggression pact, dividing up the world'.[4]

Faced with this planetary criminal alliance, the first in human history, lawful society continues to wage its little wars, splinter into a thousand ethnic fragments, haggle over legal jurisdiction and perpetuate a multitude of police agencies carefully keeping secrets from each other. Sensible crooks appear to have put such futile exercises behind them.

There is room for everyone in their expanding universe. The heroin age, which they launched in the 1960s, has made them prodigiously rich; and the tremendous upheavals of the 1990s – the collapse of communism, the falling away of barriers across Europe, the mass migration of uprooted populations – are making them more so.

The drug traffic alone, exceeding half a trillion dollars a year now, is the world's second biggest money-maker, after the arms traffic; and these syndicates engage in both.[5]

The interest they have accumulated from investment of drug profits in the last decade is approaching a trillion dollars, according to a European Community estimate ($820 billion).[6]

That doesn't count customary pursuits such as theft, extortion, gambling, loan-sharking, forgery, prostitution, pornography, money-laundering, contract-killing.

Wealth of such magnitude is a phenomenon altogether separate from the personal fortune of a cocaine baron who can keep a private zoo, or a Palermo boss who can give somebody a solid gold bathtub for a wedding present (as one did not long ago). This is the wealth of the biggest multinational in the world, with the reach and resources to act accordingly.

Using it judiciously, the big syndicates can penetrate giant corporations, manipulate the world's money markets, destabilize currencies, buy entire countries larger than Aruba, all of which they are doing or have done. 'Buying a national economy is not a criminal offence,' says a state prosecutor in Russia, where it assuredly isn't.

The fact that those who own such a weapon are manifestly pooling their strength is extraordinarily menacing. All their sources of revenue have been multiplying geometrically since the Soviet empire crashed. The story that follows has to do with the calamitous growth of criminal power in Europe, America, the world, since that epic happening.

At the start of the 1990s, the myth still prevailed that only Italy and the United States offered a natural habitat for the Mafia, and indeed for all organized crime. Evidence to the contrary was denied nearly everywhere else until the signs grew too alarming to ignore.

Sweden and the rest of Scandinavia, Finland and the Baltic states, Russia and the entire ex-Soviet bloc, Nigeria and the whole of West Africa, Australia and the length of the Pacific Rim, most of South America and every country in Western Europe have all fallen victim by now.

Sudden recognition has come nearly everywhere at once, as crime skids out of control around the globe.

Seemingly overnight, it has become the fastest growth industry in

Britain; according to a *Guardian* survey, its turnover there hit an astonishing £14 billion ($21 billion) in 1992.[7]

Holland, an island of civility on a turbulent continent, has more crimes per head now than twenty other countries, including Britain, France, Italy and the United States. Australia, Belgium and Switzerland (!) have more crime victims per head than the United States.[8]

In the deceptive language of numbers – half a billion crimes worldwide in 1990 – it is hard to distinguish between 'micro-' and 'macro-' criminality: the one largely drug-induced and poverty-driven, the other structured, efficient and increasingly international.

In the language of power, however, it is this last that has become an intolerable threat to free nations.

America, assailed by predatory gangs of staggering number and variety, is still the favourite of the international underworld. But Europe is where the high drama is playing out.

The European Community is a momentous experiment in union among twelve disparate sovereign states: Britain, Ireland, France, Germany, Denmark, Holland, Belgium, Luxembourg, Spain, Portugal, Italy, Greece. 1993 was to have been its year of triumph, with half the continent thrown open to a free market of fabulous promise. Sadly, there was no Big Bang.

Hortatory rhetoric could not conceal the qualms and second thoughts, the anxiety bordering on anguish, the hot quarrels behind closed doors, when the moment came for the twelve EC states to keep their word. In the end, the barriers went down just halfway, even this partly a fiction, for goods, services and money – not for people.

People were the EC's nightmare by 1993: migrants and crooks, both in unbearable numbers.

More than any other part of the affluent First World, the EC faced an uncontrollable invasion of migrants from every direction. The noble vision of a great European space stripped of all barriers and looking outward soon receded, as the poor, the oppressed and the upwardly mobile of four continents pushed and clawed their way in.

Half a million, then a million, then the imminent threat of three, five, ten million made the difference between gallant principles and reality. The image of a Fortress Europe defending its wealth and privilege behind high guarded walls, once abominable to EC leaders, was no longer unthinkable. By 1993, year of the single market, the military patrols by land, sea and air, the helicopters aloft around the clock, the satellite pictures, radar and infra-red night-sights, the forcible expulsions, the boat-people drowning in sight of Mediterranean shores, had made the image painfully real.

Every kind of criminal was riding in on this human tide, from the petty shill to the multinational troops of the big crime conglomerates. Some of the latter had been in for a quarter of a century. The rest started to come along as soon as they saw the gravy train ahead, in 1985.

When EC leaders decided to create a single market that year, the Community had a combined Gross National Product approaching five trillion dollars.[9] Its in-house trade ran to nearly a trillion and a half dollars, and it accounted for a third of all the world's exports and imports.

It was America's largest trading partner (a quarter of a trillion dollars both ways), largest foreign investor (over a quarter of a trillion dollars), and largest host to American investment abroad (nearing a quarter of a trillion dollars).

Once its inner borders went down, a third of a billion people would be free to circulate without passport or customs controls, carry baggage and ship goods without police inspection, live where they pleased, bank or go into business anywhere.

On the strength of this, the European Community stood to become the richest trading area on earth. Big-time gangsters could no more resist so intoxicating a prospect than anyone else on the make.

'The one will have a fatal attraction for the other,' predicted the US Justice Department's organized crime expert, Charles Saphos, in 1990. 'The multinational crime syndicates have the largest amount of expendable wealth in the world. The single market will create the largest concentration of wealth in history. Criminal money will naturally gravitate towards this immense area of opportunity. Europe will be a great place to be a crook,' he concluded.[10]

But crooks were the last item on the European Council's agenda when he said so in 1990. Engrossed in plans to make it easier to make money, EC leaders had scarcely given a thought to the opportunities for criminals to do likewise. In a warning largely disregarded, the director of the Netherlands Police Academy observed:

There is no place where expertise on police in the European countries is brought together. There is no centre where the problems and possibilities of internationalization of the police can be studied. There is no place to compare the different laws relevant for the police, no comparative study of police systems and their

peculiarities, no comparative description and evaluation of
police strategies, tactics and procedures in the different special-
izations, no compilation of information about training systems
and equipment and facilities. There is no research on the development of police work after 1992 . . .'[11]

With the single market barely two years away, the twelve EC states
had sacrificed few of their sovereign prerogatives. Each had its own
laws on extradition, rights of asylum, hot pursuit, exchange of police
and intelligence information, undercover agents, controlled drug
deliveries, jail terms for drug traffickers, money-laundering, phone
taps and listening devices, protection of privacy in data banks.

For instance, a fugitive convicted of 'association with the Mafia' in
Italy could not be extradited from the other EC states, none of which
had a similar law. Belgian police could not tap anybody's phone, native
or foreign, or use any electronic surveillance device, even on a truck in
transit.(Drug traffickers loved to do business there.) Dutch law forbids
the release of any information to a foreign agency that might lead to
the arrest of a Dutch national, and forbids a Dutch citizen even to
name a fellow citizen suspected of criminal activity abroad.

A German cop could not pursue a criminal over the Dutch border
into a disco (or any building) without a formal *lettre rogatoire*, or over
other inner EC borders for more than ten kilometres – six miles, a five-
minute ride – and that in a plainly marked police car. (A Dutch cop
could chase a criminal straight across Germany though.)[12] A French
undercover narcotics agent could entrap a drug trafficker by putting up
money, but a German narcotics agent who tried it in his country
would go to jail.

A backsliding drug trafficker risks life imprisonment in Great
Britain and Greece and a forty-year sentence in France, but an *optional*
maximum of twelve years in Holland.[13] 'The Dutch don't believe in
law enforcement to fight drugs anyway,' observed an aggrieved cop in
France, which has the toughest drug laws in Europe.

Harmonizing these regulations could take a lifetime. Indeed, hardly
any have been harmonized up to now. (It was hard enough to harmo-
nize a simple electrical item described by a German journalist as 'the
most frightful thing of all' – the SIP, the single integrated plug.)[14]

In effect, Western Europe lay like a vast open city under murderous
criminal bombardment. The speed and scope of the assault shocked
those who had trusted to ministerial wisdom and the salutary effect of
myriad ad hoc committees. Nothing in the EC's elaborate preparations

brought it remotely close to catching up with the crooks.

By an extraordinary twist of history, the ministers and ad hoc committees were planning to free up the Western side of Europe just when communism disintegrated on the Eastern side. If there was ever a chance to block a massive criminal invasion, that ended it.

Once the standoff between East and West was over, the armature keeping much of the human race in hand was gone. Boundaries started to give way everywhere; whole nations began to split up; the satellite states of Eastern Europe cracked open; the Soviet Union flew apart.

Law enforcement broke down all across Soviet territory and in Poland, Czechoslovakia, Hungary, Rumania, Bulgaria, Albania. Border controls practically ceased to exist throughout Eastern Europe, calling the whole concept of Western Europe's defence into question.

The single market was supposed to be borderless inside, but assuredly not outside; quite the contrary. Securing its outer border was an indispensable condition for removing internal impediments. This would have been hard enough if the EC states had only had to worry about several thousand miles of ragged coastline from the Greek islands to the Atlantic shores of Ireland to the Baltic Sea. Actually, they did not worry much about the rest of their outer rim.

Stern communist patrols guarded the entire length of their Eastern frontier during their planning stage. So long as the Iron Curtain was in place, the line could scarcely be breached either way. Once the Curtain fell, it simply could not hold. Germany, bordering on nine countries, had already abolished frontier controls with six of them to the west and south (Holland, Belgium, Luxembourg, France, Austria, Switzerland). To the east, it now shared not only five hundred kilometres of porous border with Czechoslovakia, but – after merging with (communist) East Germany – another as long again with Poland.

Through this huge gap, virtually unpoliced, a resourceful traveller with or without papers could travel more or less unhindered from Siberian Irkutsk to Paris or Brussels, and vice-versa.

Practically speaking, the whole continent lay open to illicit tourists. Migrants flocked to Eastern Europe from Asia, Africa and South America, joining throngs of East Europeans surging West.

Authentic economic refugees among them could hardly be distinguished from carpetbaggers, pimps, con men, loan sharks, black marketeers, forgers, money-washers, arms runners, drug traffickers. Homeless and penniless, usually smuggled in as bonded slaves, they were the new menials of the big crime cartels.

The traffic went the other way also. As always, the crooks moved faster than governments trying to forestall them. The very day the Berlin Wall came down in 1989, they were racing across the line to stake out territory in ex-communist East Germany.

There they met the Russian mafia coming West.

The implications of this encounter were deeply disquieting for every nation in and out of Europe, starting with the United States. The same crime syndicates meeting the Russians in Europe had plagued America for years: the Colombian cartels, the Sicilian Mafia, the Chinese Triads, the Japanese Yakuza.

The Colombians were supplying most of America's cocaine. The Triads were bringing in three-quarters of America's heroin. The Yakuza, specialized in gun-running, drug-running, money-washing and corporate blackmail, had made America 'a prime investment site' over the previous decade, the Justice Department said.

The Sicilian Mafia, pronounced dead by certain American enthusiasts, was still rated officially with its American offspring as the country's 'most serious organized crime problem'. According to the FBI, it was bringing in thousands of fresh forces to rejuvenate, if not replace, the American mafia's geriatric leadership.[15]

As if arranged by some malevolent hand, the Russian mafia was sending in thousands of fresh forces also, to beef up the *organizatsiya* in America. Formed by older emigrés in the 1970s – simultaneously with the Sicilians and just as invisibly – the *organizatsiya* was rising rapidly to mob stardom in the US.

Even in America, Russian gangsters stood out as truly gifted frighteners, clever, ferocious, pitiless. 'They make tons of money, they kill people, they are international, they are into drugs,' said a harried federal prosecutor, wondering 'how the hell this Russian organized crime got so big and how we can get rid of them'.[16]

Possibly the most inventive swindlers alive, their multi-billion-dollar scams – at least \$5 billion in America by 1992 – were the envy of Cosa Nostra. The fact that the two weren't fighting was a sign of the times: the Russians had simply agreed to pay a cut to four of New York's five Cosa Nostra families.

Meanwhile, Russian clans stretching across eleven time zones to the Pacific were running into the Triads and the Yakuza at the other end of the map. Russian traffickers could provide new outlets to the West for Triad heroin-moving through China. Georgian and Japanese gangs were hijacking used Japanese cars bound for Russia's luxuriant black market.

Thus the US, China and Japan were locked in to a criminal circuit reaching right around the planet.

With the closing of the circle, organized crime achieved its own world without frontiers. Of all the disastrous developments since the breakup of Soviet Russia, this was among the most hidden and insidious.

For Judge Falcone, who knew it best, the Sicilian Mafia had no equal. 'There is only one Mafia, Cosa Nostra, the most perfect and ferocious criminal organization on the face of the earth,' he said.

Towards the end of his life, however, he conceded that other big players could be called 'mafias' too, provided they were formally structured, flexible, versatile, extremely violent, capable of assuring protection at the highest levels, and very rich – as were the Triads, the Yakuza and the Russian clans, he concluded.[17]

Though none could have emerged anywhere but on its native soil, their followers have walked strikingly similar paths. Born in times of political upheaval, government oppression or foreign occupation, they started out as social rebels or patriotic folk heroes, and ended up as larcenous, murderous thugs.

The youngest, the Russian one, goes back to the 1860s, the very years when Italy's Mafia was born. Just as Giuseppe Garibaldi, hero of the Italian Risorgimento, used young Sicilian bandits to fight the Bourbon kings, so did early Russian revolutionaries use crooks to fight the tsar.

It began when a long-forgotten figure of the Bolshevik revolution named Nicholas Ishutin invented the Organization. Its open political arm did the pedestrian work of insurrectional agitation and propaganda. Its secret arm, named Hell, was devoted to spreading public disorder through assassination, blackmail, armed robbery and so on, bringing terrorists and common criminals together for the first time.[18]

Russia's legion of common criminals were the Bolsheviks' natural allies. Surly, wretched, brawling and often sodden drunk, they were nevertheless the classic rebels of tsarist society. 'Russian tradition regarded them as liberators of the people,' writes Valery Chalidze in *Criminal Russia*.[19]

Legitimized by the nation's future rulers, the thefts that Lenin called 'expropriations' – 'exes' in thieves' slang to this day – were accepted as a kind of entitlement by much of the populace as well as the thieves. Russians were traditionally inclined to regard other people's property as fair game, observes Chalidze. They were greatly encouraged in this view by a Bolshevik regime seizing everybody's property in the name of a workers' state.

Later, when communist rule was assured, Stalin bore down hard on

thieves – too late. In half a century of close association with Stalin and
his peers, Russia's criminal population had grown beyond measure,
forming an underground unique in the annals of crime anywhere.

Of all its counterparts, the model closest to Russia's was the Italian
Mafia, wrote the poet and ex-thief Mikhail Dyomin after six years in
Siberian prison camps. The main difference was a matter of politics, he
said:

> The legitimate world bears the same relationship to a Russian
> thief as a henhouse to a fox. The problems of the henhouse are
> of no interest to the fox. His only concern is to penetrate it, sat-
> isfy his appetite, and get the hell out.
>
> The Italian Mafia feels perfectly at home in the henhouse,
> where it not only eats its fill, but determines the pecking order of
> the birds themselves.[20]

These were not ordinary thieves, explained Dyomin. They were the
aristocrats of the profession, members of the 'thieves' world' (*vorovskoy
mir*): a 'solid corporation of underground establishments . . . embracing the full extent of the Soviet state, with one general code of ethics
prevailing from the Bay of Finland to the shores of the Japan Sea.'

Theirs was a wholly closed society, extravagantly depraved and
despairing, rejecting outside morality, politics, patriotism, even social
intercourse. Under Russian thieves' law, a professional criminal had no
right to work for anyone, or have any contact with the authorities,
wrote Dyomin. 'He can only earn his living with his thief's trade. A
thief thieves, a sucker plows. To each his own.'

Innumerable rules, standards and notions of propriety regulated the
thieves' world, wrote Soviet scholar D.S. Likhachev:

> The thieves' community has tremendous authority over the indi-
> vidual [whose life] is governed by a network of strict regulations
> extending to the most minute matters. Any violation of these
> rules is punished by a thieves' court . . . The penalty is always
> severe and inflicted without delay . . . A thief may escape from
> jail but he knows that it is almost impossible to escape judgment
> by a thieves' court.[21]

Thus, a thief was certain to be strangled or knifed to death if he stole
from or lied to a fellow thief, worked at a real job, tried to 'leave the
flock', turned scab or informer, or served the state in any way –

allowing himself to be drafted into the army, for instance. Serving in the army was the ultimate, unforgiveable sin. (Dyomin, who had done so, lived in dread of discovery in prison.)

Presiding over this community were men of monk-like austerity who spent most of their lives in jail: Russia's incomparable 'thieves within the code' (*vory v zakone*).

Chosen by others for their superior intelligence and indomitable spirit, they were the strategists for all undertakings in and out of prison; the clan representatives at nationwide policy meetings (*skhodka*); the keepers of the common kitty (*obshchak*) to finance operations, bribe officials and support convicts' families; the mediators of internal peace and arbiters of the code.[22]

There was a whiff of religious exaltation in their renunciation of the meanest creature comforts, and pride in self-inflicted pain. Like most of their fellow convicts, they made a point of proving their capacity to endure the unendurable.

Edward Kuznetsov, serving fifteen years for trying to hijack a plane, described fantastic scenes he had witnessed in Soviet prison camps:

> I have seen convicts swallow huge numbers of nails and quantities of barbed wire; swallow mercury thermometers, pewter tureens (after breaking them into edible portions), chess pieces, needles, ground glass, knives and spoons.
>
> I have seen convicts sew up their lips or eyelids with thread and wire; sew rows of buttons to their bodies; nail their scrotum to the bed . . .
>
> I have seen convicts cut open the skin of their arms or legs and peel it off as if it were a stocking, or cut lumps of flesh from their belly, roast them and eat them; or cut off their fingers or nose or ears or penis – there is absolutely nothing they will not do.[23]

Rather than acts of protest, these were expressions of pride and defiance, Kuznetsov thought: 'a way to carve out a slice of life'. Political prisoners, treated atrociously by most criminal inmates, often admired their bravery nonetheless. Andrei Sinyavsky, the Soviet dissident confined in Siberia for six years, describes the death of a thief named Pushkin at the hands of a prison scab: 'When the scab laid him on a sheet of iron and lit a fire underneath, he shouted out words that I would be proud to use as a motto, if only I felt worthy of them: "Hey, tell everybody I died like a thief!" '

World War II was the beginning of the end for the keepers of the true thieves' faith. The underworld survived and flourished, but the moral code of the fiercely sovereign *vorovsky mir* perished.

The war had shattered the old order throughout Europe. Criminals from East and West were criss-crossing the continent over unguarded borders, much as they do today. Russians were landing in foreign jails, exposed to the winds of change; and Western Europeans were landing in Soviet jails, where their behaviour was considered 'ambivalent and intolerable', explained Dyomin.

Sliding into crisis, Russia's thieves-in-the-code made a first portentous move to internationalize organized crime. In 1950, they convened a Europe-wide All-Thieves' Congress 'to hammer out some kind of general rule on questions of ethics'.

The meeting-place was Lvov, westernmost of Soviet cities, close to an outer frontier of forest and swamp easily crossed on foot. Heading the foreign guest-list were delegates from 'the truly thief countries of Italy and Poland'.

The ten Russian delegates included Dyomin, because 'green as you are, you've got culture. You've read all the books. You'll know how to make a good impression on Europe. You won't fall flat on your face.'

The All-Thieves' Congress was noisy and unproductive. After four days of wrangling, the delegates could agree on just one point: 'At home everybody's free to do what he wants, but on foreign soil he has to abide by the prevailing thieves' laws.'

At home, however, Russia's own criminals could no longer agree either. World War II had riven their ranks from top to bottom. Their cardinal rule – no collaboration with the state – could not withstand a call to arms by the Motherland.

Given the choice of fighting for their country or being shot, a thieves' congress had ruled that those joining the army should not be punished. Many thousands did join, only to collide violently with those who did not, upon returning from the front.

There followed a spate of terrible bloodletting spoken of as the Great Scabs' War. The traditional thieves were outnumbered; the scabs won. Before long, the ancient rule preserving a closed thieves' world crumbled away.

Stalin had always thrown political prisoners in with common criminals, hoping the latter would liquidate the former. He could count on them to terrorize dissident intellectuals, steal their food and miserable possessions, leave them to starve or freeze to death, all of which the thieves did. Under the new scabs' code, however, they could be *asked* to do such things, and more.

Allies for half a century previously, Russia's communist leaders and criminals rediscovered a curious affinity. Both stole. The criminals stole the property of private citizens and the State. So did the communist Nomenklatura, through graft, expropriation, embezzlement, wholesale extortion and 'ceiling statistics' (inflated production figures dreamed up by staring at the ceiling). Indeed, the Soviet Union was a kleptocracy, said a well-known scholar.

Over the course of yet another half century, the Soviet Union's professional criminals and communist functionaries became indispensable to one another, to their enormous mutual benefit. Like its Italian counterpart, the Russian fox came to be at home in the henhouse, not only eating its fill but helping to determine the birds' pecking order.

The Triads descend from the longest line of secret patriotic societies in history. The earliest were the Red Eyebrows, who deposed and murdered an imperial usurper called Wang Mang in the year 9AD. Others followed in succession for nearly two thousand years – the Copper Horses and Iron Shins, the Yellow Turbans, the White Lotus Society, the Incense Smelling Society, the Origin of Chaos Society – until a Triad Red Pole fighter named Dr Sun Yat-sen drove the last emperor from the throne of China.

That was in 1912. The Triads had lived for this moment since the year 1644, when Manchu invaders threw out the Chinese Ming emperor and installed a foreign Ch'ing dynasty. 'Overthrow the Ch'ing and restore the Ming' became the Triads' sworn endeavour down through the centuries.

It is still their sworn endeavour, though Mings and Ch'ings are gone forever. Distinctions between past and present, dead and living, legend and fact, mystical and real, tend to blur in the Triads' accounts of themselves.

Today's 80,000 Triad brothers do not live on ancestral memories, however. They have not been known to commit a patriotic act for almost a hundred years. Their intricate rituals, though preserved almost intact, are perfunctory. The one tradition unimpaired by time is the terrifying set of thirty-six oaths binding them to secrecy.

Like the Mafia, the Triads draw blood to frighten a brother into silence and obedience for life. The blood is drained into a bowl with the blood of a beheaded cock, and mixed with the ashes of a yellow paper bearing the candidate's name, burned in his hand. Upon drinking it, he vows to be loyal and faithful, for 'the wicked and treacherous will die like this cock'.[24]

Dying like a chicken is the least of the terrors embodied in the thirty-six oaths: to violate a single one is to be 'struck down by five thunderbolts' or 'myriad swords'.

No less than their Sicilian and Russian counterparts, Triad members risk death at every turn: for betraying the secret of the Triads' existence; for consorting with outsiders against Triad interests; for lying to, stealing from or 'committing indecent assaults upon' a Triad brother's wife; for 'trespassing upon the land occupied by my brethren'; for trying to leave the Triads, alive.[25]

Once past the frightening oaths, members come under granitic control. The brotherhood has no central government, but its guidance comes from Hong Kong and Taiwan, and its licensed branches all over the world are tightly run.

Interpol has described their structure as a several-storey building, in which the inhabitants on one floor don't know where the stairs are to the next storey.

The chain of command is vertical, much like the Mafia's: an elected Hill Chief and his counsellor (or *consigliere*); an Incense Master to initiate members and mete out punishments; a White Paper Fan to manage lodge funds and percentage points to the boss; Red Pole fighters or enforcers, skilled in kung fu.

Such was the Triads' protection against the imperial wrath of the Ch'ings, and such it remained when Triad patriots turned their minds to other things. Some were still going straight when the undoubtedly honourable Sun Yat-sen abolished imperial rule altogether, but nearly all their lodges were full of professional criminals by then.

The Triads were no worse in this regard than any number of China's secret patriotic societies, except for lasting longer. Indeed, they have been engaged in extortion, usury, prostitution and especially drug trafficking longer than any criminal organization extant.

They were in at the creation of the heroin market, and have held the key to the biggest source of supply ever since. Every turn of history has helped them, from the time they found a way to make a home of their own off the mainland, beyond the Ch'ings' reach.

In 1842, the enclave of Hong Kong became a British Crown Colony, whereupon the Triads swarmed in and took over. By 1845 they were so menacing that their organization was outlawed; by 1847 they had recruited three-quarters of the colony's Chinese population; a decade later they had an unbreakable grip on practically all its trade.[26]

In China, meanwhile, the Triads' horizons suddenly widened. Halfway through the 1800s, the British East Indies Company set out to hook the population on opium, brought in from India to pay for China's coveted tea, silk, cotton and rice.

The plan was a smashing success. Twenty million Chinese became addicts, from the lowliest coolies to the royal household. The Triads, long-time opium traders, made almost as much money as the British did.

An incredible windfall came a century later, when China, sinking under massive addiction, banned opium in all its forms. Refined heroin was soon worth its weight in gold, and the Triads had the field to themselves.

This was in 1928. The honourable Sun Yat-sen was gone, succeeded by another Triad brother named Chiang Kai-shek. The Triads, serving as his financial advisers, hit-men and dirty tricks department, had the run of the mainland. With Hong Kong besides, Asia's soaring illicit market in heroin was theirs.

From there they went wherever millions of Chinese emigrants went – practically everywhere – to do what they habitually did. From Singapore, Australia and the Philippines to Holland, Britain, Canada and America, Chinese communities were squeezed by the Triads exactly as Italian emigrés were squeezed by the Mafia: through blackmail, gambling, loan-sharking and monthly shakedowns, which they called 'dipping into the fragrant oil'.

World War II brought a fortunate split in their ranks. Some fell in with the Japanese occupation army, and so had a first fateful meeting with the Yakuza, their partners in crime ever since. Others had the foresight, or luck, to stick with Chiang Kai-shek.

When the war was over and Peking was falling to the communists, the Generalissimo took his Triad friends with him to Formosa, now Taiwan. With their help, he took along much of China's moveable wealth as well. They were amply rewarded.

While Chiang Kai-shek had fled eastward to Formosa, remnants of his Kuomintang army had retreated westward into the Shan states of northern Burma. There, in the heartland of the Golden Triangle, some 12,000 of the Generalissimo's troops joined by 10,000-odd Chinese refugees settled down among the most bounteous poppy fields on earth.

Forced to pay a deliberately onerous tax, local peasants were obliged to increase opium production from a modest 30 tons a year to 2,475 tons by latest count – well over half the world's entire supply.

No outsider could penetrate this fabulous mountain empire, commanded by the late Chiang Kai-shek's loyal generals and defended by a formidable private army. Whoever aspired to supply the heroin addict population of the United States or Europe was bound to apply to the Triads sooner or later. Only they have had privileged access to the Golden Triangle's prized commodity for the last half-century. They still do.

In the eyes of the law, the Yakuza came into existence only when it was outlawed in January 1992. Its presence in Japan over the previous two or three hundred years had never been acknowledged by the government. Though the measures finally taken against it were less than rigorous, the Yakuza sued the police for interfering with its 'right to be happy'.[27]

The official record suggested that it did have a right to be happy. Japan had next to no crime, on the books: 1.3%. The Yakuza's 100,000-odd members scarcely figured in even those statistics until 1992, when they racked up 2,000 homicides.[28]

The fact that they were listed in the phone book, handed out visiting cards and hung shingles on their office doors until that year implied that they had nothing to conceal. Indeed, a good deal of their $18 billion-a-year business is still conducted more or less in the light of day. Outlawed as the Yakuza, they have simply gone legal.

Their biggest syndicate, the Yamaguchi-gumi in Kobe, has set up a diversified holding company called Yamaki. Others have formed regularly chartered real estate companies, art galleries, high-tech consultancies, boutiques and a League of Purification to fight drugs.[29]

The Yakuza's crimes reflect a perfect understanding of the Japanese mentality, which values harmony, detests disorder and is obsessively concerned with saving face. The nation's pervasive fear of losing face has added an extra dimension to *omertà* as Sicilians know it, compounding shame with fear, enabling an organization of vicious delinquents to hold an entire country to ransom.

Every human frailty, social breach or surreptitious taste brought to light means losing face in Japan: not just gambling, prostitution, porno-tourism and drugs, but making debts, disturbing the peace, or appearing in court. The very act of denouncing a crime to the police means losing face.

Rather than risk such disgrace, Japanese governments have preferred not to reveal the Yakuza's true strength to the outside world until very recently – still less admit that it has hooked 600,000 Japanese on 'ice' (crystal methamphetamine), a world record.[30]

Giant corporations have preferred to pay a fortune in blackmail to avoid commotion at stockholders' meetings. Politicians and business-men have made regular payoffs in expensive gifts, known as *jumkatsuyu*, 'oil that lubricates society'.

Victims of extortion, fraud, terrifying harassment and scandalous usury (1% *a day*) have preferred to suffer in silence, or worse. The Yakuza's *sarakin*, or loan sharks, drove 2,300 Japanese to suicide some years ago. Another 7,300 gave up their jobs and families in despair.[31]

Thus, the Yakuza's own prey have helped to perpetuate its knightly self-image and glowing legends.

The Yakuza Man immortalized in a thousand novels and films (usu-ally financed by the Yakuza) is a gentleman crook of unfailing chivalry and suffocating virtue, who plunders the rich to feed the poor, just like Sicily's Mafia Man.

He dwells in exemplary togetherness with his Yakuza family. His body is covered with excruciatingly painful tattoos to demonstrate manly courage; and his small finger is often severed at the joint, to atone for an error.

'The actual procedure is to take a little silver knife on a table and you pull it towards you and bend over and your body weight will snap your finger off,' a former boss has explained.[32]

The origins of this gallant brotherhood are hopelessly buried in folklore. It is said, without proof, to have emerged in the early 1600s, when young townsmen banded together to resist the depredations of roving samurai warriors.

It is likelier to have appeared a century or so later with the *bakuto* gangs, as authors David Kaplan and Alec Dubro say in their fine book *Yakuza*. Gamblers working the nation's medieval highways, the *bakuto* used the word *yakusa* for a losing card combination (8-9-3, or ya-ku-sa).

Even that far back, the *bakuto* gangs were organized in tight, secret hierarchical families, vowed to silence, bound by a code replete with the usual death sentences for betrayal or disobedience.

Theirs was a primitive generation of gangsters, in a dark age of feu-dalism. By the turn of the century, however, Japan was moving fast into the rich industrial world, and the Yakuza with it. The traditional sword and martial arts gave way to the handgun and sunglasses. The new Yakuza Man was all business.

The years between the two world wars were a prelude to the Yakuza's explosive appearance on the international crime scene. Its 3,000 gangs came to control casinos, houses of pleasure, white slavery (foreign girls 'selling Spring'), porno-tourism, nightclubs, theatrical agencies, movie studios, publishing houses (largely cranking out Yakuza folk tales), professional sports, trucking, earth-moving, loan-sharking, money-laundering, drug trafficking and gun running.

Its collusion with bankers and brokers yielded billions of yen in unsecured loans and secret kickbacks on the stock market. One of its deals caused the near-collapse of the world's largest brokerage, Nomura, in 1991. (Nomura had turned over an amazing 25 billion yen, $180 million, in kickbacks to the boss of the Inagawa-kai, Japan's second largest Yakuza formation. He used the funds to expand operations in South Korea and the United States.)[33]

Its powers of corruption surpassed even the Sicilian Mafia's. The longtime grey eminence of Japanese politics, Shin Kanemaru, was exposed in 1992 for having taken a $4 million bribe from a Yakuza-run company. One hundred and thirty members of the Diet, Japan's parliament, proved to be on its payroll that year.[34]

Above all, its talent for blackmail could bring Japan's giant corporations to their knees. The technique, doubtless the envy of the international underworld, plays on Japan's fear of losing face.

Professional *sokaiya* buy a few company shares, demand a huge pay-off and, if refused, turn up at the next stockholders' meeting to spill company secrets or make a scene – shout, kick furniture, slap the chairman of the board. Thirty of Japan's largest corporations are among those who pay up. (Not all are so resigned. In 1991, 1,700 Japanese companies tried holding all their stockholders' meetings on the same day, hoping the *sokaiya* would run out of personnel. They didn't.)[35]

Until just a few years ago, this malignant growth on the body politic was a secret Japanese affliction. The Yakuza was all but unknown to the outside world, though it had long been at work there.

World War II had taken its gangsters wherever Japan's occupation led, all over Asia. Apart from meeting up with the Triads in Hong Kong, they made contact in Korea with local gangs eager to learn how to manufacture 'ice'. (Korea's White Tiger Gang was once invited to Tokyo for a ten-day seminar on how to behave like a Yakuza. 'They studied the rigid Yakuza code, took a night course on shooting firearms and came home sporting the close-cropped hairstyle of the Japanese mafia,' reported Kyodo News Service.)[36]

Similar connections established Yakuza colonies in Taiwan, the Philippines, Indonesia, Malaysia, Thailand, Singapore.

After the war, they hit the West. As Japan reached out with a new policy of *kokusaika* – 'internationalization' – Japanese businessmen took to the road, and the Yakuza followed. Within two decades or so, they were entrenched in Paris, London, Rotterdam, Sao Paolo, Honolulu, Los Angeles, San Francisco: blackmailing Japanese companies, running drugs and arms, laundering billions of dollars for themselves and their friends.

As if they'd all been to the same school, the Yakuza behaved much like the other mafias abroad. They took menial jobs as waiters and busboys, sheltered among and preyed pitilessly upon their own nationals, invested judiciously, bribed copiously, and managed to stay out of the cops' line of vision.

3

Crime Without Frontiers

In June 1990, the prime ministers of the European Community set aside two hours at their Dublin summit to consider the Sicilian Mafia, on the insistence of Chancellor Helmut Kohl. He feared that it would infect the entire continent once EC frontiers went down – that what had happened to Italy would happen to Germany and all Europe.[1]

For all he knew, it was happening already, he told me in a long evening's talk that spring. Over a broad round table giving on to his garden in Bonn, the Chancellor and his Interior Minister, Wolfgang Schäuble, spoke of their deepening worries for the coming single market: the nearly perpendicular rise in drug addiction; the drug traffickers' seemingly impenetrable cover; the banking system's permeability for money-laundering; the potential for extortion, fraud, penetration of legitimate business, corruption of the police and judiciary, political pollution.

The Mafia was the obvious threat, he said, if only because it *belonged* in the European Community. With a home seat in Sicily, its members had all the privileges of what would come to be known as the EC's thirteenth state. They alone, among all the world's big crime syndicates, would have the legal right in the single market to move their men, money and goods around the entire western half of the continent without impediment.

Before long, Kohl thought, the Mafia – and not just the Mafia – would be using both sides of the continent interchangeably: buying up property in the East, expanding the drug market there, laundering money, bribing bureaucrats and border guards, recruiting new talent. Among others, half a million unemployed agents of the communist security police would be for hire, he noted.

I mention this interview because it was the first indication of governmental concern in Western Europe. Nobody outside Italy was really looking at the Mafia in the spring of 1990; not many were doing so inside Italy either, at government level.

Chancellor Kohl had forced the matter onto the agenda of the Dublin summit over stiff Italian resistance, I learned later. Italy's Prime Minister, Giulio Andreotti, and Foreign Minister, Gianni De Michelis, had not only jibbed at discussing it but did not even want the word 'mafia' used.

If Italian government leaders were stubbornly reluctant to talk about the Mafia, their EC partners still tended to wonder if it was real, had no idea how to detect it at work, and had certainly not done much to keep its larcenous hands off their territory. Worse, such defences as they had counted on were caving in.

This was the stupendous year ending communist rule in Eastern Europe. Law enforcement was practically gone along the European Community's entire eastern perimeter. Men, money and goods were beginning to move back and forth with ease where the Iron Curtain had been.

Yet, moving into the final year of preparations for the single market, leaders of the European Community still radiated confidence in their immunity to the ills of pathologically distressed countries: the United States, say, or their own unfortunate Mediterranean partner.

When they finally began to take notice, halfway through 1990, they could not make up for five lost years. What Chancellor Kohl feared had happened already. Not only was the European Community infected, but the carriers were spreading east, and a virulent new pest was coming west.

Even as EC leaders met in Dublin, an underground counter-summit was held in East Berlin. Agents of the Soviet Interior Ministry had tracked ranking 'thieves-within-the-code' when they travelled out from Soviet Russia to meet with 'international mafia groups' and leaders of the Russian mafia operating abroad – in Germany and the United States especially. (This has been confirmed by Alexander Gurov, head of the Ministry's Sixth Department to Combat Organized Crime at the time.)[2]

The Russians had been trapped behind the Iron Curtain since the

All Thieves' Conference in Lvov, nearly half a century before. Now they could renew old ties with colleagues from 'the truly crook countries of Poland and Italy', and establish others. Crossing the frontiers of a crumbling Soviet empire had become a kid's game, to quote the head of Interpol Moscow, and the great criminal clans spanning Soviet territory from the Pacific to the very centre of Europe were free.

This was the summer when the last borders went down for the international underworld: well over a year ahead of the European Community's, rendering most of its strategy for defence obsolete.

The Russian mafia's appearance on the international scene coincided with an explosion of crime, starting along the geopolitical line once separating East from West. The perpetrators were a miscellaneous crowd on both sides, indigenous and foreign, revelling in the utter breakdown of law enforcement after the communist collapse.

They were soon using both sides of the continent interchangeably, just as Chancellor Kohl had predicted. As if in a self-fulfilling prophecy, his own country was the frontline state.

Apart from its wealth and power, Germany had strict bank secrecy, no currency controls, unbending rules protecting privacy, a severely hobbled police force, unwary politicians, Europe's most hospitable laws of asylum, and a commanding geographical position astride the continent.

Its borders were already down by mutual agreement with most of Western Europe; and after merging with ex-communist East Germany, its new border with Poland became a freeway to and from all Eastern Europe.

The 431-kilometre Oder-Niesse line is not much in the way of a frontier. The Niesse River is only ten metres wide, and the Oder is often shallow enough to wade across. Frankfurt-an-der-Oder, chief checkpoint on the German side, was manned in 1990 by a demoralized and virtually decapitated *Bundesgrenschutz* (border guard). The checkpoint on the Polish side was scarcely manned at all.

This was where the huge hole began, known in Euro-speak as the EC security deficit. After seventy years of communism, it could not be sealed.

The whole eastern end of Germany, formerly a rigid communist police state, was virtually unpoliced. Stasi's hundred thousand agents were gone, the Vopos were gone, customs officers, courts and magistrates serving the old regime were gone, and could not be replaced for years.

Germany wanted and needed to keep the border open anyway. Poland, the first satellite state to fight free of the Kremlin, had strong moral claims on all its Western neighbours. A prime victim of Hitler's occupation army, it had a particular claim on the German conscience. 'Never again barbed wire, an army, a wall –never again!' exclaimed a captain at *Bundesgrenschutz* headquarters in Berlin.[3] Perhaps more to the point, Poland was the gateway through which Germany now hoped to gain economic ascendancy over central Europe. Therefore Chancellor Kohl's government could not and would not put up a high fence against it.

Nothing short of that was likely to avert onrushing disaster. Poland's new democratic order, destitute and exceedingly fragile, could not even begin to deal with the policing of its frontiers in any direction.

Like Czechoslovakia, lower down on Germany's eastern flank, post-communist Poland offered marvellous opportunities for crime. The collapse of the most efficient, brutal and oppressive police system ever created had left a terrible void.

Policing under the communist regime had consisted largely of suppressing political dissidents. Those who had been good at it were opting for hasty retirement. Few breathing the bracing air of freedom cared to take their place.

'Not only do we have no computers, no faxes, no cars and no money, but we have no training and no manpower,' said Commander Marcinkowicz, Warsaw's Deputy Police Chief. 'We have 30% vacancies in the police force. People can't forget the secret police. Even though our civilian police were never political under the communists, that's the image. The spirit of liberty rules. Nobody wants to be a cop.'[4]

Apart from a severe shortage of personnel, Poland had no visa requirements for the rest of Eastern Europe, and no hope of plugging the leaks in a thousand-kilometre frontier with Russia.

Here was Europe's swinging door, the sole Soviet bloc country offering practically free passage from the rest of the bloc to the West and vice versa. 'We cannot control our borders; in effect, we *have* no borders,' said an Interior Ministry spokesman.

Desperate migrant populations from everywhere were already forming a critical mass in the country, soon to burst upon Western Europe. A sizeable criminal contingent moved among them.

By 1990, two million itinerant Soviet traders were quartering Polish territory, destined to become seven million in barely another year.[5]

With 'personal invitations' bought or forged, they were crossing over at Brest-Terespol, Mosciska-Medyko, Grodno-Kuznico, by car, train, bus, truck.

Bivouacked around the Palace of Culture in the capital and pushing out to the remotest provinces, they were hawking shoddy Soviet goods for the miraculous Polish zloty – the sole Soviet bloc currency freely convertible to dollars. 'For Russians, even Poland is a paradise,' a saddened Polish reporter observed.

The Russian mafia was collecting payoffs from all of them, said Poland's former Prosecutor-General, Alexander Herzog.

> We've known for many months that the Russian mafia is operating here. We know these traders have to pay the mafias in Moscow, Leningrad and Minsk, through their bases in Warsaw.
>
> Even in everyday life we see that this flow of traders is not spontaneous. In a small village in the south, where I would not imagine it could happen, I saw busloads of Soviet citizens arriving from Lithuania, Belorus, Russia, Georgia, Mongolia – two or three buses a day. They knew exactly where to peddle, where to sleep: they were organized.
>
> This mafia is bringing violence we've never seen here before. Shootouts with machine-guns, gas guns, bodies dumped from cars, car-bombs . . . We never catch the killers; their own people are afraid to testify, just like in the movies.
>
> We expect that to grow. Because our police are not prepared to fight such crimes – not here or anywhere in Eastern Europe. And Europe's borders are loosening: this Russian mafia is ready to move on.[6]

In the course of 1990, the Russian mafia moved on to Berlin. It was descending on Germany in force. Criminal bands erupting in all the ex-satellite states were drawn inevitably into its orbit: Rumanians, Hungarians, Czechs, Bulgarians, and especially Poland's own expert crooks. As if cloned by the Nomenklatura of Brezhnev's day, the Russians were quickly gaining dominion over organized crime throughout Eastern Europe.

Berlin, where their thieves-in-the-code gathered that summer, was their natural destination. A sizeable Russian emigré colony there offered what captive emigré colonies everywhere offer predatory countrymen: excellent camouflage and a steady income.

This particular colony also contained many fugitive crooks from the old country, who had their own protection racket going and controlled 85% of Berlin's gambling halls. The new Russian mafia was soon blackmailing the old Russian mafia fugitives, and selling protection to Russians already paying the old fugitives for protection.[7]

In addition, Germany had inherited a quarter of a million Red Army troops in the eastern Länder, due to remain for another four years. No sooner were these regions annexed to Federal Germany than the Red Army's camps became a grand bazaar. Sixty thousand Kalashnikovs disappeared from its armories within a few weeks; anti-air missiles were selling for $450.[8]

A Russian 'business mafia' began to collect state tax refunds on non-existent imported goods for the troops, bring pinball machines into the officers' mess, trade in black market alcohol and cigarettes, and strip the barracks of anything not welded to the floor.

Meanwhile, a Russian-Polish 'car mafia' appeared, stealing only the biggest and best: 24,000 Mercedes, Audis and BMWs went east that year: ten hours to Warsaw, another ten to Moscow.[9] Drivers ordered to stop at the Polish border simply crashed through the barrier and drove on.[10]

In those early days, German authorities were no more aware of the Russian mafia's presence *as a mafia* than of a whole submerged community of foreign crime groups in place for years.

Germany had nearly five million guest workers in dozens of emigré colonies. Apart from the Russian one, there was a small but fast-growing Chinese one, notable for its proliferating Chinese restaurants – 3,000 by late 1990 – with few customers and visibly affluent proprietors. Much larger communities of Italians and Turks had settled in over the years, along with Yugoslavs, Rumanians, Kurds, Afghanis, Sikhs, Tamils, Palestinians, Iranians. They all had wolves among the sheep.

Defeated by a babel of strange tongues and the usual wall of silence, German police had neither the fortitude nor will to try singling these out. Few believed in the bogeyman of organized crime up to then. The very phrase, *Organizierte Kriminalität – OK –* was alien and frightening in a country convinced that it had none.

I had experienced the smiling scepticism of Germany's famed criminal police, the *Bundeskriminalamt* (BKA), in Wiesbaden, when I came across the Turkish mafia myself in the mid-1980s. Germany teemed with Turkish drug traffickers at the time, accountable to the Bulgarian secret police and the godfathers of the trade in Istanbul. They had been working the German scene since at least 1975, when Turkey's mafia went into partnership with Sicily's: the one to supply morphine-base for heroin, the other to refine it.[11]

The two had then carved up the European market, leaving the continent's central and southern tiers mostly to the Sicilians and the northern one largely to the Turks, West Germany included.

From zero in 1975, West Germany reported 623 heroin overdose deaths just three years later. Thanks largely to Turkish-Sicilian persistence, the ODs doubled over the next decade (and would triple by 1990).[12]

Yet, coming from Istanbul with a thick file of evidence in the 80s, I ran into a polite blank at the BKA. The senior officials I met, in a cheery conference room curtained in flowered cretonne, assured me that the biggest traffickers on my list – among the Turkish mafia's top men in Germany, all indicted or convicted at home – were respectable businessmen above suspicion.[13]

Unused to criminal conspiracy, German police saw none in a singular configuration of Italian criminals either. If the Mafia existed at all – they weren't sure – it was Italy's problem. The odd Sicilian crook in Germany was only to be expected. The names called to their attention now and then by the Italian police rang no bells, tending to run together in a blur of Italianate vowels.

Actually, Germany had been the Sicilian Mafia's second home in Europe since the 1960s. The same bosses running the Sicilians' heroin network in America had used German territory all along to hide out from the law (or each other, when they fought), expedite drug shipments, wash money, and park their hit-squads or sleepers.

(A Sicilian drug trafficker caught in Germany in 1992, resident in the country since 1970, had been photographed by the FBI at a Mafia meeting in New York in 1946.)[14]

Exactly as they did in Brooklyn, they took cover among 70,000 Italian *Gastarbeiter* in the country, worked hard, and opened chains of pizza parlours wherever they went.

It was exceptionally difficult to mistake the distinctively felonious spoor of the pizza parlour. From the early 1960s onward, nearly all Sicilian mafiosi slipping in to America had gone into the pizza business, sheltered behind it, washed their drug money through it, skimmed the cash take, worked it to extort payoffs by arson, acid, bombing and murder, and shifted dope from one of its kitchen doors to another.[15]

They were doing the same in Germany for a quarter of a century before anyone caught on. The Mafia's footprints were all over the country, in small towns like St Ingbert or Dormagen, in big industrial cities like Frankfurt, in Baltic beach resorts and southern health spas like Baden-Baden.

Agostino Flenda, the Sicilian Mafia's pointman for heroin in northwest Europe, had operated out of a dingy Munich pizzeria since the early 1970s.[16] Roberto Palazzolo was living in Munich when he was arrested for massive money-laundering in the Pizza Connection case: reportedly as much as $5 billion.[17]

Agostino Badalamenti, whose uncle Gaetano had headed the Mafia's governing Cupola in Palermo, was shot and chopped to pieces in Solingen in 1984.[18] (His uncle Gaetano, among the biggest international drug traffickers alive, was 'revered as a god on earth' by his Mafia subjects, said the first famous Sicilian defector Tommaso Buscetta.)[19]

Giovanni Caruana, whose family was intermarried with the unforgettable Cuntrera brothers of Siculiana and Caracas, was shot and nearly killed in St Ingbert in 1975; four of his nieces and nephews had pizzerias in Germany. One, Alfonso Caruana, began washing narcodollars there in 1978. (He arrived that year with $600,000 in a suitcase, after paying a fine in Switzerland for failing to declare them.)[20]

Alfonso's brother, Pasquale, was picked up in Weil am Rhein a decade later, on an Italian warrant for drug trafficking. His travelling partner, Giuseppe Cuffaro (not the Aruba Cuffaro), was caught soon afterward in Baden-Baden, overseeing heavy heroin shipments in transit from Thailand to America.

Directing the Mafia's heroin traffic to the West since 1970, the Cuntreras had strategic forces positioned wherever strategy so required: Montreal, Miami, London, Brussels, Geneva, Malta, and Germany of course.

They had actually *invented* their money-laundering system in Germany, and so had an obvious interest in it when Pasquale Caruana was arrested there in 1988.

He had been cruising the German countryside for six weeks at the time. His partner had spent 220 days in Baden-Baden, clocking 33,000 kilometres for side trips in a rented Mercedes. (Between jaunts, Cuffaro had flown four times to Thailand, once to Venezuela and again to Canada, and made phone calls to Thailand, Canada, the US, Venezuela, Belgium, Spain, Luxembourg and Italy.)[21]

Interrogated by an Italian magistrate, Pasquale Caruana said he intended to establish residence in Germany, which the judge took to mean that he intended to 'create operative bases for the Mafia's drug traffic and money-laundering' there.[22]

All of Italy's crime groups were paying serious attention to Germany by then. Totò Riina in person visited often on 'fact-finding missions'. Lorenzo Nuvoletta, a top Camorra boss and a made member of the Mafia as well, had an official residence in Karlsruhe, near Baden-Baden. The Camorra's super-boss, Carmine Alfieri, maintained a home in Nuremberg.[23]

They had wonderful facilities in Germany by the late 1980s: a point-to-point circuit of pizza parlours, several thousand resident Sicilian mafiosi and Neapolitan camorristi without rap sheets; straw men to buy real estate or rent warehouses; and plenty of throwaway Italian helpers – kanonenfutter, cannon fodder, Germans call them.

The BKA had nearly all the pieces of this picture, but could not see the whole. Its director, Hans-Ludwig Zachert, a trim, closely-barbered and faultlessly tailored executive, is competent, conscientious and generally on top of his job. Until the autumn of 1990, however, he lacked the indispensable key to detecting the Mafia's presence.

Alessandro Pansa, one of Italy's most gifted cops, calls it 'a reciprocal knowledge of reality': an instant perception beyond Italy's perimeters of how mafiosi think, infiltrate, camouflage their operations and deploy their forces abroad.

For instance, says Pansa: 'Early in 1990, we informed the BKA that a suspected Sicilian mafioso had bought three hotels near Frankfurt. They checked him out and said he was clean. We advised them to watch out for arson in the neighbourhood. A couple of months later, six nearby hotels were burned down.'[24]

Arson, as Pansa knew but his German interlocutors did not, was standard Mafia practice for frightening businessmen into making the monthly payoff that had provided its basic income for nearly a century: the pizzo, which means 'wetting a small bird's beak'.

When, over the following year, 142 pizzerias and hotels were burned down in just two regions – Lower Saxony and Rhine-Westphalia – the BKA was not so easily gulled. 'We're 100% sure the Mafia was behind them,' Director Zachert told me then.[25]

The BKA's long voyage of discovery did not begin until the autumn of 1990. That September, two Sicilian waiters working in a pizzeria called Ai Trulli in Leverkeusen flew to Sicily, shot a judge dead, and flew back to wait on tables the same night. A witness actually saw them ambush Judge Rosario Livatino along the road to Agrigento on the southern Sicilian coast, chase him through a field, and shoot him in the mouth when he tripped.

The Ai Trulli had been on German police blotters since 1986, when a group of Sicilian mafiosi gathered there for a 'dinner of reconciliation'. The dinner had ended with a car trip to a nearby forest, where one of the reconciled diners was tied to a tree and burned alive.[26]

Four years after what had seemed like an isolated episode, this finally registered as part of an ongoing, sinister design. Two of Judge Livatino's killers, swiftly caught and arrested, proved to belong to a whole team of Mafia hit-men nesting in Germany – one of many.

Their home town was Palma di Montechiaro in the province of Agrigento, centrepiece of Tommaso di Lampedusa's classic work, *The Leopard*, and famous even in Sicily as an area of high Mafia density.

A thousand Sicilians from Palma di Montechiaro lived in Mannheim, among 15,000 Italian guest workers. Dozens were thought to be commuting from Germany as 'groups of fire' in Palma's endless Mafia feuds.

A *carabiniere* sergeant stationed in Palma since 1960, Giuliano Guazzelli, could guess the identities of Judge Livatino's killers merely from a meagre description of 'two tall young men who didn't even look like Sicilians'. He was killed for that a year later.

Some weeks after Livatino's death, the BKA invited Judge Falcone to Wiesbaden. Chancellor Kohl had been pressing for more information on the Mafia since the Dublin summit the previous June, Dr Zachert told me. Falcone brought 'a burst of light', he said.

The Mafia was not an association of independent families, Falcone explained: it was 'one and indivisible', with 'extremely rational and functional rules'. The threat it posed, therefore, was not so much in its numbers as in its 'structure and capacity to put a unified strategy into place'.[27]

'He gave us a picture of what Italian investigators were learning about the Mafia's network in Germany – much worse than we dreamed,' Zachert said. 'He warned that we should expect a still bigger invasion because the Mafia was looking for new markets in Eastern Europe.

'He turned over names of people in seventy-six Mafia families. We set up a SIMA computer network to check this with our own criminal files. The computer threw up 480 of these Sicilians in our files, some going back a quarter of a century. Now we're checking 4,000 more . . .'[28]

Eventually, the BKA's list of suspected mafiosi on German soil ran to twenty-seven typed pages. Sixty-eight Italian crime cells were detected across the country: around Munich and Frankfurt, along the Rhine, in Cologne, Hannover, Stuttgart and Berlin, Leipzig and the outlying eastern Länder.[29]

New settlers kept arriving, sent up from Sicily with seed money to expand operations, as Italian investigators were told by the endlessly informative Mafia defector Leonardo Messina.

Looking back, the BKA realized what all this meant. The Sicilian Mafia had 'chosen Germany as its operative base in Europe for the years to come,' declared BKA Director Hans-Ludwig Zachert.[30]

These were the years, starting January 1, 1993, for which the Mafia had been preparing. 'They're going to open the frontiers: if Italy is big, Mr President, imagine how big Europe is. That's why we had to think ahead,' explained a major defector, Antonino Calderone, to the Italian parliament's Anti-Mafia Commission.

Thinking further ahead, Men of Honour were staking out territory in Germany's new eastern Länder well before 1993. Only hours after the Berlin Wall came down late in 1989, a mafioso positioned in West Berlin got his orders to cross over. Italian police were listening in as Giovanni Tagliamento, member of the powerful Morabito family of Catania in southeastern Sicily, called with the instructions:

'Go in there and start buying.'

'What should I buy?'

'Everything – restaurants, discos, pizzerias – everything!'[31]

Chancellor Kohl knew next to nothing of these matters when we talked in Bonn, just months after the Wall fell. The awakening came afterward, when a horde of newcomers from every corner of the planet – racketeers, con-men, contract-killers, gamblers, pimps, car thieves, burglars, swindlers, counterfeiters, money-washers, arms runners and drug traffickers – swept into Germany like an army of omnivorous ants.

A rolling criminal tide hit the country, stirring a diffuse sense of uncertainty and unease. The crime rate doubled in Berlin in barely six months. Car thefts shot up to 46,000 over the next year and 87,000 the year after, nearly one in every five stolen all over Western Europe. Prospective buyers took to crossing over from Poland and photographing the car of their dreams in some East German driveway, for delivery to Warsaw the next morning.[32]

Fraud, forgery, arson, smuggling, prostitution, gambling, daytime burglary, spread like a monstrous inkblot. A million stolen car radios were shipped out of the country in containers, bound for Poland, Russia, Hungary and Czechoslovakia. Over 125,000 credit cards were filched.[33]

The *pizzo* – *schutzgeld*, rakeoff – was replicated in a dozen languages: four out of five Italian businessmen in Frankfurt were paying it, as were similar proportions of Yugoslavs, Turks, Russians, Chinese. Violence erupted: bodies in cement coffins, murder on the steps of a court-house, muggings, break-ins, shootouts in broad daylight.

An estimated two billion deutschmarks' worth of narcodollars washed through German banks within the year.[34] (An American mafia courier was picked up with $1.2 million at Los Angeles airport, heading for Frankfurt.) A torrent of counterfeit dollars poured in.

Seizures of heroin quadrupled in 1990, the bulk coming from Czechoslovakia and Poland. Overdose deaths rose by 50% in a single year (from 989 to 1,500). By the year's end, Germany was said by Interpol to have become 'the main point of transit for the entire European heroin market'.[35]

An incredible two-and-a-half tons of cocaine were confiscated that year – 'Certainly more than our German market could stand, *so they are creating demand*,' said the BKA's man for narcotics.[36]

This was not just the work of lawless foreigners, though these became the pretext for ugly racist violence. Germany's own criminals, many and tough, actually accounted for nearly two-thirds of all the crimes on the books in 1990.[37]

Increasingly in partnership with the big foreign syndicates, they were up to the eyes in some of the biggest operations across the coun-try. In a single two-ton shipment of cocaine, German traffickers were entangled with those of eight other nationalities: Yugoslav, Dutch, Austrian, Chinese, French, Venezuelan, Uruguayan and Sicilian. (The Sicilians were giving the orders, though.)[38]

For all the pickings in Federal Germany, the big crime groups were unmistakably focusing on the new eastern Länder.

Barely a year after the communists' fall, intelligence analysts in the *Bundesnachrichtendienst* (BND) sent a disturbing position paper to Chancellor Kohl. The international drug cartels were 'setting aside as much as half of their income to develop new markets in the European Community,' the BND said.

In particular, the Mafia, the Yakuza, the Colombians and the Turks were investing in government bonds, real estate, building societies, hotels and casinos, finance and leasing companies, banks and insurance companies; buying up airlines and trucking concerns to handle their own distribution; acquiring shares in newspapers, radio and TV stations; donating to political parties.

Though all twelve EC states were targeted, the 'heaviest concentration' was in eastern Germany, the BND found. The Italian Mafia alone had invested 50 billion deutschmarks there, it said.[39]

Some of this appeared to be guesswork. Investigators in those early days were just picking up the first stray signs of an unknown animal, moving through dense undergrowth and exquisitely gun shy.

Regular police in the BKA could not find proof of anything like a fifty-billion-DM Mafia investment, for instance. But they did find 'clear structures of organized criminality' emerging in the eastern regions:

> Criminals from organized crime strongholds have been buying fixed assets, founding firms, and buying into existing companies on former East Germany territory. Dummy enterprises are used to get licences, especially for sex shops, video-tape libraries, restaurants, amusement arcades . . .
>
> The goal is not merely to invest laundered profits, but to use legitimate enterprises for criminal operations.[40]

The BKA did not know then that the Mafia was penetrating major legitimate enterprises in the West of Germany as well as the East.

In the summer of 1990, Italy's *Guardia di Finanza* had uncovered a disturbing Mafia deal with Philip Holzmann Ag of Frankfurt, a colossus of the German construction industry. Holzmann, beating out a Fiat subsidiary, had won a six-million-dollar contract to build a dam in Corleone, Sicily: home of Totò Riina and of Luciano Leggio, the notorious *capo di tutti i capi* preceding him.

The contract, awarded in 1988, had been hailed as marking Sicily's entrance into the Common Market. In fact, the Mafia had procured it for Holzmann in exchange for getting all the sub-contracts.

Italy's parliamentary Anti-Mafia Commission found a number of things wrong with the whole dam project: the absence of inert materials anywhere in the area, for example, and excessive delays in expropriating the land.

Despite the German firm's known efficiency, construction costs kept rising. The dam was nowhere near completion two years later.

Mafia salesmen had been making similar offers all over Western Europe, the Guardia di Finanza discovered. Over 600 charges were brought against a Mafia holding company, distributing the sub-contracts throughout Italy.[41]

Nobody knew how far the Mafia infection was spreading. Before much longer, however, its powers of corruption would appear to bear out Chancellor Kohl's blackest premonitions.

Germany had its share of homegrown corruption. By authoritative estimate, four out of five public works contracts in Frankfurt, the quintessence of free enterprise, were 'decided in advance'.[42] As Kohl had told me, however, he *knew* that kind of graft. It was some unknown foreign kind that he feared.

In fact, Germany in 1990 was like a flowerbed ready for Mafia planting. Twenty or thirty years of patient cultivation were paying off for the Sicilians' underground crime colony. Mafiosi washing and re-investing billions of dollars there could not imaginably be doing so without buying help from politicians, businessmen and forces of the law.

They 'probably had relations and connections' with the German establishment, admitted BKA Director Zachert two years later. 'We have suspicions, not proofs, that our institutions are compromised,' he told a conference in Rome.[43]

There was no longer a doubt then that Germany's police were beginning to succumb. In heavily populated North Rhine-Westphalia, beset by Yugoslav, Turkish, Polish, Russian and Italian as well as German hoods, one in every five organized crime cases coming to court involved bent cops.[44]

Within a remarkably short time, all the Chancellor's presentiments were coming true. Germany was 'the face of a criminal Europe without frontiers', warned an association of Italian businessmen in a chilling survey of the continent's underworld scene.[45] More perilously exposed than any of the EC twelve save Italy, it embodied their paralyzed state of unreadiness to meet the enemy.

Apart from reasons of self-interest, common to all, it was a victim of its admirable intentions. Repelled by memories of Hitler's brutal police state, German lawmakers had gone as far as they could in the opposite direction.

'Why did your people choose Germany?' Zachert would ask the Sicilian defector Tommaso Buscetta, after discovering the Mafia's shocking strength there. Because of Germany's 'excessively punctilious legislation' and 'total lack of regulations for money-laundering', was Buscetta's reply.[46]

Indeed, Germany's legal code was an iron defence of the individual's right to be safe from government intrusion. *Datenschutz*, the basic law protecting privacy, was sweeping, rigid and seemingly unalterable.

German police could not use phone taps save in life-threatening or serious property damage situations. They were flatly forbidden to put a bug in a wall. They could not wear body mikes except in self-defence, or present such tapes in court even then.

They could not effect surreptitious entry under court order. They could not infiltrate an undercover agent without risking his likely death, since he could do nothing illegal such as trespassing, or betting in a poker game with the mob.

They were obliged to report a crime on sight: 'to strike before the iron is hot', as a sympathetic American colleague put it. They could not make a move without convincing evidence that a crime was about to be committed. They could not check a suspect's bank records. They could not investigate tips on money-laundering, which was not a criminal offence.

Such strictures meant that the BKA, though forewarned, could not listen in when delegates from the American mafia's Patriarca family of Boston met with German counterparts in a Wiesbaden hotel to talk about gambling casinos.[47]

Nor could it open a file on the Sicilian mafioso with orders from Palermo to buy up everything in East Berlin. Nor, despite urgent signals from the Italian police, could it go after a lengthening list of others investing dirty money in the eastern Länder; the source of the money could not be questioned.[48]

An American judge's request to freeze $20 million of suspected drug money in a German bank account could not be granted.[49] Two Turkish drug traffickers caught by border guards with $700,000 in cash could keep the cash and run. (They did not even lose their social welfare cheques as registered political refugees, since cross-information among German agencies was not permitted.)[50]

These laws, sacrosanct in a resolutely free society, were being used to beat the law and savage the society. With exemplary intentions, Germany had become a privileged sanctuary for every kind of international crook.

The fact that many of the crooks invading Germany answered to one or another of the big international syndicates was just beginning to register, but not the fact that the syndicates were joining forces.

Secret criminal brotherhoods in planetary communion might have been a script for a bad movie. Most Western investigators would have taken the idea for fiction in 1990. A handful, mainly Italian, had reason to know better.

Early that year, Italy's parliamentary Anti-Mafia Commission had sent an urgent message to the UN Assembly. Organized crime was 'taking on the characteristics of an extremely dangerous world calamity', the Commission said:

> International criminal organizations have reached agreements and understandings to divide up geographical areas, develop new market strategies, work out forms of mutual assistance and the settlement of conflicts . . . and this on a planetary level.
>
> We are faced with a genuine criminal counter-power, capable of imposing its will on legitimate states, of undermining institutions and forces of law and order, of upsetting delicate economic and financial equilibrium and destroying democratic life.[51]

The report dropped like a lead balloon at the time.

Later, when the signs grew more insistent, the press took to speaking of a 'Euromafia', presumably under the Sicilian Mafia's command. This was unfair to the Mafia's big league colleagues. Obviously, the criminal legions advancing on Europe were not solely under Sicilian command.

But they *deferred* to the Sicilians. The Mafia's structure, sophistication and connections in the outside world, its lines of command binding Europe to America, the subtlety of its hold on men and its extraordinary staying power, came closer than any to meeting the needs of the times. It was organized crime's 'role-model for the year 2,000', Italy's Interior Minister said.

Part 2

A Meeting of
Like Minds

4

The Sicilian Mafia
Looks East

'If you want to know if I worry about dying, I began to worry as soon as I joined. Everybody worries about dying in Sicily. Once the bosses used to die in their beds, now nobody dies in his bed any more.'

This was Leonardo Messina, the Man of Honour with impressive credentials and exalted connections, describing the Sicilian Mafia's long slide into manic distrust and coarse butchery.[1]

He was testifying at a time of intense drama, in the months following the terrible murders of Judges Giovanni Falcone and Paolo Borsellino in the spring of 1992.[2] Not in over a hundred years of killing had the Mafia killed with such satanic ferocity: half a ton of explosive to blow up Judge Falcone, his wife and three bodyguards; a bomb for Judge Borsellino blasting the walls of four apartment buildings up to the tenth floor.

Two hundred and eighty Men of Honour had broken their blood oath of *omertà* since then, and crossed over to the side of the law. Some were sickened by the Mafia's growing savagery; others were simply running for their lives.

They described a criminal fraternity in the grip of a tyrant bent on destroying all that preceded his rule – a whole generation of Mafia bosses and soldiers, a timeless family structure, a fruitful partnership with Italy's governing class going back half a century, indeed the very survival of what Messina called 'historical memory' in the ranks of Cosa Nostra.

The tyrant was Salvatore 'Totò' Riina, nicknamed the Beast, soon to fall into the hands of the state he had plundered, manipulated and humiliated for twenty years.

Chosen heir of the notorious Luciano Leggio, imprisoned since 1974, Riina had presided over the longest era of ferocious bloodletting in Mafia history. The Great Mafia War of 1981–83, which he won, had left over a thousand of his enemies dead: shot, strangled, burned, beaten, tortured, dismembered, beheaded, trussed like goats, hacked with axes, dissolved in acid, barbecued on a grill, thrown to the pigs.

The Mafia's parallel war against the Italian state in those years, which he led, had featured the murders of five judges, a prosecutor-general, a state prosecutor, two police chiefs, a colonel and a captain of the *carabinieri* (Italy's elite paramilitary police), a crusading journalist, the Christian Democratic Party's provincial secretary, the Communist Party's regional secretary, the president of Sicily's regional government, and the Prefect of Sicily, General Carlo Alberto Dalla Chiesa, the state's highest representative on the island.[3]

Neither war ever ended. Other judges, prosecutors, journalists and policemen were murdered periodically before Falcone and Borsellino went down; and after finishing off his enemies within Mafia ranks, Riina took to killing off his allies.

Nobody was safe from his corroding suspicion after the earliest defectors appeared. By order of the Cupola in 1982, the death sentence for them was extended not only to their close relatives, including mothers, sisters and aunts, but to their friends and mere acquaintances. Agents of Riina's personal intelligence service were planted secretly among Sicily's 150 Mafia families from then on.[4]

Riina's Mafia was more frightening and mysterious than anything in Italy's experience when the new defectors appeared. Exposed briefly to the light after the Great Mafia War, it had quickly snapped shut again.

Earlier defectors in the 1980s, known as *pentiti*, had had their day in court. Judge Falcone and his small pool of investigators had sent 474 Mafia defendants to trial. Tommaso Buscetta and a score of others had testified against them; 323 had been convicted and sentenced to some twenty-six centuries in jail.

By rights, Sicily's 5,000 made mafiosi should have been in full retreat when the verdict came down in December 1987.

They had taken rough punishment in New York's Pizza Connection trial that same year. Betrayed and debunked by their own members, raked over in the press, damned in millions of pages of courtroom testimony, they appeared to have lost it all: their heroin network in

America, their heroin labs in Sicily, their money laundries in Switzerland, the cream of their leadership. Even the head of their governing Cupola – Michele Greco, 'the Pope' – was behind bars for life.

Yet barely a year after Palermo's historic maxi-trial, it might never have happened. Judge Falcone's anti-Mafia pool was dismantled, investigation was at a standstill, and the Mafia was going from strength to strength.

In a grotesque parody of justice, Italy's Court of Cassation, highest court of appeal, had overturned 480 Mafia convictions since 1986. Only 60 of the 342 mafiosi found guilty in the maxi-trial were still in custody (down to ten by 1992).

The others had either got out provisionally and vanished, or had got out, period. (In January 1992, a member of the Cupola sentenced to life imprisonment for ninety-nine murders strolled out of a Palermo hospital in his pyjamas, leaving his cellular phone on the bed.)[5]

The fact that these criminals could walk free was not just a joke on Italian justice. The entire structure of Mafia power depended on it. One reason was its need to project an image beyond human reach: a disembodied, malevolent power emanating death and destruction, impervious to the law. But its more pressing need was to protect its own men.

Sicily's Men of Honour had to be sure they would not go to prison, or if they did, would not stay long. Their methods of assuring this had worked smoothly since the mid-nineteenth century (except for a brief interlude under Mussolini).

Today we know the secret of their seemingly miraculous recovery from every legal affliction. The fix was in. The new *pentiti* have explained exactly how it was done.

The trials were 'adjusted', Messina said:

Why didn't Cosa Nostra give a damn when the maxi-trial began? Because we knew it would end in a soap bubble; that was the word passing around to tranquillize our men.

The word was out that this trial, like all the others, would go a certain way in the lower court . . . But everybody knew it would have to go well in the Court of Cassation . . .

Why did we kill Judge Scopelliti, who was going to be the prosecutor in the Court of Cassation? Because he was talked to, and he wouldn't promise to take the right line.

When a Man of Honour has to go on trial, everybody on the

bench and on the jury is 'talked to'. We talk directly to the judge. There are judges who've been contacted by Cosa Nostra, who wouldn't promise to let us off. They were killed on the street . . .

When they can't control judges, they kill them. Look how many have been killed – count them . . .[6]

So, while a handful of judges and cops laid their lives on the line to fight the Mafia, its men could feel free to kill them off with impunity. 'If I'm a mafioso killer and I know the trial can be *adjusted*, I'll get more arrogant, no? That's why we're so arrogant, because we always knew the trials could be adjusted,' testified Gaspare Mutolo, another important defector.[7]

In January 1992, however, this time-tested arrangement broke down. The Court of Cassation upheld the verdict in Palermo's maxi-trial.[8] Men of Honour convicted but out of jail were hauled back in. The politician serving as the Mafia's main liaison with Rome had failed to deliver.

The Mafia's first response to this electrifying event was to kill the politician who had failed to deliver. Salvo Lima, Sicily's top Christian Democrat and longtime spokesman for then-Prime Minister Giulio Andreotti, was gunned down on the streets of Palermo.

The death of Salvo Lima was an arrow in the heart of the Italian establishment. Many believed it was a direct message to Andreotti, the most powerful politician in the country since World War II.

It was primarily because of his enduring relations with Lima that Andreotti came under judicial investigation afterward for an allegedly 'positive contribution', neither 'episodic nor marginal', to the Mafia's 'interests and aims'.[9]

Lima was a made member of the Mafia, a secret revealed months after his murder. Guarantor of Andreotti's electoral base in Sicily for a quarter of a century, he was described by several important defectors in 1992 as 'our best guarantee that everything could be settled in Rome'.[10]

The verdict in Palermo's maxi-trial was by far the most urgent matter to be settled in many years. When the Court of Cassation upheld the verdict instead of reversing it as expected, the Cupola decided that Lima 'was no longer any use to us', Messina said. 'We had to show that anyone who doesn't keep his word must die; Cosa Nostra is like that.'

Salvo Lima could not keep his word because the *Palazzo*, the faceless command of the Italian establishment, could not keep its end of the bargain any more.

With the collapse of communism in Eastern Europe, the whole structure of political power in Italy was coming undone. Fear of communism had held the governing parties together and kept them in office since the start of the cold war. Once the fear was gone, they were fair game.

For fifty years, they had preferred to co-exist rather than collide with the Mafia. Some politicians might have hated the thought, while managing to live with it. But those who ran the Palazzo were active accomplices, providing political and judicial cover in exchange for votes, power and a share in Mafia payoffs.

By court estimate, the Mafia had upwards of half a million captive votes in Sicily alone: one in every five or so on the island, one in every two polled by Christian Democrats, the swing vote for a tenth of the national electorate. With its allies on the southern Italian mainland, it controlled or conditioned around three-and-a-half million votes altogether – a third of southern Italy's.[11]

Regularly, at election time, the top Mafia brass decided how to hand the votes out, as the *pentito* Calderone has explained:

> The families vote for all the parties except the communists and the [neofascist] MSI . . . Before the elections, we'd get the signal for certain names and parties, and our provincial commissions would take charge. Every family's members, relatives and friends could amount to thousands and thousands of votes – two hundred thousand just for the province of Catania.[12]

Since the Mafia always collects, it was paid off in a thousand ways, with rigged public contracts, giveaway state credits, pork-barrel jobs, plummy government posts, golden gifts of silence, and 'adjusted' trials guaranteeing its perpetual immunity .

In this it was helped by a singularly potent deviate wing of the Masonry. In 1977, a covered Masonic lodge had formally invited the Mafia to enrol two members from each of its provinces in Sicily, guaranteeing secrecy. The invitation was debated at a regional conference and finally accepted, on condition that the Mafia should learn the Masons' secrets, but not the other way round. Nearly all the top bosses had joined, defectors revealed.[13]

'Men of Honour who get to be bosses belong to the Masonry: this must not escape you,' Messina told the parliamentary Commission. 'Because it is in the Masonry that we can have total contact with businessmen, with the institutions, with the men who administer power . . .' Indeed, Messina added, this secret Masonic connection is 'an obligatory passage for the Mafia on a world level'.[14, 15]

Through any of Palermo's fourteen covered Masonic lodges, among others, the Mafia could in fact reach up to Licio Gelli's now defunct Propaganda Due, the P2, and so to the topmost levels of the Palazzo. (A stupefying list of P2 members found in 1981 included seventeen army generals, four airforce generals, nine carabinieri generals, eight admirals, the heads of all three secret services, thirty-eight deputies and senators, fourteen magistrates, three cabinet ministers and five prefects.)[16]

No amount of rumour and speculation over the years could match the reality, as the new *pentiti* provided a lengthening list of politicians, judges, policemen and intelligence agents forming an intricate web of complicity enmeshing the Mafia with Italy's governing class.

Clearly this was why, despite Totò Riina's unrelenting assault on the state, the Italian establishment was compliant throughout his long reign. But even a governing class so deeply compromised could no longer resist the pressure for change by January 1992, and not just from its own electorate.

Chancellor Kohl knew by then that the Sicilian Mafia was using Germany as its operational base for Europe. He was not the only one leaning hard on Andreotti's government to bear down on it. The whole European Community was doing so.

The Community's inner borders would be coming down in just another year. Foreign Minister De Michelis, confronted by blunt-spoken colleagues in a swing around EC capitals, came back shaken in 1991. Italy, 'cradle of organized crime in Europe', was 'the biggest single risk to the Community's security in an open market', declared a majority of the European Parliament's deputies that year.[17]

Starting in the winter of 1992, therefore, the government moved to close some legislative loopholes, coordinate police work, protect defectors turning state's witness, close down dubiously elected city councils in the south and bar Mafia-prone politicians from office.

Somebody also saw to the Court of Cassation when the maxi-trial came up on appeal. The Court's incorrigible sentence-basher, Corrado Carnevale – the untouchable judge who had thrown out 480 Mafia convictions since 1986 – was taken off the case.[18]

Carnevale had been 'Cosa Nostra's guarantee' in Italy's highest court, the *pentiti* said later. 'When we were told "Carnevale's there," we'd say "Jesus be praised!" ' Mutolo declared. 'This defeat was like a poison to us. We had to overturn everything – the judiciary, the political world.'[19]

Upon Carnevale's removal and the subsequent court ruling,

therefore, the Mafia broke off relations with its old political partners.

The Cupola's choice of strategy was an ultimate declaration of war, the supreme expression of Totò Riina's preference for military force over other forms of persuasion.

The Mafia was dismissing the politicians and parties it had used for half a century, and setting out to find new ones who would get the point – come to terms, give up all thoughts of resistance, back off.

The strategy was worked out at a conclave of top bosses lasting some three months, in the Sicilian province of Enna.[20] The death of Salvo Lima immediately afterward was a warning. The real message came when the highest symbols of resistance to the Mafia, Judges Falcone and Borsellino, were literally blown away in a deliberately terrifying show of strength.

Totò Riina, all modesty in his wilted shirt and crumpled pants, rising to his feet deferentially to answer a judge's questions, looked as if he needed help to read and write. Yet during his reign the Mafia grew into an impenetrably complicated corporate monster.

Contrary to the school of wishful thinkers, the Mafia has not been crowded out of the heroin trade. Though its dominion over the worldwide market is gone, it still has 'the central role in controlling the internal market and traditional traffic with the United States', says Italy's Interior Ministry.[21]

While heroin and cocaine are still 'its principal source of income at home and abroad', however, the Mafia has diversified sideways, upward and outward.

Its strength can no longer be measured by conventional crime statistics in a single country, certainly not in Italy alone. It operates in dozens of countries, and spreads its wealth among them in a thousand undetectable ways.

The days are gone when its finances were entrusted to a couple of identifiable crooked bankers like Michele Sindona and Roberto Calvi, both of whom died in the end for failing to deliver.[22] Today the Mafia not only uses hundreds of bankers, but buys banks.[23] Its members take along financial advisers in their travels abroad, and live in good part on the income from a mountain of accumulated capital.

'Drugs have made us immensely rich,' testified Leonardo Messina. 'When a heroin deal is on, the families are asked if they want to chip in. There are some who chipped in 200 million lire long ago and in three years they had 25 billion. The fathers die and leave it to their sons.'

By now, therefore, the Mafia has reached a 'third level' in its financial affairs, say Italian authorities. It no longer depends wholly on crime for a livelihood. Half of its revenue comes from laundered capital re-invested in legitimate enterprises around the globe: financial and leasing companies, real estate, commerce, industry, agro-industry, gold mines.[24]

Not that the Mafia is going straight, 'either today or tomorrow', Judge Falcone explained shortly before he died. 'A mafioso never ceases to be a mafioso,' he said. Legitimate enterprise is used to cover the illegitimate kind, as always.

Since such foreign revenues are largely untraceable, the only estimates available are those of its Gross *Domestic* Product in Italy: $20 billion to $25 billion a year.

Drugs account for only a fifth of that. Extortion, public works contracts, bank robberies and theft account roughly for another fifth each, and fraud, gambling, prostitution, smuggling for most of the rest.[25] The fraud includes swindling the EC out of a quarter of a billion dollars just for grain in 1992.[26]

The Mafia's worldwide money laundries and arms traffic are not included.

The figures are supposed to take in four Italian organized crime groups, but the four are really one, defectors say. 'There is only Cosa Nostra; the others are simply a manner of speaking,' declares Messina:

> You can call it Camorra or 'Ndrangheta or Sacra Corona Unita [the younger United Sacred Crown], but those are just expressions. The structure is always Cosa Nostra . . .
>
> The people you call camorristi belong to Cosa Nostra. The summit of the Camorra is Cosa Nostra, the summit of the 'Ndrangheta is Cosa Nostra. The Mafia *invented* the Sacra Corona Unita. The 'Ndrangheta is only a name; the Sacra Corona is a nickname . . .[27]

'Forget about the Camorra and the 'Ndrangheta. They don't exist. The Mafia exists. Cosa Nostra exists,' was Tommaso Buscetta's way of putting it.[28]

Together, the Mafia and its wards have around 15,000 members and perhaps ten times as many helpers, occupying the contiguous regions of Sicily, Calabria, Puglia and Campania, surrounding Naples. These are called the 'regions at risk', in that the Mafia controls the territory there: the entire southern third of the country, in which the government cannot enforce the law.[29]

Controlling the territory means 'knowing and preventing the manoeuvres of an adversary, exercising dominion over the population, practising extortion, imposing recognition as the authority that knows everything and can do everything,' says the Italian parliament's Anti-Mafia Commission.[30]

In this third of Italy, three in every four businessmen pay the monthly *pizzo*. They have even been assured officially that it is legal. In a ruling that scandalized the press and public, a Sicilian magistrate has held that owners of a business have a right to avoid 'conflictuality', by which he meant being burned down, bombed out or shot.

'Whoever doesn't pay should know what happens sooner or later. Somebody in the Rinascente department store group refused to pay, and 40 billion lire went up in smoke. If everybody did that, all Sicily would go up in smoke,' the magistrate said (whereupon Palermo's Chamber of Commerce proposed to make the *pizzo* tax-deductible).[31]

This is no longer the old-fashioned shakedown; it is the way in for a commercial kill. 'First they ask you for money . . . maybe 400, 600 or 800 million lire ($700,000). Then they offer you loans at low interest or none, they tell you what suppliers to use, they make you hire their friends. Finally they tell you they're joining your company. Then they take everything,' says the president of Catania's Association of Industrialists.[32]

Or else, they buy up all the company's outstanding debts, and then come around with their enforcer-bailiffs to collect or take over. (Perhaps they learned this trick from the Yakuza, who have done this for years.)

Nobody in the Italian south gets a public works contract unless the Mafia says so: this up to now, though it may be changing like so much else in Italy.

Until its exposure in 1993, Sicily's entire multi-billion-dollar public works programme was controlled directly by the Mafia, through a regularly constituted company called Sirap. Founded a decade earlier in the office of Salvo Lima, who headed it, Sirap awarded the contracts, collected the rakeoffs and parcelled them out in fixed percentages.

The contracts were allocated in Lima's office and rubber-stamped by city councils or Sicily's regional assembly. Consenting politicians got their cut, but a Mafia 'ambassador' dispensed it, answering directly to Totò Riina.[33]

There were no competing bids. 'If somebody gets in the way, he dies,' explained Leonardo Messina. Northern companies coming south had to 'adjust to Cosa Nostra's ways', Messina added, and they did.

Fiat, building a six-billion-dollar car plant in San Nicola di Melfi, paid a 7% commission at every stage of construction. The Roman earth-moving company laying down the plant's sewer network shelled out $200,000 up front and $16,000 monthly thereafter.[34]

The Mafia could get away with this for fifty years because many northern Italians saw it as a peculiarly Sicilian phenomenon; it was dangerous, violent, grasping, stifling, arrogant, but workable only in the poor, backward, derelict south.

Once it became a national incubus – the source of a nationwide narcotics epidemic, an arbiter of the nation's finance, a direct menace to the nation's governing class and threat to its credibility in Europe – opinions changed.

As all Italy knows now, the Mafia has been implanted in every major city north of Naples for a long time. In the course of 1992, police uncovered a cell in wealthy Bologna led by Totò Riina's eighty-four-year-old uncle, in command of all Mafia cells in the region for two decades.

Another cell, near civilized Florence, managed a weapons supermarket. A third, in the prosperous Tuscan town of Prato, operated a busy money-washing machine.

A joint police survey throughout affluent Tuscany found Mafia investments in factories (Prato), hotels (Versilia, Montecatini, Chianciano), fisheries (Viareggio), marble (Carrara), and the splendid vineyards around Siena.[35]

A consortium of all four crime groups was found to be running drugs and arms for the entire north out of a Milanese car park that autumn; a ton of cocaine was on the way there when police arrived.[36]

Milan has always been the big attraction. Capital of the wealthiest region on the continent, this is the most sophisticated and European of Italian cities: the nerve centre of industry and banking, the nation's window on the financial world, the natural channel to the money markets of Frankfurt, London, Tokyo, New York.

Here, in the early 1970s, the notorious Luciano Leggio, passing as Baron Osvaldo Fattori, created a whole new Mafia condominium for theft, extortion, building rackets, gambling casinos, a muscle market for southern immigrants and kidnapping on a grand scale. (This was when Paul Getty Jr had an ear cut off by 'Ndrangheta kidnappers, holding him for a million-dollar ransom in Calabria's bleak Aspromonte mountains.)

Then, at the end of the 70s, the Mafia and Camorra jointly set up a high-powered financial centre in Milan. Working through a front company called CITAM, its 160 stalwarts included the Cuntrera brothers of Caracas, the Zaza brothers of Naples, Tommaso Buscetta and leaders of the Pizza Connection circuit in New York.[37]

Their activities eventually filled two thick volumes of a Criminalpol investigation.[38] Tapping their phones pointed police to money laundries in Canada, England, the Caribbean, Switzerland, Sicily and Milan itself. Mafia money-washing through CITAM invaded the Milanese stock exchange, bought into legitimate industry, enriched the banks.

Leaders of the ring were on the verge of buying the city's San Siro racetrack and Hilton Hotel for around $100 million when they were found out. Tried and predictably acquitted, they dropped out of sight and, for many, out of mind.

A decade later, however, Milan had become a crossroads for Europe's drug traffic and the epicentre of its arms trade, racked by violent crime and awash in dirty money.

Some 25,000 picciotti – helpers, peons – are working the region for the Mafia and its affiliates today, says Italy's parliamentary Anti-Mafia Commission.

Narcodollars are flooding through its banking system, stock market and legitimate business: 'rivers of it', according to Confindustria, the Italian manufacturers' association.[39] 'If not a single dirty lira remained in the stock market, trading would drop 15%,' an authoritative source told the Anti-Mafia Commission.[40]

Huge amounts are invested in anonymous government bearer bonds; the Mafia's way of conditioning the value of the lira, says Italy's Interior Ministry.[41] 'There are operations here forcing the money market up and down to recycle dubious capital,' says Milan's Prosecutor-General, Francesco Saverio Borelli.[42]

The Mafia is 'taking over the market, taking over commerce, taking over real estate, taking control of the territory,' says the Italian Federation of Bar and Restaurant Owners (FIPE).[43]

Half of FIPE's 210,000 members are paying the pizzo – more than half, in Milan and its hinterland. Their stories have a dreary sameness: threats of an 'accident', then the broken windows or burned cars, the loans at low or no interest, the demand for shares in the company, the takeover: just like in the south.

Many victims are driven to the edge of bankruptcy, FIPE reports. 'They're taking 30% of everything out of my pocket,' testifies a Milanese restaurateur. 'When I tried to say it was ruining me, they left a pack of bloody syringes at my door with a note saying "Be good or next time we'll put Aids under your skin." '[44]

No judge seemed able to lay a finger on them until 1992. (Among other things, they had assured the destruction of incriminating records in Milan's courthouse, by leaving bits of cheese among the pages for resident rats: so we are told by the president of the Chamber of Commerce.)[45]

In 1992, however, a spectacular court case known as the Duomo Connection exposed the workings of just one crime ring in Milan. Its leaders were ranking members of Cosa Nostra and the 'Ndrangheta, connected to the Cupola in Palermo and the powerful clan of Santo Pasquale Morabito in Calabria.

With kidnap ransom money from Calabria, they were paying for cocaine imported from Argentina, laundering the proceeds in Switzerland, and re-investing the money in Milanese real estate. At the same time, they were bringing in heroin by TIR truck from Turkey, and importing weapons from Switzerland for distribution to the Camorra in Naples: Kalashnikovs, Uzis, Walthers, carbines.

Meanwhile, they had set up thirty finance and real estate companies, running at a generous profit from no apparent source. With part of the proceeds, they had built an entire residence complex in a Milanese suburb, after bribing officials to falsify papers, speed up their permits and alter the city's whole urban development plan.

In violation of the city plan, furthermore, they got permits to build thirty hotels for the World Soccer Cup, only one of which was open in time for the games.[46]

To be fair, they were not the only ones. Milan, known now as Tangentopoli for its generous political *tangenti*, or rakeoffs, has turned out to be one of the planet's leading payola capitals.

Exposed in 1992, it touched off the most thunderous judicial investigation in Italian history. 'Operation Clean Hands', led by three unflappable young magistrates, showed that practically all of Milan's officials from the mayor down were on the take. Eventually, the same pattern emerged up and down the country.[47]

In or out of office, politicians on the mainland were doing exactly as the Mafia did. For at least a decade, they had exacted a percentage on all public works contracts, based on a sliding scale, the money divided with mathematical equity among governing and opposition parties.

Spreading from Milan to Venice, Turin, Rome, Naples and Reggio Calabria, Tangentopoli has became legitimate Italy's own monster.

Five former prime ministers, a host of former cabinet members and nearly 3,000 other politicians and businessmen had been accused, indicted or jailed by mid-1993; the nation's entire governing class has been devastated.[48]

In the south, from Naples down, the graft proved to be under joint management by politicians and the Mafia, Camorra or 'Ndrangheta. In Milan, however, only a tenuous if intriguing connection has come to light. Both the city's bent politicians and the Mafia were using the same Swiss office, Li-Mo, to launder their money, it turned out.[49]

If nothing else, however, the Mafia could turn the pandemonium in Milan to good use.

Major industries engaged in public works were paralyzed when the Tangentopoli story broke; hundreds of large and small companies came to a standstill. As a first batch of company directors and politicians were led off to jail, the President of Milan's Chamber of Commerce set alarm bells ringing. 'The banks are cutting off credit to the companies in trouble. But the Mafia has the money to buy them out. It is happening in these days, in these hours,' he warned.[50]

Italy became too small for the Mafia long ago, but no government anywhere knew how far it was spreading abroad until the 1990s. Even then, most were inclined to say it was all Italy's fault. Actually, the Mafia's men have found sanctuary, complicity and safety from the law wherever they've gone, in Europe especially.

Europe's guilt, going back decades, should have shamed its leaders in 1992, in a case provoking some hilarity instead.

That winter, Italy's Finance Minister took an outraged but futile swipe at the Camorra, by banning the sale of Philip Morris cigarettes. The Camorra has had a black market monopoly on Philip Morris tobacco in Italy since World War II, more or less the size of the state's monopoly and growing.[51] Several million Italian smokers are pleased to dodge a 65% tax on their favourite Marlboros; nearly half a million earn a living by selling them; 25,000 smugglers bring them in by speedboat and TIR truck.

Consequently, popular fury erupted when Marlboros disappeared from state tobacco shops, and the Camorra's street corner stands came under astounding police scrutiny. The foreign press jeered. The Philip Morris Company appealed indignantly to the European Commission in Brussels. The Commission, at its bureaucratic worst, pronounced the ban in contravention of free trade.[52]

Forced to back down, Finance Minister Formica made one last

try: he offered a government job to any tobacco smuggler willing to go straight. Just one took him up; not enough money, the others said.

Colossal stakes were riding on this seemingly comic exercise: a billion-dollar-a-year profit on black market tobacco, another billion in lost taxes for the state, an international narcotics trade worth far more, and an exceptional international chain of money laundries.[53]

The Camorra's contraband tobacco moves through an elaborate circuit from Switzerland, Belgium and Holland (producing states) to Hungary, Rumania, Bulgaria and Turkey (storage depots) to Yugoslavia and Albania (staging areas for the final run across the Adriatic into Italy).

This circuit in reverse constitutes the famous Balkan route. The biggest two-way trade in arms and drugs ever uncovered has depended on it since the 1960s. Three-quarters of the heroin reaching Western Europe and a substantial portion of America's travels along it.

It was the Balkan route, and the money in Marlboros, that brought the Sicilian Mafia into partnership with the Camorra in 1974. The capital was needed to bankroll the Mafia's grand entrance into the worldwide heroin market. The smuggling circuit was tested, manned and demonstrably safe from surveillance across nine national frontiers.

A year later, the Sicilians sealed their pact with the Turkish arms-drugs mafia in a village near the Yugoslav-Italian border, whereupon morphine-base and heroin started to roll back over the same frontiers.[54]

In the two decades since then, smuggled tobacco has kept moving more or less freely over these nine frontiers. Police and customs agents look for the heroin; the tobacco usually passes.

The billion-dollar cash flow finances an army of drug couriers, heavy investments on the French Riviera, and the extravagant plans of the Camorra's tobacco kingpin, Don Michele Zaza, a wonder at staying out of jail.

Known as Michele 'U Pazzu – Crazy Michael – the not so crazy Camorra boss is also a ranking member of the Sicilian Mafia, sworn in by the Cupola's 'Pope' himself in 1974. Indeed, defectors have fingered Zaza as the Mafia's liaison with the Camorra for their shared traffic in heroin and cocaine.

Falsely humble, illiterate, shifty and garrulous, Don Michele got his start in black market cigarettes at the age of six, he once told a quizzical Italian magistrate:

First I'd sell five cases of Philip Morris, then ten, then a thousand, then three thousand, then I bought myself six or seven ships that you took away from me ... I used to load fifty thousand cases a month ... I could load a hundred thousand cases, $10 million on trust, all I had to do was make a phone call ...

I'd buy $24 million of Philip Morris in three months, my lawyer will show you the receipts. I'm proud of that – $24 million![55]

Nevertheless, it was for heroin that he was picked up in 1982, when a Rome narcotics squad trailed him to a Paris dinner party with members of the Sicilian Cupola, discussing a ninety-three-kilo shipment to America.[56]

Transferred from jail to a Rome clinic for his perennially and usefully ailing heart, he walked out casually and moved to France for good.

The Camorra and Mafia have been installed along the French Riviera for decades. From there, reported a special Commission of the French parliament in 1993, Zaza 'led an organization grouping some thirty companies in Europe, the United States, South America, Panama and the island of Saint Martin, with perfect logistics for transport over a good part of the planet.'[57]

The Caribbean island of Saint Martin is also known as Saint Maartens. Formerly under French and Dutch colonial rule, the island is divided into two sovereign states under the respective wings of their former rulers. Each has privileged access to the European Community, meaning free entry with no police checks or customs clearance. Both have fallen into Mafia hands since the conquest of nearby Aruba, which also enjoys free access to the EC. Saint Maartens is largely used to move drugs, Saint Martin to launder the proceeds.[58]

Saint Maartens was a key port of call in Don Michele Zaza's new itinerary for shipping dope. His containers of cigarettes travelled in TIR trucks as far as Marseilles, where the cigarettes were offloaded and replaced with heroin. Then the containers were shipped on to Saint Maartens, for relay to the easily accessible American mainland.

Calling in at Panama and Venezuela on the return trip, the same vessels were taking on cocaine bound for Spain and Italy.[59]

Zaza had five companies in the port of Marseilles for this purpose, the French parliamentary commission found: 'one for transport, one for customs clearance, one for maintenance of the containers, one for transporting the containers, and one for the organization's own trade' – heroin going out and cocaine coming in.

There was 'good reason to believe that the organization also controlled several shipping companies, such as the Dutch-owned Nordana
Lines,' the commission said.

To launder their profits, Zaza's Camorra-Mafia crowd in France
used to operate through luxurious private clinics around Marseilles,
until the DEA came nosing around. In the autumn of 1989, therefore,
bosses of the Camorra, the Mafia and the Corsican Milieu gathered in
Marseilles to plan a switch to casinos.[60]

Using a front company called Sofextour based in Monte Carlo,
they were going after eight major casinos along the French coast,
starting with the famous one at Menton, to be flanked by new luxury
hotels equipped with fruit machines, loan sharks and girls.

Even without fixing the games, they would have netted close to a
billion dollars a year, and washed as much or more through the most
elegant set of laundries on the continent.

Everything was lined up by the spring of 1991 – real estate, banks,
notaries, accommodating police inspectors, croupiers – when a thousand
land, sea and airborne troops of the French and Italian police made a
dawn raid on Paris, Marseilles, Nice, Cannes, Menton and Naples.

Fifty men were arrested, not including Don Michele: he was in a
French jail already for running a truckload of Marlboros (471,000
packs) from Holland through France on the way to Portugal.

With thirteen previous convictions in Italy for drug trafficking,
multiple homicide and so on, 'U Pazzu had been a fugitive in a manner of speaking since 1984. From then until 1989, he had travelled
around undisturbed in his bullet-proof Rolls Royce, dividing his time
between a million-dollar mansion in Beverly Hills and a sumptuous
villa on the French Riviera.[61]

Repeated Italian requests for his extradition had failed to move
French authorities, who showed no particular interest in his Marseilles
drug business either. He got just three years in France for running
tobacco, and was out in two, for 'certified heart trouble'.

During his short stay in jail, he had continued to collect rent from
the French consulate in California for his million-dollar Beverly Hills
mansion.[62]

Back in his sumptuous villa on the Riviera, Don Michele took up
just where he'd left off. For the next two years, he ran a two-billion-
dollar Camorra-Mafia money laundry, through a huge network of
legitimate French and Italian companies.[63]

The French sent Zaza back to jail in the spring of 1993, an apparently sincere if belated act of penance. It was no longer possible to

ignore the dangerous presence of the Mafia and Camorra in France or anywhere in Europe.

Starting that spring, they lost their lifelong immunity in Italy itself.

Up to then, Mafia bosses supposedly in hiding were visiting colleagues in Palermo's Ucciardone prison, walking freely around the island's capital, dining in de luxe restaurants, living within blocks – yards – of their family homes.

In 1993, they were picked off one by one. Totò Riina was the most spectacular catch. But police also caught up with Riina's number two, the purely vicious Nitto Santapaola of Catania, who once had four kids strangled for snitching his mother's purse.

Riina's number three, Giuseppe Madonia of Gela, was intercepted as he was slipping off to Germany with a suitcase full of deutschmarks.

The boss who had walked out of a clinic in his pyjamas, Pietro Vernengo, was recaptured within a few months. Gaetano Fidanzati, a fixture in the intercontinental dope trade for forty years, was tracked down in Argentina. The Cuntrera brothers were flown back from Caracas in handcuffs.

Francesco 'Ciccio' Madonia, whose emissary had set up the Colombian deal in Aruba, was not only captured but stripped of his worldly goods – 250 bank accounts, 202 buildings, 62 commercial companies, 262 cars including a Ferrari, a Maserati and a Rolls Royce, 43 valuable real estate plots and 6 yachts anchored in the Gulf of Palermo.[64]

The Camorra lost not only Zaza in France but its reigning prince in Naples, Carmine Alfieri. A self-made billionaire who read Dante and collected Impressionist paintings, Alfieri complimented the police for finding him in a hidey-hole under the floor of his villa. His own number two, Pasquale Galasso, was captured soon afterward and talked, ending the careers of nearly all the politicians who mattered in the city.

For the first time since the birth of the Sicilian Mafia nearly a century and a half before, Men of Honour who went to jail realized that they were going to stay there.

In the course of that year, the crime-rate in Italy fell by 20%. The drop in Italy's southern 'regions at risk' was 38%.[65]

These seemingly miraculous achievements were all the more extraordinary for coming at the worst moment in Italy's postwar history. The economy was in deep crisis, the lira was in a free fall, the Tangentopoli scandal was at its height, and the parties governing Italy for forty years were hitting bottom.

Whether because or in spite of its approaching demise, the old order in the Palazzo surrendered. Unseen but insurmountable obstacles to a resolute war on the Mafia fell away; the police and judiciary were free to do what they proceeded to do superbly well.

They were spurred by a popular revolt such as Italy has rarely seen. Not only grief but cold anger swept over the country when Judges Falcone and Borsellino were killed – everywhere, but especially in Sicily. Sicilian students, schoolchildren, housewives, tradesmen marched in the streets, hung out sheets in mourning, spoke out on television. Many started to help the police, defying Sicily's ageless law of *omertà*.

Having brought this on itself, the Mafia appeared finally to have gone too far. But it is not an impulsive organization.

As if defining the terms of his own death, Falcone had once explained that 'Mafia violence must not be considered as a manifestation of gratuitous or unmeditated cruelty, even in its most shocking forms. The Mafia always obeys a rigorous logic, or else it wouldn't be the formidable organization it is.'

Therefore, it must have calculated the odds.

The Mafia was 'moving on a worldwide chessboard' in 1992, said Italy's Interior Ministry. This is where it stood when it killed Judge Falcone, the Ministry reported:

> It was taking on major new commitments in the drug trade; modernizing its 'circuits of investment in legal enterprises'; expanding its extortion rackets; investing 'hundreds of billions of lire' in government bearer bonds, bought through foreign banks. It was strengthening ties with other mafias abroad for drug trafficking and money washing, 'especially on the American continent'; using Germany and Austria as 'bridgeheads' to the east; 'expanding massively' in Eastern Europe and Russia; reaching agreements with the Russian mafia and American cosa nostra for economic fraud there; bringing 'colossal sums of dirty money' into Russia; trading narcodollars for rubles; going into 'multiple ventures' in real estate throughout the former USSR.[66]

In short, the Mafia was in a phase of intensive growth at home and imperialist expansion abroad. Therefore, it could not afford to be *seen* to be on the defensive. Its first, imperative priority was to put on a show of overpowering strength.

The point, then, was not merely to kill the Mafia's two strongest adversaries in Italy, but to do so to maximum theatrical effect. The deaths of Giovanni Falcone and Paolo Borsellino were meant to impress a worldwide audience, and did.

Italy's response may have surprised, perhaps stunned, those who planned the attacks. The wave of defections and secrets betrayed, the rejection symptoms in their own Sicilian hinterland, the national army sent in to patrol Sicilian streets, the drastic new government decrees, incredible arrests and appalling confiscation of their wealth – three billion dollars seized that year – these things had to mean that the Mafia was hurting.

Some defectors even thought it could be destroyed at last. 'You must give them no room. You must give them no time. You have to crowd them. If you want to, you can win right now!' testified Leonardo Messina.

But the Mafia is not beaten yet, nor has it shown a sign of retreat. Men of Honour and their *picciotti* are still doing nearly everything they were doing before, says Criminalpol's Alessandro Pansa.

Experts believe they are already finding new political partners in Rome. Judging from their military preparations, they have plainly set out to frighten the judiciary, the police, the Palazzo and the public into surrender.

In 69 raids on their various arms caches during just the last four months of 1992, police found 377 machine guns, 291 pistols, 195 bombs and rocket launchers, and a land-to-air missile, all made in Russia or elsewhere in Eastern Europe, along with over a ton of explosive and half a mile of fuse.[67]

Mysterious bombings, anonymous threats, planted rumours spreading fear and confusion, all point to a new strategy of terror – possibly, this time, with the help of what Italian authorities call 'occult international forces', meaning the Mafia's powerful criminal confederates around the planet.

5

The Russian Mafia
Looks West

There are fifty ways of saying 'to steal' in Russian, and the Russian mafia uses them all. Frustrated citizens claim it is the only institution that works in post-communist Russia. In any event, it is the world's largest, busiest and possibly meanest collection of organized hoods.

By last count, it consisted of 5,000 gangs and some 3,000,000 helpers, controlling the territory in all fifteen of the former Soviet republics, covering eleven time zones and a sixth of the earth's land mass, now foraging far beyond as worldwide barriers fall.[1]

Its alarming proportions affect the whole tormented question of what the West should do about or for Russia and the rest of the ex-USSR. The mafia intrudes in every field of Western concern: the nascent free market, privatization, disarmament, conversion of the military-industrial complex, foreign humanitarian relief and financial aid, even state reserves of currency and gold.

Furthermore, it has begun to intrude directly on the rest of Europe and the United States: 'Looking at the West as a wolf looks at sheep,' an analyst observes.

This mafia is not the old nebula of common criminals, familiar since tsarist times, or even the more accomplished crooks of Brezhnev's day. It is a union of racketeers without equal.

Unlike the true Mafia in Sicily, it has no home seat or central command, no hierarchical structure, ancestral memories, common blood-lines, sworn-in members. Yet its proliferating clans are invading every sphere of life, usurping political power, taking over state enter-prises, fleecing the nation of its natural resources, engaged in extortion, theft, forgery, armed assault, contract-killing, swindling, drug running, arms smuggling, prostitution, gambling, loan sharking, embezzling, money-laundering and black marketing – all this on a monumental and increasingly international scale.

Rising from the ruins of the Soviet empire, the new mafia has far outclassed the one flourishing under communist rule. That one, the Brezhnev solution for a stifling centralized economy, had provided illicit goods and services – firstly but not only for the Nomenklatura – by stealing from the state, buying protection, smuggling, cheating, bullying and bribing its way straight into the Kremlin.

A team of a hundred investigators uncovered it, set loose by the KGB just before Brezhnev died, probing for the next five years. 'We have run into a mafia,' announced the team leader Telman Gdlyan finally to *Izvestia* in 1988. There followed the trial of the USSR's Interior Minister and his Deputy, Yuri Churbanov, Brezhnev's son-in-law. Putting him in the dock caused a sensation. But Churbanov, greedy and foolish, was merely a political collector's item.

His loot came from the mafia of Uzbekistan in central Asia, three thousand kilometres from Moscow. Every party apparatus from the district *oblast* up to the Central Committee of the Soviet Union was hooked in to the Uzbek mafia. The first to be caught was the head of the Soviet Interior Ministry's anti-corruption squad in the Bukhara Region; stashed at his home were diamonds, rubies, blue jeans, thou-sands of Swiss watches, a million rubles in pocket money and a full mile's length of gold brocade.[2]

His mafia boss, chairman of the presidium of Uzbekistan's Supreme Soviet, had squirrelled away over 200 pounds of gold bullion, 5,000 gold coins of imperial mint, 12,000 precious jewels, five cars, eleven TV sets, and hundreds of expensive furs.

The Uzbek mafia used to provide, for a fee, everything from military medals, decorations, dachas and cemetery plots to Party membership cards, government posts and seats on the Presidium. Through faked 'ceiling statistics', it extracted a quarter of a billion rubles from the state for a million tons of non-existent cotton.[3]

Competing for pride of place with the Uzbek mafia was another in Azerbaijan on the Caspian Sea. This one, headed by the Soviet Union's First Deputy Prime Minister – Geidar Aliev, a full member of the Soviet politburo, restored to power in Azerbaijan in 1993 –

presided over a 'petroleum mafia', a 'fishing mafia', a 'fruit and vegetable mafia', a 'caviar mafia', a 'railroad mafia', an 'export mafia', a 'customs mafia' and a 'militia mafia' operating inside the Interior Ministry's Division for Fighting Violators of Socialist Property and Speculation.[4]

Through these various branches, the Azerbaijani mafia earned a king's ransom by poaching sturgeon, packing and exporting clandestine caviar, running underground factories with stolen state materials and shipping its black market goods all over the Soviet Union.

All the regional mafias of Transcaucasia ran such illicit factories – often inside the state's own factories, but free of taxes, overhead costs and impossible production norms. 'In my time, I estimate that about a third of the clothing and shoes in the Caucasus were made underground,' says the former head of the Prommontazh Trust Order Department. 'During my career I bribed 1,600 people, of whom twothirds were Party, Soviet and state enterprise officials. Criminals keep track of such things.'[5]

Nobody was happier with the system than Brezhnev, comforted by a miraculous supply of consumer goods, glowing production figures, and due tribute for a ruler of his mould.

Among the gifts showered upon him by Azerbaijan's mafia boss was an outsized diamond ring encircled by smaller diamonds for each of the fifteen Soviet republics, symbolizing 'Brezhnev the Sun King'. The boss of Uzbekistan gave him a solid gold bust four feet high.[6]

These revelations in 1988 were followed by a purge of over 100,000 police officers: 15% of the entire Soviet police force.[7]

This was korruptsiya communist style, a shared monopoly of power between politicians and crooks. Liberated Russia deserved better. But yesterday's politicians are still largely in place, yesterday's crooks are today's free entrepreneurs, and korruptsiya, spreading uncontrollably as things fall apart, has become the curse of a stricken nation. 'Corruption is devouring the state from top to bottom,' exclaimed Boris Yeltsin after watching it grow for a year.[8]

Everything about the former USSR seems so much larger than life – its geography and ethnic diversity, its gifts from nature and man-made calamities, the dramatic sweep of its history, the magnitude of its misery – that facts and figures strain credibility. Some may think there are three too many zeros or a misplaced decimal point in what follows. The numbers in this story of crime and corruption are bound to look unreal.

In 1991, year of the communists' fall, the All-Union Research

Institute of the Soviet Interior Ministry estimated that half the income of an average government functionary was coming from bribes, compared to 'only 30%' before 1985.[9]

Some time before, the Soviet prosecutor-general informed the 2nd Congress of People's Deputies that 'a third to a half of all heads of cooperatives' in most regions of the USSR were probably embezzling funds. His office had indicted 225,000 officials on this charge, he said. Of seventy found guilty in a single case, eighteen worked for the Department to Combat Embezzlement.[10]

Some 20,000 police officers were being fired yearly for collusion with the mafia by 1991, double the rate under Brezhnev.[11] Moscow's Policeman of the Year was convicted for bribery.[12]

Four out of five agents in the Soviet Interior Ministry s militia were thought to be on the take: this according to the then head of the Ministry's Sixth Department to Combat Organized Crime, Alexander Gurov. 'There's no doubt that a third of the mafia's profits go to militiamen and our functionaries,' he said.[13]

These were merely symptoms of a malignant growth pervading the economy, the banking system, the body politic. Millions of ordinary citizens have succumbed, making off with state property, black marketing, swindling, buying or selling protection. Obviously they aren't all tied to the mafia. Russia is so chaotic and broke that hardly anybody can stay honest and survive.

'You Westerners may call this corruption, but we say *nishinstvo* in Russian, a term describing a poverty so desperate that one loses one's shame and moral compass,' said Moscow's police chief in that first tremendous year of freedom.[14]

If not every lawbreaker is a mafioso, however, the mafia swims among them like a great predatory shark, recruiting some, exacting payoffs from others, frightening away any rival eyeing its prey. Insatiable and seemingly invulnerable, it is swallowing up factories, co-ops, privatized enterprises, real estate, raw materials, currency, gold: a quarter of Russia's economy in 1991, between a third and a half by 1992, according to Russian authorities.

By the end of that year, 'Nearly two-thirds of Russia's commercial structure had ties to the growing criminal world': this according to President Boris Yeltsin himself.[15]

Between 1989 and 1991, the last years of communist disintegration, the mafia's turnover shot up from less than a billion rubles to 130 billion – the size of the national deficit – reported the Interior Ministry's Alexander Gurov. 'In the next few years, its turnover will reach 200

billion rubles; organized crime will then control approximately
30–40% of the country's GNP,' he warned at the time.[16]

The accompanying kill-rate has climbed to a world record. Once,
Soviet leaders had taunted America for its sixty-odd murders a day, a
mark of capitalist depravity. By 1993, murders in the Russian Republic
alone were running to over 80 a day: this not counting the other fourteen ex-Soviet republics.[17]

By then, Russia was getting to be such a dangerous place that its
own Prosecutor-General, Valentin Stepankov, advised every citizen 'to
defend himself by every means, and we won't ask if he's exceeding the
limits of legitimate self-defence . . .

'It is very difficult to do work like mine in a country which has the
most profound lack of respect for the law,' he observed.[18]

Many of the dead were victims of drunken brawls, racket-enforcers,
armed robbery or gang warfare, but murder by contract was coming
into use simply as a way of climbing the free enterprise ladder.

Fifteen hundred contract-killings were racked up in 1992. The following summer, the president of Russia's Young Bankers' Association
sent an anguished appeal for help to President Yeltsin. Ten directors of
the country's largest commercial banks had been murdered in the previous weeks, presumably for failing to extend still more outrageous
loans than those they had granted already.[19]

A disturbing number of other victims were policemen. Lost amidst
all the rest of the doom-ridden news from Russia is the fact that its
mafia has become the world's leading cop-killer.

Neither in Sicily nor even in Colombia have so many policemen
fallen under criminal fire: 186 in 1989; 193 the next year; 300 the year
after, and as many again the year after that. Another 719 were
attacked by gunmen just in St Petersburg in 1991.[20]

This was the year when the Soviet Union's outer borders opened up,
while inner borders closed around fifteen newly sovereign ex-Soviet
republics. All nationwide Soviet institutions were gone by the start of
the next year, including those for law enforcement. The Soviet-wide
Sixth Department, created by Gorbachev barely three years earlier for
a concerted assault on organized crime, was dismantled.

No central authority remained to coordinate police intelligence,
order arrests, control 36,000 miles of Soviet land and sea frontiers, or
movements of men, money and goods from one to another of the new
Commonwealth of Independent States. No laws governed passage
from one to another. The only organization fully operative across the
length and breadth of the late USSR was the mafia.

In just two or three years, it had doubled in size (from 2,500 to 5,000 clans) and increased its business activities more than a hundredfold. Its leaders had established contact with their Western counterparts, and thousands of its members had expanded operations in the United States and Western Europe.

It was moving heavily into the international drug trade, and had mastered the complexities of shady international finance. By all odds, it was the fastest-growing crime consortium on the planet.

And it was still a shared monopoly of power between politicians and crooks.

There are elaborate theories to explain how so commanding an organization can seemingly have neither head nor tail, and manage to be everywhere and nowhere.

Indeed the Soviet mafia is a hybrid monster hard to describe. 'Brigades' emerge and disappear, leaders come and go, bands migrate from the Caucasus to Moscow or to Vladivostok on the Sea of Japan. Some are known by nationality: Chechen, Armenian, Azerbaijani, Georgian, Russian, Ukrainian, Uzbek, Ingushy. Others are known by occupation: the drug mafia, the gambling mafia, the taxi mafia, the gold mafia, the currency mafia, the stolen-car mafia and so on.

Territories may be staked out by a tribe, a region, an urban neighbourhood or simply a marauding and charismatic boss.

A single gang raided in 1992 was found to embrace 500 members of smaller gangs, equipped with 'firearms and knives, ammunition, modern means of radio communication, foreign cars and half a billion rubles in cash'.[21]

A 'Big Urals' gang absorbing six smaller ones works the entire ex-Soviet territory from Moscow to the Baltic states to the Far East.

Myriad organized gangs may be mistaken for the real thing, from Asiatic bandits to a Russian version of Hell's Angels. Lines are indistinct between mafiosi and ordinary swindlers or black marketeers. Often there is no discernible line at all between mafiosi and their political confederates.

Nevertheless there really is an authentic criminal organization known as the Russian mafia, richer by far than forces of the law and much better equipped in weapons, communication systems, transport.

It admires and copies the Sicilian Mafia as the highest standard of excellence. 'Now, my dear friends, we are living the most solemn moment here in Diomga, our little big Palermo,' said the flamboyant 'Dzhem', boss of Komsomolsk in the Far East, toasting his mafia's 'immortal ties' to the Sicilian confraternity at a grand wedding.

Five hundred mafia heavyweights gathered there from Siberia, the Caucasus, Cecenia, Tatarstan and Uzbekistan cheered him on. (Police have a secretly filmed video of this memorable event.)[22]

Members of this mafia are admitted only with a mafia sponsor, and only after proving their valour by killing somebody on order, preferably a friend or relative – exactly like their admired Sicilian colleagues.[23]

Once in, they still live largely by the code of the old Thieves' World, risk its abundant death penalties, communicate in their private jargon and flout their tattoos: a spider web for drug traffickers, an eight-point star for robbers, a broken heart for district bosses.

Loosely articulated, they form something like the classic criminal pyramid. Common thugs make up the base at street level, under gang leaders running their territory like military boot camps. Above are a 'supply group' and a 'security group', the one largely a conduit for communication with the other.[24]

The security group forms an umbrella of respectable citizens – journalists, bankers, artists, athletes, politicians of the old and new Nomenklatura – providing intelligence information, legal aid, social prestige and political cover.[25]

Above are the godfathers: the indomitable *vory v zakone*, thieves-within-the-code who still command the heights of the Thieves' World, preserving its 'thieves' ideology', administering justice, plotting strategy.

There are seven hundred known thieves-within-the-code by now, at large or in prison.[26] Guiding rather than governing, they provide most of the brains for their subalterns.

Though far from being absolute rulers over violently unruly and fiercely competitive gangs – there is no Totò Riina among them – they are 'the mafia's politburo', to quote a captain in the Sixth Department, the arbiters of the criminal world.

'Our thieves-within-the-code are vital to the mafia's internal order,' says I. Pavlovich, deputy chief of the Russian Republic's Sixth Department. 'Each sphere of influence is under their control. They meet periodically, settle territorial disputes, decide on operations, make policy . . .'[27]

The power emanating from these mafia conclaves inevitably surpasses a fragile Russian government's, in that their edicts are instantly transmitted, unmistakeably enforceable and almost universally obeyed.

In January 1991, for instance, the most authoritative thieves-within-the-code gathered from all over the country to discuss a financial emergency: so we are told by Alexander Gurov, head of the Sixth Department at the time.

Soviet Premier Pavlov had suddenly withdrawn all 50- and 100-ruble notes from circulation (see Chapter 9). Everybody in the mafia kept illicit cash reserves in these notes, the largest denomination issued up to then.

'My operational report showed that these thieves-within-the-code – the supermen, the big-time mafiosi – got together to discuss ways of selling off or exchanging the banknotes for new ones or getting them out of the country,' Gurov said later on national TV. 'The thieves-within-the-code decided where the rubles had to be exchanged or smuggled out. Then they gave permission to set aside a quarter of the entire sum for bribing the administration.'[28]

The underworld mobilized overnight. 'Black market currency sharks vanished from Moscow,' Gurov declared. The ruble notes were rushed to corruptible state factories and banks in remote regions to be exchanged under the counter.

The Konkuret co-op, with only 1,000 rubles in its account, handed in 190,000 rubles in 50s and 100s. A shop in Novosibirsk taking in 10,000 rubles a day 'contrived to hand in' 240,000. Hundreds of millions of rubles were washed with little trouble. Unlike the poor, who lost lifetime savings they'd been hiding under a mattress, the mafia came out very well.

The godfathers met again in the winter of 1991, to consider Gorbachev's 500-day programme for transition to a free market. They liked it. A free market in the USSR meant not only mobility, relaxed borders and dollars from abroad but a chance to mount the most colossal criminal buyout in history.

For all the wreckage of Russia's economy, it still had the world's richest natural resources. And once privatization got under way, the whole country would be up for sale.[29]

Though few realized it then, the Russian mafia was about to make a big strategic leap: from merely feeding off the economy to owning it. To prepare for privatization, however, the godfathers needed time. Accordingly, they decided to stall the entire government programme until they were ready. In the event, they stalled it for a year.[30]

Late in January 1992, Tass-Krim Press reported that the godfathers had reconvened at a dacha near Moscow. 'Therefore, privatization of the capital's trade and service sectors, delayed because various mafia clans were resolving the distribution of enterprises among themselves, is likely to go ahead soon,' the Russian news agency said.[31]

First, the godfathers had to impose a new peace among Moscow's eternally warring clans. The truce they had worked out in 1988, at Dagomys on the Black Sea, had ended in an orgy of bloodshed after barely a year. But the first stage of privatization was, in effect, an imperative call to order.

'The Yeltsin government is selling state enterprises amounting to 92 billion rubles this year. Organized crime is putting 50 billion rubles through the banking system. So the mafia can buy up more than half,' said the Russian Interior Ministry's top social economist, Tatjana Korjagina, leader of the first parliamentary Anti-Mafia Commission in Soviet history.[32]

The logic of peace was unarguable. Once inner harmony was restored, the godfathers divided zones of influence, and went after the 6,000 properties coming up for auction in Moscow. The rules for privatization were fluid, bent officials were easily come by, and most Russians had no money to speak of. In a matter of weeks, the mafia had the city sewn up.

'According to sources who spoke on condition they were not identified, the mafia has already privatized between 50% and 80% of all shops, storehouses, depots, hotels and services in Moscow: the biggest enterprises providing for the city's vital activities,' reported Tass-Krim Press.[33]

Where standard bribery failed in the course of the takeover, the mafia had only to apply a little force. To acquire a popular Gastronom in the capital, it simply prevented employees from bidding by locking them up for an entire afternoon.[34]

(In another year, it would be grabbing enterprises by killing off its own more successful businessmen instead: the young director-general of a prosperous real estate agency, the director of a metal factory, the director of a brokerage, the vice-president of Tekhno-bank. 'They were dressed by Valentino and Calvin Klein, but underneath they had tattoos on their chests,' wrote *Komsomolskaya Pravda*.)[35]

In the end, the Moscow properties were sold off for only 200 million rubles, whereas the city had been expecting 1.6 billion.[36] Asked how he felt about the whole larcenous affair, the head of the city council's privatization committee replied: 'Why not? If the mafia guarantees law and order, food in the shops and washed floors, then I'm for the mafia.'[37]

There was no protest from Moscow's Mayor Gavril Popov, who had outdone the mafia if anything. In November 1991, the Mayor had actually signed over an entire district of the capital to a French-

Russian joint venture called UKOSO, in which he and his minister for the Municipal Economy were accused of holding 40% of the shares.

The 'October' district covered 4 million square metres of choice real estate from the splendid Gorky Park to Gagarinsk Square, occupied by academies, monasteries, a hospital and 220,000 residents including Mikhail Gorbachev. It was worth around $30 billion, but UKOSO got it on a 99-year lease at $10 a year.

I was among the incredulous readers of this improbable news story. Later, however, it was confirmed to me by an impeccable source. The eminent economist Tatjana Korjagina lives in the 'October' district, and pays her rent to UKOSO.[38]

To suggest that the Mayor was a still bigger crook than the crooks is to draw too fine a distinction. Popov, who resigned eventually but kept his loot, was 'selling the city's best real estate and historic landmarks to foreigners, censoring all criticism of the criminal activities of the city's leadership, and mixing executive power with criminal elements, creating a unique mafia network which controls the life of the city,' as a top Russian manager put it.[39]

Mayor Popov was never taken to court because, like two and a half million government office holders in the former USSR, he had official and unconditional immunity.

Russia had no law to punish corruption anyway. It had no law permitting access to Popov's or any bank accounts, no mechanism for controlling private banks, no sanctions for money-laundering, no screening for civil service applicants, no inspectors to check the source of foreign capital, no tax audits, no legal provisions against organized crime, and no protection for government witnesses (whose names *and* *addresses* had to be listed in indictments).

Under a Supreme Court ruling, furthermore – rigged in 1986 to protect the Uzbek mafia, and modified later only in part – a defendant in a criminal case could not be convicted unless he pleaded guilty. 'This is a disaster from which we cannot recover,' says the prosecutor-general's Chief Investigator for Big Crimes, Boris Uvarov.[40]

The lack of a legal framework to fit a wholly new political structure, a desperately urgent problem, was one of too many to be dealt with by a frail and uncertain government.

On top of it, the KGB was in a state of penury and purge; and the militia, facing an army of dedicated cop-killers, struggled with ancient telephones, ageing patrol cars, no gas, no computers and no money. Earning around $10 a month besides, their sporadic raids were understandably half-hearted.

On one occasion, 24,000 militiamen rounded up 7,709 presumably dangerous criminals in the capital, of whom 479 were charged with petty hooliganism, 1,520 for lacking residence permits, 147 for drunken driving, 519 for just being drunk, 165 for vagrancy and 14 for brewing illegal vodka. 'The inhabitants of Moscow can sleep more soundly now,' said the militia's crime prevention chief without a shade of irony.[41]

So, singularly free from harassment, the political-criminal condominium called the mafia has in fact come to control the life of Moscow, and of all Russia and the other Commonwealth States.[42] Its terrible strength emerged in the desperate winter of 1990–1991 when, with a free market on the way, food vanished from Soviet shelves. The food was there, but not in the shops.

An Italian TV crew filmed twenty heavily loaded trucks leaving Moscow's wholesale produce market, not one of which unloaded at a retail outlet. Hidden in the basement of Shop No. 19 in the October district police found 700 kilos of chicken drumsticks, 400 kilos of butter and nearly two tons of meat.

At the Nizhnedevitsk slaughterhouse in the Voronezh region, 1,707 kilos of meat and 50 sheep carcasses were dumped and covered with earth; 110 tons of rotted vegetables were discovered at a storage facility in the Odessa region. Similar reports came from Syktyvkar, Chernovtsy, Perm, Vladimir, Suzdal.[43]

Foreign food aid approaching $13 billion over the next winter ran into inexplicable delays. Trainloads from Western Europe were shunted to sidings in Moscow and left there. Britain's 120-ton shipment of frozen meat was rejected altogether at Moscow's Sheremetyevo airport, allegedly for being infected with mad cow disease (it wasn't).

A 'consistent part' of European Community shipments were 'systematically stolen by organized bands', said Larissa Pikhacheva, directing foreign aid for Moscow. Red Cross offices in Moscow's Perovsky and Proletarsky quarters found aid cartons 'systematically opened and stripped of coffee, biscuits and chocolate'; (200 grams of coffee were selling on the black market for 300 rubles, an average month's salary).

Fifty-four planeloads sent in America's spectacular airlift, Operation Hope, had to be escorted by Red Army troops and kept under armed guard around the clock. Of 80,000 packages sent to St Petersburg by the German Arbeiter Samariterbund, only 10,000 reached the population; another 30,000 were blocked in the harbour. A caravan of

German aid trucks was forced to turn back at the border after failing to find a customs agent to clear them; others passing through were stoned. 'An adventure in peace looked more like a mission of war,' said a young Russian interpreter in the caravan.[44]

The strangling of the nation's food supply was a gargantuan operation to force up prices and expand the black market in foodstuffs. Millions of citizens had a hand in it, but Boris Yeltsin himself spoke out angrily against 'the mafia that controls the markets'.[45]

Not all the black marketing is so closely held. Much of it is really a free market for anything sold off the books, from a used can-opener or Red Airforce uniform to computers or dented samovars.

Russians travel for six days on the Trans-Siberian railway to Peking, to trade Russian watches, cameras and exotic puppies for Chinese clothing and bicycles; Vietnamese buy Russian bicycles and tea kettles to sell in Hanoi; Mongolians pick up cheap Russian food blenders and fake Johnny Walker whisky to peddle off a fruit crate in Warsaw. The mafia's 5,000 gangs don't necessarily run this vast itinerant army, but they rarely fail to collect their cut.[46]

Moscow is smothered by them. Twenty criminal 'Brigades' hold the city, with their 6,000-odd armed thugs. Everybody in some kind of business – restaurants, food markets, gas stations, flower stalls, news stands, casinos, beggars' corners at the Kremlin – is 'under somebody' who collects a monthly payoff.

The Dolgoprudnaya, who drive around in Volvos with preheated seats, have a corner on the best protection rackets. The Lyubertsy run prostitution; the Solntsevo control slot machines; the Ingushy smuggle contraband leather and skins to northern Italy; the Azerbaijani keep a corner on the drug trade by turning their rivals in to the cops, and so on.[47]

Then there are the Chechen, with their own army of 600 killers in Moscow. Natives of a self-proclaimed sovereign enclave in the northern Caucasus (pop:700,000), they are the most notorious and versatile of all Russia's mafiosi at home and abroad.

There are many Chechen gangs, not necessarily friendly to each other, but uniformly vicious and assured of perfect sanctuary in their tiny mountain republic. Upon declaring its independence in 1991, its President, General Dudaeyev, opened its prison gates, let everybody out, and closed the prisons down.[48]

The Chechen are hated and feared in Moscow, but cannot be dislodged. Their swaggering toughs are also taking over the streets in Berlin, Warsaw and Prague, stealing cars in Germany, Austria and

Sweden, running drugs into Western Europe, working fraud and currency scams in the United States.[49] Wild, cruel and impenetrably secretive, they are singularly frightening villains.

Chechen gangs do almost anything imaginable that is illegal, starting with 'protection', the Russian equivalent of the *pizzo*. Protection is the racketeer's 'main function and service', explained a Chechen entrepreneur to the *Chicago Tribune*'s Thom Shenker:

> No businessman wants the Militia interfering in his affairs. Nor does he want riots with 100 people from opposing groups brawling over his restaurant or enterprise. Our function is to control the criminal situation, prevent unrest and acts of vandalism. We provide favorable conditions for development of business and the prosperity of businessmen in Moscow.[50]

I ran into Chechen controlling the criminal situation on another beat, when two agents of the Sixth Department took me on a crook's tour of Moscow. The place was Uzhny Port on the river, terminal for stolen cars from all over Western Europe.

Here, among humbler models on a vast, icy used car lot, stood rows of Audis, BMWs and Mercedes: the cars mourned by so many of the 85,000 Germans who lost theirs in 1991.[51]

(Another mafia ring, from Georgia, was pirating used cars shipped from Japan to Russia's Pacific coast, attacking caravans with razors, knives and machine guns.)[52]

We got no welcoming salesman's smiles from the stonefaced, heavy-browed Chechen in greasy leather coats, watching us as we watched half-frozen militiamen lift car hoods, peer inside and move on. The Chechen were paying $1,000 a month for that blind policeman's eye, my guides said.

Every kind of scam awaited the unwary customer: a Mercedes refitted with an East German Trabant motor, or a cash payment vanishing with a uniformed 'cashier'. A Moscovite rummaging for spare parts in a mountain of junk would not leave his own car unguarded, the agents said, for fear of its being not only stolen but *sold* behind his back.

The tour led from Uzhny Port to the Polayana Dom in front of Moscow's planetarium, for the electronic goods mafia; the Lazurit jewellery shop on Sirenevy Boulevard for the gold mafia; the Hippodrome, built by Tsar Nicholas I and transformed into the glittering Café Royale Casino, for the betting and gambling mafia; a billiard parlour next to gracious Ostanskinsky Park reserved for 'the intelligentsia of the underworld' ('because gambling needs brains').

Then came the Foreign Trade Bank, for the hard currency mafia; the Intourist Hotel in sight of the Kremlin, for the prostitution mafia and a dozen others; the Danilovsky market for the Azerbaijani drug mafia . . .

The Danilovsky market, though a beacon for addicts, can hardly convey the magnitude of the drug mafia operating across Russia and all the Commonwealth States.

Nature, more generous than man to this Soviet land, has endowed it with a prodigal source of narcotics. The ex-USSR produces twenty-five times more hashish than the rest of the world. Cannabis grows wild on seven-and-a-half-million acres of its territory, in Kazakhstan, Siberia, the Far Eastern republics, the lower Volga River basin, the northern Caucasus and southern Ukraine. (Truck drivers cut it to dry on an outward journey and gather it to smoke on the return run.)[53]

Opium poppies flourish anywhere in Kazakhstan's Chu Valley, 60,000 kilometres square. Luxuriant poppy fields sprawl over Uzbekistan, Turkmenistan and Tajikistan.[54] The latter three Islamic republics have the same soil and growing conditions as contiguous Afghanistan and Iran, with whom they are inevitably in league. Afghanistan has just overtaken Burma as the world's largest opium-producing country. With Iran, it forms the Golden Crescent, the world's second largest source of supply.

In the old days, Tajikis would set out pots and pans at nightfall and pick them up filled with Afghan dope in the morning. Trained driverless donkeys with 100-pound loads would cross over from Iran to Tajikistan.[55] Even these precautions are no longer needed; the borders between these Moslem states have been abolished altogether.

For once, organized crime was late in spotting a potential bonanza – the chance to create and feed a huge addict population and export for dollars. The possibilities were overlooked, perhaps deliberately so; Soviet controls were severe. Opium and hash, used for centuries in the harsh mountains and deserts of central Asia, were largely consumed where they grew.

When Soviet controls fell apart, things changed. By 1992, family-sized poppy fields yielding two crops a year were rationalized and under heavy armed guard. New plantations in Uzbekistan increased by a thousand per cent. Around 200,000 acres were planted to poppies in Kyrgyzstan. The number of opium growers tripled in Kazakhstan's Chu Valley. Plantations were springing up in Tajikistan. Others were spreading over a thousand square kilometres of empty radioactive terrain around Chernobyl.

Altogether, the 1992 crop was expected to be worth $5 billion.[56]

There was no proof up to then that the opium was being converted into refined heroin for export. But that was bound to come, and was 'probably happening' already, said the UN's anti-drug chief in Vienna.[57]

Meanwhile, an ant army of heroin couriers was moving up from the Golden Crescent through Tajikistan, Uzbekistan and Turkmenistan with forged papers, radio telephones and paramilitary protection, crossing the breadth of Soviet territory bound for Odessa on the Black Sea, for Finland, the Baltic states, Poland, Western Europe, America.[58]

Similar movement was under way from the Golden Triangle in southeast Asia, the heroin travelling across southern China into Kazakhstan and Kyrgyzstan.[59]

The drug mafia was taking over horizontally and vertically, from production and processing to transport, distribution and marketing.[60] Free of centralized surveillance, it moved largely unhindered across the crazy-quilt of internal Commonwealth borders, ignoring ethnic tensions.

'Our thieves-within-the-code have ruled that nationality conflicts should not be allowed to interfere in the work of the professional criminal core,' said Alexander Gurov, when the Union of Soviet Socialist Republics came crashing down.[61]

Apart from heroin and hash, underground laboratories started to produce synthetic drugs such as krokodil and chert (devil), a thousand times stronger than heroin. The most lethal, methyl-fentany – diluted in proportions of 1 to 20,000 –was made exclusively in Russia. These were cheaper than homegrown natural drugs, themselves two hundred times cheaper in Russia than in the West.

Soviet cities had always been a market of sorts, expanding as soldiers got hooked on heroin in the Afghanistan War. But galloping addiction set in only after traffickers mounted their assault around 1985. From then on, the addict population doubled yearly.[62]

By 1992, Russia had 1.5 million registered addicts or occasional drug users, according to General Alexander Sergeev, the Russian Interior Ministry's anti-narcotics chief. The figure was all the more startling for the carefully preserved fiction that socialist Russia had no addicts whatever. In fact, some Russian experts thought the 'real' figure was 'at least three to four times higher'. St Petersburg's anti-narcotics chief thought it was ten times higher.[63]

In that one year, the drug mafia's profits increased fourfold from 4 billion to 15 billion rubles: this even before its first harvest of modernized, commercialized crops.

Thus Russia had the rare distinction of being at once a user country, a transit country, and a producer country, all three on its customarily extravagant scale.

Russian traffickers were known to have been working heroin with Western counterparts, the Sicilian Mafia especially, since 1985.[64] By 1992, they were delivering heroin to Sicilian mafiosi in New York, selling amphetamines on the American market, and were said by Interpol Poland to have reached 'precise agreements in Warsaw with big German and Dutch cocaine traffickers, and Colombia's Cali cartel'.[65]

That year, in fact, a shipment of pure Colombian cocaine shaped into 34,000 pairs of Peruvian-made plastic sandals was sighted in Moscow, heading for Warsaw.[66]

Even then, the US State Department did not list Russia among forty-eight producer or transit countries, in its International Narcotics Control Strategy Report for 1992. No Western government publication did. In another year or so, they would. 'Russia may well become the bridgehead for all European traffic in drugs – be warned!' said the head of the Russian prosecutor-general's Research Institute, Vitaly Karpetz.[67]

Of all the Russian mafia's occupations, the biggest by far had to do with plundering the economy through multifarious, unbelievably lucrative fraud. This is where a prostrate country lay open to the international underworld.

A gluttonous horde of foreign carpetbaggers, speculators and assorted felons showed up as soon as Russia began to look West. 'It's like the old Texas oil-boom towns, a constant parade of con men, promoters and shady customers . . . the greatest collection of sleazebags in the world,' remarked US ambassador to Moscow Robert Strauss.[68]

The foreign invaders might be skinned by Russian partners, or walk off with the store; one American skipped with nine billion rubles – around $60 million at the time – while his Chechen partners awaited him in Moscow with axes and hatchets.[69]

Nevertheless there was money for all, in a partnership joining Western dollars with Russian expertise.

Russian criminals are unrivalled in the art of turning a dishonest dollar after seventy years of communist rule. Nothing is too small or too big, from selling unpaired shoes to clearing 100 billion rubles with fake Visa credit cards. The latter was just one of their more glittering operations in 1992.[70]

That spring, the Chechen mafia stole 30 billion rubles outright from the Russian state – roughly $200 million in mid-1992.[71] A straw bank in the minuscule Republic of Chechenia sent bogus 'credit advisories' for that amount to Russia's Central Bank: statements saying it had the sums on deposit. On the strength of this, the straw bank asked for a credit line in Moscow to import computers. The money didn't exist, nor did the bank in Chechenia, but Russia's Central Bank 'had no time' to ask questions, observed Big Crimes Investigator Uvarov, for whom this was the biggest crime yet.

The Central Bank sent the money to a dozen commercial banks in Moscow : 'the real money', Uvarov explained. Then, informed that the computer deal had fallen through, the commercial banks obligingly allowed the cash to be withdrawn and sent back to Chechenia, minus their cut.

Soon afterward, another fake credit advisory from Chechenia cost the Central Bank another 1.5 billion rubles. The money, invented again, was meant to pay for 500 imported Chrysler jeeps.

This time, an American named Kenneth Stebbins made off with the money. President of the American Grain Company and head of a Russian-based joint venture called BOL-CO, Stebbins was supposed to buy the jeeps in the US. Instead, he used the rubles in the Russian account as security to get a line of credit in dollars in his own American account, and vanished.[72]

Over the next months, the Central Bank was swamped with phony credit advisories from St Petersburg, Novgorod, Volgograd, Chelyabinsk, Daghestan, Perm, the Tatar Republic, the Chuvash Republic and elsewhere.

Altogether, announced the Russian Interior Ministry, the Central Bank converted 270 billion rubles from fake paper to cash in the course of 1992: around $1.8 billion snatched from an exhausted Treasury, nearly twice the total foreign investment in all joint ventures up to then.[73]

During the same year, Russia's Foreign Trade Ministry 'lost' $2 billion, Boris Yeltsin told a special conference on crime and corruption; the funds had simply disappeared from the Ministry's balance sheet.[74]

Officials of the Defence Ministry were 'stealing entire ammunition depots without fear of being caught,' Yeltsin said. Criminals were bribing heavily to get export licences, buying petroleum and precious

metals with rubles and selling these resources abroad for hard currency 'at a huge profit', he added.[75]

Petroleum, in the country with the world's biggest reserves, was
among the hotter items in what had become one big bargain basement
of Russian resources. Almost anybody properly connected could loot
the store, but the unique Soviet version of the joint venture was the
best way in.

Conceived as a magical bridge to capitalism, the joint venture was
supposed to transform the Soviet economy with model factories using
Western money and expertise. Dismayed by the unsteady Russian
scene, however, serious Western investors held back. Shady investors
had fewer qualms, especially with a smart mafioso for a partner.

Despite the ancient stricture of the Thieves' World – a death sentence for working 'outside' – half the mafia's thieves-within-the-code
were going directly into some new joint venture upon getting out of
jail. (The other half were unemployable invalids.)[76]

With them were the stars of the old Nomenklatura, unfailingly
summoned as 'consultants'. Even hardlining ex-Premier Valentin
Pavlov, jailed after the failed August putsch of 1991, was offered such
a job once 'certain legal and physical aspects' of his situation were
resolved.[77]

Under these auspices, the magical bridge to capitalism quickly
became 'a crooked world of rampant bribery and financial manipulation, aimed mainly at finagling permission to export cheap Soviet raw
materials for enormous profit,' wrote investigative journalist Elmar
Guseinov, in a major exposé in *Izvestiya*. 'The joint ventures we have
now are contemptible and must die – will die,' he concluded in 1990.[78]

Instead, they grew so pervasive and prosperous that even those
under unmistakeable mafia management – especially those, for their
energy and resourcefulness – were seen by many as the only way to
effect Russia's transition to capitalism.

Some said without blinking that the mafia should actually be legal-
ized to speed up the process. ('These people are insane,' said Big
Crimes Investigator Boris Uvarov.)

Capitalism generally starts out with a generation or two of piratical
robber barons who build railroads or drill oil wells and end up as the
backbone of the nation, the argument went. They create wealth first
and then pick up acceptable ethics to go with it, as John Rockefeller
did with Standard Oil in America. Such reasoning implied that people who fought America's robber barons a century ago were not only
wasting their breath and often their lives but actually getting in the

way of progress. Put baldly, it suggested that a democratic society is not necessarily menaced and may indeed be strengthened by a rising class of businessmen-hoods.

If any new democracy offered monumental proof to the contrary, it was Russia. While its cleaner joint ventures contributed marginally to the economy, those under criminal management contributed nothing, produced nothing, risked nothing, created no wealth save for the country's 100,000 new millionaires, who simply robbed what was there.

The case of Artjom Tarasov, free Russia's first accredited ruble millionaire, showed what a sharp businessman could do with a joint venture and sheer brass as free enterprise got under way in Moscow.

Tarasov, a young, dapper and fast-talking deputy in the Russian parliament, formed an independent joint venture called Istok in 1989. Founded by the Moscow Innovation Commercial Bank, it was authorized by the state to conduct various export-import transactions in raw materials, and 'provide assistance in organizing barter deals with foreign partners'.[79]

As Tarasov has said himself, he could only carry out such transactions 'by using *untraditional methods*' (his italics):

> Untraditional methods entailed very difficult work, which Istok did. To explain the essence of this work, let me propose shipping a small amount of fuel oil. No one will let you have the oil, the money for the purchase must be borrowed on interest from a commercial bank, no one will provide transportation, and if you find it, carloads are lost mandatorily on the way, the port does not even want to talk because it is overloaded with planned shipments, you find a tanker yourself and finally, no one will let you export fuel oil on a Russian licence, and no one on the foreign market wants to buy it since its quality is low-grade. We solved all these 'little' intermediary problems, and that is why we were untraditional.

Tarasov has never disclosed how he solved the little problems, leaving the Russian press to draw its own conclusions. This is *Izvestiya*'s version, among others:[80]

Soon after forming Istok, *Izvestiya* said, Tarasov went after Russia's petroleum. On behalf of an American associate wanted by the FBI – the biggest tax swindler in American history, indeed – he got 4 million tons of crude out of Russia on a legal export licence: buying at 50 rubles a ton ($5 on the black market then) and selling at $140 a ton abroad.[81]

In the summer of 1990, Tarasov asked the Premier of the Russian Republic, Ivan Silaev, for a licence to export 500,000 tons of heating oil, on the grounds that Russia had too much of it and lacked storage facilities. (Actually Russia had a cruel shortage of heating oil the following winter.)

The licence granted, Tarasov got government credits to pay for the heating oil. The head of customs was directed to accelerate shipment, while the Ministry of Transport provided the necessary railroad tankers.

By the time the presumably unsaleable low-grade heating oil reached the port of Odessa bound for the West, it was found to be 'a higher quality than indicated in the export contract – almost high-quality gasoline! – raising its sale price by a factor of two', Tarasov conceded.

Then Tarasov asked Premier Silaev for permission to put the proceeds of his heating oil/gasoline sales into an Istok account in a Western bank; this would dodge a 40% tax on hard currency imposed by the central Soviet government – the Enemy for the Russian Republic's government in 1990.

With the Russian Premier's permission, he opened an account in the Monaco branch of the French bank Paribas, sold the oil in Western Europe at a record price – $176 a ton, because of the Gulf War, he says – turned over $9 million of the proceeds to the Soviet government, put the rest into his Paribas account, and left Russia.

How much stayed in the Paribas account has never been established. According to Tarasov, '$11 million remained in Monaco'; *Izvestiya* spoke of $46 million; Tarasov's successor at Istok referred to a 'shortfall' of $27 million. [82]

Whatever the sum – and it must have been substantial – the balance did not go back to Russia, nor did Tarasov. Though it might be argued that no law had been broken, he nevertheless told *Izvestiya*: 'I assure you, I am ready to fly back tomorrow, but I am not sure that I would not be arrested right in the airport.'[83]

Prospects like these inevitably brought Russia's talented crooks and their political accomplices into burgeoning partnerships with Western counterparts: manipulating the country's currency, destabilizing its fragile economy, stripping it of its oil, gold, timber, copper, cobalt, aluminium, titanium, steel, uranium, plutonium and rare-earth metals.

Describing the scene in the summer of 1992, Moscow Interpol's deputy chief, Anatoly Terechov, declared:

> Less than half of our joint ventures work. Only a quarter deal with their declared activities. Two or three out of five are financed with money of dubious origin.
>
> Many joint ventures are fictitious. Often they're one-man operations to swing hard currency deals. Four thousand of them have right of access to the foreign market.
>
> At least 500 of our mafia groups use them to link up with international crime – in the United States, Italy, Germany, Austria, France, Canada, Poland . . .[84]

Six months later, Boris Yeltsin himself adjusted this last estimate upward. 'At least a thousand mafia groups have contacts with international organized crime,' he said.[85]

The American and Sicilian mafias were the first in, by way of what was arguably the biggest black market currency swap ever perpetrated (see Chapter 9). As they and others moved in deeper, their Russian confederates moved out farther.

For Big Crimes Investigator Uvarov, Western authorities still didn't realize what was going to hit them. 'Naturally it's wonderful that the Iron Curtain is gone, but it was a shield for the West,' he says. 'Now we've opened the gates, and this is very dangerous for the rest of the world.

'America is getting Russian criminals; Europe is getting Russian criminals. They'll steal everything. They'll *occupy* Europe. Nobody will have the resources to stop them. You people in the West don't know our mafia yet; you will, you will.'[86]

Part 3

The
Pax Mafiosa

6

In Europe

The map of the underworld in 1993 was full of surprises. The Russian mafia turned up in Sweden, Belgium, Holland, Luxembourg, Britain and several new American cities. The American mafia appeared in Russia. The Sicilian Mafia was in Russia also, working with both the Russians and the Americans.

American and Sicilian mafiosi had a 'South Russian International Bank' going in Sverdlovsk, heart of Russia's military-industrial complex.[1] Russian and American mafiosi had a 'Himbank' in Rochester, New York.[2] An 'Ndrangheta clan in Calabria was buying $2 billion worth of rubles from a German bank to buy a bank of its own in St Petersburg, along with a Russian steel mill and an oil refinery.[3]

The Russian mafia's Chechen were setting up a financial base in the City of London.[4] The Colombians had an 'office of representation' in Warsaw,[5] and a spectacular cocaine deal with the Russian mafia in St Petersburg.

Sicilian Mafia families were suddenly found to have a considerable presence not just in Germany but in France, Belgium and Holland. Other Sicilians appeared to be taking over at least two American mafia families (in Philadelphia and Boston).

Yakuza leaders came out from Tokyo to confer with their Western counterparts in Milan, Venice, Geneva and London.[6] The Triads were bringing massive reinforcements from Hong Kong to America, Britain and Holland, and filtering into nearly every state of Western Europe.

These were visible signs of the planetary attack force forming up among the most powerful crime syndicates on four continents: a phenomenon the world has never known. Free nations, slow to perceive it, had nothing like the strength needed to resist it – not in Europe, not in America, not anywhere.

Germany was the critical battleground. Criminals of seventy-nine nationalities were now operating on its territory. More than half were in mixed international groups with triangular connections: from Berlin to Russia and America, from Frankfurt to Italy and America, from Munich to Thailand and America.[7]

Distinctions between Europe and the United States were meaningless in this kind of criminal warfare. The Bundeskriminalamt (BKA), much the wiser since the fall of the Berlin Wall, could prove it in a hundred ways.

Proof was hardly needed for the Sicilian Mafia, commuting between Germany and the US since the 1960s. The startling performers were the Chechen, the Georgians, the Ukrainians – the whole villainous crew invading Germany from the former USSR

The Russian mafia was doing just what investigators in Moscow had been predicting since Soviet frontiers gave way. Barely three years after reaching Berlin, it had transferred $7 billion illicitly from Russia to Germany, and was reportedly notching up almost a third of the organized crimes there: this according to the Russian Interior Ministry.[8] Some 300 Russian gangs inside Germany were dealing in drugs, weapons, radioactive materials, antiquities, stolen cars, money-laundering and blackmail, with hooks out in every direction.[9]

The BKA had watched the pattern unfolding since the summer of 1991. The Chechen and Georgian clans, working their rackets inside the Russian emigré colony – blackmail, extortion, prostitution, gambling – were hardly noticed until they started to fight over turf.

That June, the Chechen shot the Georgians' leader, Tengis Marianashvili, in Berlin; he didn't die, and shot back. The following April, the Chechen killed him in Amsterdam. Three months later, a Georgian avenger killed one of the Chechen shooters, in New Jersey, USA. Half a year afterward, the Chechen killed an aide of the dead Georgian leader, in Luxembourg.

What were the Chechen doing in Luxembourg, Amsterdam and New Jersey? They were *travelling*, says the BKA. Everybody in the Russian mafia travelled.

One of their interests came to light in February 1993, when over a ton of cocaine was intercepted in St Petersburg. The largest shipment ever seized in Russia and the second largest in Europe, it marked the Russian mafia's maiden appearance on the big-time drug scene.

The Cali cartel had made the arrangements with Israeli traffickers in Colombia, who worked with a Russian mafia gang in Belgium, who worked with other Russian hoods in Amsterdam, who sent their people to pick up the cargo in St Petersburg and ship it on to Germany.[10]

Five or six of the Russians in the case were involved in much deeper matters. The same men were among the Russians watched by a special BKA team for over a year.

As soon as Germany's eastern borders went down, Russian crooks settling into Berlin had begun to set up an intricate web of interlocking joint ventures with Moscow, the BKA team had found. The parent 'export-import' companies were always in Berlin; 'daughter companies' cropped up in Belgium, Holland, Luxembourg, Hungary, South Korea, New York, Los Angeles and Miami. By the winter of 1993, new daughter companies were spreading to all three Baltic states.

'The same owners and managers appear over and over again,' the head of the BKA team, Wolfram Bieling, told me. 'Five or six run the show abroad, and they are very, very busy. They have ties with diamond dealers in Antwerp, and with the Russian mafia in Brooklyn. They have contacts all over Eastern Europe. They go back and forth to Russia. We know they're in permanent and close contact with the biggest mafia bosses in Moscow and St Petersburg . . .'[11]

The BKA could not break through their cover. They must have been swindling, which Chechen crooks did everywhere, and were bound to be laundering. (Two fellow-Chechen had settled into London with a million pounds sterling in cash to establish a base in the City. Both were murdered in their opulent and atrociously furnished London flats on the same day, in March 1993).[12]

They were almost certainly moving heroin. Their companies were shipping regularly by airfreight from southeast Asia to the US, ostensibly in transit for Berlin; but what usually reached Berlin was a cheap leather jacket or coat in an otherwise empty container.

While the BKA couldn't prove the heroin, it did find proof that they were manufacturing amphetamines. Two of their front companies, American Eagle and MS International, were importing the basic materials from Eastern Europe, and using chemists from Stasi, the former communist secret police. The refining was done inside Red Army barracks in Germany.[13]

Stranded when the Soviet empire fell apart, the Red Army's 280,000 troops in the eastern Länder were patsies for the Russian mafia. A good number were actually part of it. Four hundred and twenty Red Army gangs in Germany were working for mafia dons in Moscow by 1991, according to Soviet military intelligence. Some of their highest ranking officers, reportedly including their commander-in-chief, were involved in 'economic irregularities'.[14]

They were an inexhaustible source of every material item that a quarter of a million troops might possess. 'The Russian barracks are wide-open. Anybody can load up with booze, cigarettes, furniture, weapons, ordnance . . . It's a nightmare,' said an American customs agent back from a visit.

Newly established in-house companies like Russobalt West and Nevikon Share Holding were selling off weapons in bulk: Kalashnikovs, rockets, mines, anti-tank missiles. Fragmentation hand grenades were on sale for 5 DM apiece ($3.00).

Safe from government intrusion, the troops had duty-free clearance for these and all army supplies, and their own private border-crossing into Poland, at Katnin-Swinemunde, solely under Russian military control.[15]

Such rare opportunities for contraband and fraud brought out the very best in the Chechen. Fraud was what the Russian mafia excelled in, and its feats in Germany were hair-raising.

These things did not show up in official crime statistics. Though the fact seemed contrary to their nature, the Russians looked better on paper than most. The bodies they wrapped in concrete were fellow-Russians; the people they terrorized were Russian emigrés. They weren't laying a finger on German citizens, or killing rival foreign crooks, or joining multinational gangs, aside from stealing cars and smuggling, largely with Poles and other East Europeans. (The Italian end of the stolen car traffic was mostly handled in Italy.)

Their main source of revenue was defrauding the German government, with little need for violence and practically no risk. They used the Red Army to smuggle alcohol, cigarettes, videos, TVs, computers and weapons in and out of the country free of inspection and customs duties. They faked army commissary receipts and demanded tax refunds on enormous non-existent consignments. They stole consignments actually sent, and collected the tax refund. (Two hundred tons of pure alcohol shipped to the troops in Germany ended up on the Polish black market.)

Above all, they claimed hard currency from the German central bank for fictitious trade with the ex-Soviet bloc – the transfer ruble scam, their master stroke.

The transfer ruble was not currency, but an artificial paper price agreed upon for trade within Comecon, the Soviet bloc's soft-currency common market. It made no economic sense in a free market, where it spread havoc for two years after the Soviet bloc collapsed.

While East Europe's communist regimes started to go under in 1989, their central banks were obliged to honour the transfer ruble until it was formally abolished in January 1992. This window of opportunity allowed the Russian mafia and the KGB, among others, to rob the banks blind.

In Poland, whose zloty was convertible, 158 phony export-import companies appeared out of the blue, presenting bills for 2.5 billion rubles' worth of fake shipments to Russia. Several turned out to be KGB fronts; the Polish Interior Ministry thought the rest were either KGB or Russian mafia, or both.[16] Whoever they were, they collected $3 billion in dollars from Warsaw's Banku Handlowego in 1991, forty times the rubles' worth by then.[17]

Germany was hit much harder. After forming a monetary union with communist East Germany, the German central bank had to pay double for the transfer ruble, since it was paying in Federal deutschmarks worth twice East Germany's.[18]

Here the Russian mafia and KGB were joined by the former East Germany's Stasi. Three ex-Stasi agents alone were accused of faking transfer rubles to milk the Bundesbank for anywhere from a third of a billion to two billion dollars.[19]

Nevertheless, Russian crooks stood out as always. 'They *romped* through this scam,' said the BKA's organized crime expert Jurgen Maurer. 'They worked through the Deutsche Augsenhandelsbank in East Berlin, using forged contracts with Russia, forged documents for goods "Made in the German Democratic Republic", forged bills of lading, etc. The bank accepted any piece of paper. There were Russian murders here for the transfer rubles . . .'[20]

Thousands of fraud charges started to back up in the Berlin prosecutor's office. Russian crooks were still forging back-dated documents to file new claims in 1993. Sixty prosecutors expected to be working on such cases for the next ten years.

Altogether, the bill for scams in this category amounted to four or five times more than all the damage inflicted by domestic and foreign organized crime in Germany by 1993. ZERV, the special commission investigating unification frauds, put the estimated loss at seven billion deutschmarks just for transfer rubles, and twenty billion DM for all the scams combined – about thirteen billion dollars.[21]

The damage could not be reckoned merely in money. The Russians and criminals of seventy-eight other nationalities were inflicting severe psychological injury on the country.

Though they represented only a fraction of Germany's five million resident foreigners, they were now committing half the nation's crimes.[22] Highly visible and dangerously provocative, they provided the excuse for an eruption of vicious racism such as Germany had not seen since Hitler's fall.

Crime was becoming an obsessive German concern. Six million incidents of criminal violence in 1992, a 'dramatic deterioration' of law and order and 'an enormous increase in aggression', every third family with a crime victim, 232,000 emergency calls to the Berlin police alone, SWAT teams going in against killers with Kalashnikovs and pit bulls, 140,000 actual criminal acts, 623 organized crime cases before the courts, 130,000 stolen cars, a steady rise in new heroin users, 2,091 overdose deaths, three murders a day: this, for an orderly population of eighty million, was 'getting close to an American level', observed an indignant editor.[23]

The big players were growing bigger and more efficient.

The Turkish mafia was bringing in three or four hundred kilos of heroin at a time, nearly all on the new Balkan route through Eastern Europe. Kurds in the communist PKK, financing their terrorist assault on the Turkish government, were bringing in a ton a year.[24]

Powerful Triad structures were forming in Hamburg, Hannover, Mannheim, Frankfurt and Stuttgart, with connections to Amsterdam, London, Hong Kong and Macao. Triad gamblers, arsonists and killers were drifting into the country with forged British passports: passing counterfeit currency, stealing credit cards, bringing in Oriental prostitutes, dipping into the fragrant oil in Germany's small Chinese colony.

Within barely a year, they had smuggled in at least 10,000 illegal immigrants from Hong Kong, Macao and the Chinese mainland. Nearly a thousand a month were being *caught* at the east German border by 1993.[25] Some were used as enforcers or drug couriers, others as indentured servants paid $1.00 an hour in Chinese restaurants, the Triads' version of the Sicilian Mafia's pizza parlour. Germany had 3,000 Chinese restaurants by 1992, up from 900 the year before.

Mixed teams of various nationalities with a hundred members or more were emerging across the country. They did heroin and cocaine, burglary, theft, prostitution, and so on, and they didn't fight. 'The killings are always within each of the big groups, not across lines. Italians kill Italians, Russians kill Russians, but they don't kill each other,' says the BKA's Jurgen Maurer.

Maurer and his colleagues had learned a lot since the shock of exposure in 1990, about the Italians especially. The more they discovered, the larger the Mafia loomed as the most dangerous threat of all.

The Sicilians and their associates on the Italian mainland were increasingly present, and known to be present, yet maddeningly elusive.

Four out of five Italian businessmen in Germany were paying the *pizzo*, now spreading for the first time to German citizens in Frankfurt. Killer-commandos answering to Palermo, or Catania, or Palma di Montechiaro were parked in a dozen German cities or small towns.

Nearly every important drug bust revealed a shadowy Sicilian figure somewhere in the background. A major Sicilian-German drug ring was moving cocaine directly from Colombia to Frankfurt to Milan. The Russo brothers of Gela, wanted in Sicily for extortion and multiple murder, had an arms-drugs gang of a hundred members in Dortmund, seat of a ring linking Germany to Italy and Belgium.[26]

Counterfeit currency, stolen credit cards, burglary, gambling, loan sharking, sex shops and porno, passing stolen cheques and bonds, running stolen cars into the country and weapons out of it: all this was in their range.

And they were swarming over Eastern Germany.

Two thousand Camorristi were working the eastern Länder, according to Naples police chief Umberto Vecchione. These were the *magliari* – sweater-peddlers, a term of contempt – using the same cover here as everywhere; they ran cheap leather and textile shops, and hawked tatty clothes with big labels.[27]

The Mafia was sending new men up from Sicily, with 150,000 DM in seed money to open discos, casinos, pizzerias. 'After a short while, they set up chains of pizzerias that hardly make a profit. But they drive around in big cars and they're big spenders. So they're washing money,' a BKA agent explained.

Leipzig and Dresden, the two key cities of eastern Germany, were practically sewn up already. The Mafia's Morabito family of Catania, related by blood to the 'Ndrangheta's notorious Santo Pasquale Morabito, was said by German intelligence to have bought $100 million worth of real estate in Leipzig – not just any real estate but the choice part in the city's historic old quarter.[28]

Dresden was falling, or had fallen, to the family of Gaetano Fidanzati, the Mafia's one-time ambassador to the Camorra in Naples, one of the most assiduous drug traffickers extant.

From their bases in eastern Germany, the Italians were spreading eastward over an open border to Poland and Czechoslovakia. The Camorra's Licciardi clan had built up a heavy trade with Warsaw and Moscow, and particularly close ties to the Chechen.[29]

Germany had no laws to stop them. Rumours had the Mafia buying real estate up and down the Rhine Valley and along Frankfurt's 'noble mile', washing a fortune in narcodollars through German banks, and investing it in east German land, buildings and factories privatized by Treuhand, the national agency in charge.

Almost none of this could be proved, however. The BKA was still too hobbled to go after dirty money. A new law in September 1992 made laundering a criminal offence, but hardly improved the chances of detecting it.

No investigation was permissible without convincing evidence that the money to be laundered came from a specific crime, or that the crime of laundering itself was about to happen. In effect, this meant no investigation.

BKA agents could not check out a Sicilian suspect on a police tip from Italy; they could only work from police records. They could not begin to investigate one known Sicilian mafioso – convicted in Italy – without strong evidence that he was on the verge of committing a crime. 'He's just a guy who lives in Germany,' responded a prosecutor who refused to open the case.

Agents could not use any instrument of surveillance, even a spy-glass, unless its use was specified by law; anything else was an invasion of privacy. They could not hire non-German agents to deal with crooks who spoke no German. They could not bug a hotel room under any circumstances, or even make practical use of an undercover agent.

Undercovers were still forbidden to commit any criminal act, such as trespassing or playing a hand of poker with the mob. The new law made a single exception, allowing them to use false papers. Thus, the agent could set up an undercover company that seemed *ready* to launder drug money, in order to entice a real launderer. But he could not *actually* launder it without being guilty of laundering himself.

A lot of money was still being laundered safely in Germany, therefore. The BKA, too severely restrained to investigate deeply, could only guess how much. Though intelligence analysts spoke of fifty billion deutschmarks invested by the Italian Mafia, they couldn't prove it. 'We tried for a year to check this out, and we couldn't find any sources to confirm it,' Jurgen Maurer told me.

That didn't necessarily mean there were no big investments, he added: quite the contrary.

The newly-annexed eastern side of Germany was a magnet for German criminals, Asian and African criminals, the American mafia looking at casinos, the Russian mafia looking at everything west of Russia – the whole international crime set. It was now part of an opulent nation with the softest laws on crime in Western Europe; it was an open door to Eastern Europe; and its entire economy was up for sale.

Normal capital was holding back, put off by administrative confusion and uncertain property rights. But illicit capital didn't mind. ('No stockholders,' says Maurer.) In the view of authorities like Maurer, the big crime cartels had 'very big possibilities' for investment in the east German Länder.

The fact that Germany couldn't find the dirty money was not just a matter of permissive laws for criminals and restrictions for cops. Most Western states had tougher laws by 1993 and couldn't find the money either.

Yet it was there, more than $120 billion a year of criminal capital moving around the world according to the Group of Seven's financial task force, GAFI: four-fifths of it in the West, festering in free societies like a wasting disease with few outward symptoms. 'We can't say where it is; we think nobody can,' says Jurgen Maurer. 'No agency knows how much is invested in Germany, or in Europe, or in America.'[30]

Europe's single market was only a few months away when a Japanese passenger of evident means and sober bearing was picked up at Charles de Gaulle airport in Paris and shipped home. He was Masaru Takumi, underboss of the Yamaguchi-Gumi, the Yakuza group with 30,000 members, by far the strongest in Japan.

Takumi had just got out of jail in Osaka, where he had been detained for five days on a charge of illegal currency dealings in Canada. Free to travel despite his brush with the law, he had taken off for France to keep an appointment there with two other members of the Yamaguchi-Gumi hierarchy and its all-powerful top boss, Yoshinori Watanabe.

From Paris, they were planning a swing around Europe – London, Geneva, Venice, Milan. After Takumi's run-in with the French police, the trip was called off.

That was just one trip, however. Five hundred members of the

Yakuza travelled west in the course of 1992, according to a deputy police commissioner in Tokyo. 'They were going to visit their mafia colleagues for the first time,' he said.[31]

But it was not the first time. A similar delegation had made almost exactly the same swing around Europe in 1984 – Paris, London, Geneva, Rome. Indeed, the Yakuza had been working the West for years.[32]

The US, their prime target since the 1970s, was a long while spotting them, but European authorities took still longer. Aside from one seemingly minor episode, not a single Yakuza operation had caught police attention on the continent for a decade.

The apparently minor episode happened in Paris, in April 1992, shortly before Yamaguchi-Gumi's aborted visit. A hundred and fifty orientals laundering for the Yakuza were rounded up at one go. They were 'worker ants', shopping daily at Hermès and Louis Vuitton boutiques for expensive items to be resold at a discount in Japan.

Four Japanese and two Chinese money-washers had recruited them through newspaper ads and supplied them with the necessary cash. The money was coming into France by way of the Channel Islands, Luxembourg and Switzerland.[33]

The trick looked very nearly harmless, particularly since nobody knew where or how the money had been made in the first place. If the Yakuza were running true to form, however, the money was likely to have come from trafficking in guns or amphetamines, loan-sharking, high-stakes gambling, the sex trade or multinational corporate blackmail. (The Yamaguchi-Gumi also had an overseas department renting out killers.)

Such activities had been impressed upon the minds of American authorities since 1984, when an *oyabun* of the Yamaguchi-Gumi described its spreading subterranean operations in the US to the President's Commission on Organized Crime.[34]

Two years before that, Japan's police commissioner had bumped accidentally into a number of Yamaguchi-Gumi members in Paris, running guns. That year, a member of the Yakuza's Kyosei-kai was picked up in Japan for smuggling in 300 Garesi handguns from Milan.

During the previous year, one of the Yakuza's most polished *sokaiya*, Seiji Hamamoto, had set up a 'foreign correspondent office' in London to blackmail the big Japanese companies there.[35]

By 1984, another *sokaiya* group, Rondan Doyukai, was storming the heights of European finance. Departing from custom, they took on three un-Japanese firms, all powerful and immensely rich: Rotterdamsch

Beleggings Consortium, Compagnie Française des Petroles, and Compagnie Financière de Paris et des Pays Bas, known as Paribas.

Not all of the *sokaiya's* traditional methods were workable here. Shouting, throwing furniture around or slapping the chairman of the board were less likely to cause shame than shocked outrage in these boardrooms, followed by a rude journey to jail.

But other classic methods might work: a threat to circulate rumours of company malfeasance, or raise incandescent questions at stockholders' meetings, or publish falsified statements of corporate earnings, in several thousand copies. The *sokaiya* have tried these tactics on some of the biggest corporations in America.[36]

Doubtless it was with something of the sort in mind that the Rondan Doyukai *sokaiya* bought thousands of dollars' worth of shares of the three companies in their sights. They were moving in for the kill when somebody in Paris spotted them.

These details, published in the fine book *Yakuza* in 1986, were practically unknown to European authorities until five years later, when a European Parliament report mentioned the Paribas affair. 'The attempt to take over Groupe Paribas was only just avoided,' the report noted.[37]

Soon afterward, Germany's BND warned that the Yakuza was investing heavily in all the EC states. Two senior Japanese police officers confirmed that it was 'laundering money everywhere, in every kind of financial institution or industry, legitimate or illicit' – just like the Sicilian Mafia, they agreed on a visit to Italy.[38]

Alas, the two mafias had much in common, observed Palermo's police chief. In fact, they were working together on at least one project by then: in a Yakuza-backed construction company, engaged in building projects in Australia.[39]

The Yakuza's silent invasion of Europe has continued undisturbed nonetheless. No agency on the continent keeps a close eye on it even now.

The FBI does, convinced that syndicates like the Yamaguchi-Gumi are riding on the backs of Japan's giant corporations to build a singularly seditious power-base in America (see Chapter 7). Yet the true relationship between Japan's crooks and capitalists abroad is hardly much clearer to the FBI than to its opposite numbers in Europe.

Nobody knows which of Japan's corporations in the outside world may be secretly at the Yakuza's mercy, how much money it may be extracting from them or investing through them, what hidden pressures may be at work behind politely closed doors.

*

In the summer of 1992, a Chinese girl living in Rome called Lyao Zing Yang was kidnapped in Paris. Her Triad captors demanded a ransom of 400 million lire, about $350,000. But Lyao Zing Yang jumped out of a bathroom window and escaped, whereupon they were arrested instead.

This might be a humdrum story, if not for the Triads' whereabouts. Most people thought they were just in New York, Amsterdam and London, where they had been implanted for a hundred years.

In fact, they had snatched the girl in Paris to avoid drawing police attention to Rome, where a flourishing Triad group calling itself Red Sun worked in tandem with others in Florence, Milan, Padua and Turin, linked to still others in Paris, Marseilles and Barcelona.[40]

Red Sun's supreme leader in Rome, arrested some months later, turned out to have been the resident of a small but swiftly expanding Chinese emigré colony there.

The Triads had smuggled 8,000 illegal Chinese immigrants into Italy in just two years, nearly half again the size of the country's entire Chinese community. Around 800 more a month were arriving in Milan, authorities thought.[41]

The same passports were used over and over again to sneak them in. Some were blanks sent out in bulk from China in cartons of ginseng and kung fu slippers. Most were stolen from Japanese tourists by lightfingered South Americans, who sold them to the Triads. Replacing the photographs was no problem: Chinese often look alike to Western eyes (and vice versa).

Those 'in search of the full moon' were charged up to $25,000 just to get out of China: to Moscow by train (six days), to Budapest by bus, to Yugoslavia by taxi (for an extra $5,000), or straight to the Italian border by train again.[42]

Whoever couldn't pay up was put to work as a bonded slave in Italy's proliferating Chinese restaurants, or in Florentine sweatshops stitching expensive handbags.

Two thousand Chinese illegals worked eighteen hours a day in eighty cramped shops like these along the Via Pistoiese, in the Florence suburb of Dannino. Taken over from Italian owners for considerably more cash than they were worth, these shops were now under Chinese management.

Surprising amounts of capital were also going into new Chinese restaurants with empty tables. Police were particularly intrigued by one in Rome's historic centre that cost $17 million.[43]

What worried Italian authorities more were the better-heeled young Chinese in snappy suits and dark glasses, arriving in the hundreds.

These were the *cho-hai*, the sharks – killers, enforcers, pimps, dippers into the fragrant oil, those who beat up recalcitrant Chinese businessmen with chains or kidnapped their wives and daughters.

The *cho-hai* were mostly coming down from a booming Chinatown in Paris, where affluent newcomers from Hong Kong were buying up shops around the Place d'Italie for well above the market price, paying cash.

Others were putting cash into more ambitious projects, such as a shopping centre and two luxury hotels on a 300-acre plot along the River Seine, 100 kilometres from Paris.[44]

Several were found to be working with the Medellín cartel's men in a ring that laundered a third of a billion dollars (1,500,000,000 francs) in 1991, through exchange bureaux in the Basque provinces of southern France.[45] (Police had got on to these bureaux because clients came at midnight with suitcases full of cash.)

France and Italy appeared to be the Triads' new countries of choice: so the police of both agreed at a crisis meeting in Lyon. But the *cho-hai* were fanning out across all the rest of the continent. Like the Yakuza, their closest friends, the Triads were flocking to the honeypots of Europe.

This was no reflection on America. No country compared to America, where the Triads were now the Justice Department's 'Number two priority after La Cosa Nostra'.[46] They were on a roll everywhere, but Europe figured large in their plans.

The tens of thousands of Chinese illegals smuggled by Triad 'snake-heads' were not only more profitable than heroin; they were a practical necessity.

Hong Kong, the Triads' window on the world for over a century, would revert to communist China in 1997. They might go back to the mainland they had fled after the communist takeover – many were in fact going back – but it would never be home.

They were still enjoyably free in the British Crown Colony, despite being outlawed. The law provided only a six-month mandatory sentence for Triad membership, a one-off offence. 'Once you get convicted, you can't be charged again. It's fashionable to get convicted; you just do your time,' says Paul Nesbitt, a Hong Kong police officer on loan to Interpol.[47]

Here, for all the efforts of a frustrated police force, they refined and shipped dope, worked gambling, usury, extortion and vice, laundered and invested ten-digit sums, and made the most of awakening China's insatiable hunger for the baubles of an affluent society.

For instance, they were averaging a million dollars a night smuggling stolen luxury cars to the Chinese mainland – Mercedes, BMWs, Toyota Crowns, ferried across in super speedboats (1200 horsepower, 140 kilometres an hour).[48]

Though unlikely to find such working conditions elsewhere, they had to move their money out, organize new refineries, relocate terminals for their underground communications and banking system, and build up more and bigger Chinese colonies to insulate their bases abroad. This was an immense undertaking for one of the six biggest crime cartels on earth – the only one soon to be without a country of its own.

The Triads had grown beyond recognition since the start of the heroin age. Once they had merely preyed on their countrymen in the Chinatowns of Amsterdam and London, San Francisco and New York. By the 1990s, they had outposts on three of the four continents.

A hundred thousand members were spread out in loosely associated gangs across the Chinese mainland, southeast Asia, Western Europe and North America.

Great umbrella groups held smaller gangs together. The Sun Yee On had 40,000 members positioned all over the map from Australia, Thailand and Vietnam to the United States. The United Bamboo Gang had 15,000 reaching from Taiwan to Saudi Arabia to Los Angeles. The 14K had 24,000 strung out from China, Taiwan, Macao and the Philippines to the US, Canada, Australia, New Zealand, Germany, Britain, Holland, Italy and France.

Like the Sicilian Mafia before them, they were rising to the heights of the underworld on heroin.

Despite their privileged access to the poppy fields of Burma, the Triads had yielded to the Mafia for twenty years. While they had a handle on two-thirds of the world's heroin supply, the Sicilians had the market. Since they were not good at operating outside the Chinese community, they left it like that.

The two brotherhoods had always got along. In New York, where Little Italy and Chinatown are back to back, one or the other 'only had to cross the road from Mott Street to Mulberry Street and make contacts with people interested in the narotics business,' a DEA agent once observed.

'Maybe the Chinese had two, three, four, five Italians that they trusted, and the Italians trusted *them*. You would never, never hear of a Chinese guy being arrested and giving up an Italian. You would never hear of an Italian giving up a Chinese, never.'[49]

So, for two decades, the Triads let the Mafia buy all the southeast Asian heroin it wanted in Thailand – China White, the addicts' favourite – and the Mafia let the Triads bring in about a fifth of America's.

By 1983, Thailand swarmed with Sicilian traffickers, whose Chinese suppliers were selling to them by the ton. One alone, called Koh Bak Kin, consigned 3,750 kilos of morphine base on his first delivery to Palermo from Bangkok – enough to produce nearly four tons of heroin, out of the six consumed yearly in America. He was filling orders for another ton or so when he was arrested.[50]

Halfway through the 80s, however, Italian and American authorities cracked down on the Sicilians' network. Though far from wrecked, it was disrupted, whereupon the Triads set up their own refineries in Thailand and elsewhere and filled the breach.

In the space of just a few years, the roles were reversed. The Triads came to provide nearly four-fifths of the heroin reaching New York, and about a fifth of Europe's on top of that.

Obviously Europe was next. Its market was going through the roof – the EC's addict population hit a million in 1992 – and the Triads were going after it. Their conduits were London and Amsterdam, which had the largest and oldest Chinatowns in Europe. London was getting tough for them, but Amsterdam was now the hinge of the entire continent's heroin trade.

Nearly everybody dealing dope passed through its Schiphol airport, a notorious pushover, or the docks of Rotterdam, or along the Balkan route, which ended in Holland. From there the junk went one way to New York or the other way to Germany, Belgium, Italy, France.

Competition was especially fierce from Turkish traffickers, whose countrymen in Holland outnumbered the Chinese four to one; (400,000 to 100,000, of which nearly half were illegals). The Triads couldn't hope to overtake the Turkish mafia in Europe anyway.

Nevertheless, they had an airlift going from the Far East to Schiphol airport, new refineries and shipping routes on the Chinese mainland, and thousands of captive Chinese helpers arriving on the continent.[51]

East Europe was opening out to them, or their potential captives. 'More and more Chinese' were coming to Poland, reported the head of Interpol in Warsaw. Trainloads of Chinese illegals were crossing Ukraine into Hungary, now offering residence permits to any Chinese citizen of Hong Kong for $100,000. (The Hungarian airline, Malev, carried the ad.)[52] Others were slipping into Austria, Scandinavia, Spain.

Doubtless the Triads weren't winning, but they were gaining.

The Sicilian Mafia did not fight them in America, nor was it fighting them in Europe; it was brokering for them. Partnered with Turkish traffickers for twenty years, it was brokering for the Turks too.

Like their opposite numbers in Russia, Sicilian mafiosi *travelled*. Who would expect them to turn up in Sverdlovsk, deep in the Ural Mountains, a thousand kilometres from Moscow? Yet Russian intelligence agents came upon one in February 1993, when he and an American mafia partner opened the 'South Russian International Bank' there.[53]

What the pair had in mind can only be guessed. Sverdlovsk is at the centre of the famous military-industrial complex that once drove the Soviet economy and equipped the Red Army. Its factories are still turning out tanks and sophisticated weaponry that the Red Army can no longer afford to buy. Others can buy the weaponry freely and legally, however, provided the transactions are not for direct export.[54]

Quantities are exported indirectly and illegally, reaching world markets through front companies in northern Italy, by way of a KGB agent's network in Vienna (see Chapter 11).

Sverdlovsk is also the region embracing Tyumen, which has more petroleum reserves than the entire Middle East. Furthermore, Sverdlovsk is the home base for the Big Urals, the consolidated Russian mafia gang now operating across ex-Soviet territory from the Baltic to the Pacific.

Perhaps the South Russian International Bank will have yielded its secrets by the time this book is published; perhaps not. Detecting the crimes of a crooked bank in today's Russia is extremely difficult; nailing the crooks even more so.

Other mafiosi, Sicilian and American, were certainly operating in the ex-Soviet republics by 1993. Documented evidence pointed to connections of some sort with the Madonia and Troia families of Palermo, the Santapaola family of Catania, the Cuntrera family of Siculiana and Caracas, the Morabito family of Calabria, the Licciardi clan of Naples, the American mafia's Biondo family in Detroit and Gambino family in New York. Their partners in the Cali cartel were present too.[55]

Nobody in authority could determine how many were actually on the Russian scene or, with a few interesting exceptions, what they were doing there.

Italian investigators looking for the tracks of Italian crooks in

Former Prime Minister Giulio Andreotti
(left) with his longtime spokesman in Sicily,
Salvo Lima, known now to have been a made
member of the Mafia. Lima was shot to death
by a Mafia hit team in early 1992 when he
could no longer deliver judicial protection
for Mafia bosses.
(Publifoto)

Pasquale Cuntrera, the most
powerful of the three Cuntrera
brothers, who directed the Sicilian
Mafia's North American heroin
trade from Caracas, Venezuela, for
nearly a quarter of a century. He is
photographed here in the VIP lounge
of Rome's Fiumicino airport,
following his expulsion from
Venezuela in October 1992.
(Mario Proto)

The bold and inventive Marat
Balagula, who towered over the
Russian mafia in Brighton Beach,
Brooklyn, during the 1980s.

Russian Mafia boss Evsei Agron,
who wielded a cattle prod to keep his
Brighton Beach subjects in line until
his murder in 1985.

Judges Giovanni Falcone (left) and Paolo
Borsellino, intimate friends and staunch
allies, both murdered by the Mafia in
Palermo in 1992.
(Publifoto)

Mr. ██████████████
AMBERHAVEN LTD.
July 9, 1990
Page Two

    However, as any good smuggler can tell you "Nothing is impossible". We will instead have the PROMSTROJBANK issue a letter that the checks are unencumbered.

Now: "Let's you and I knock the flies off", and find solutions to this valid transaction. I believe we are all singing out of the same "hymn book", but one of us is "tone deaf".

Respectfully submitted.

Jack Tremonti

Jack Tremonti/ by ██████████████

A piquant phrase in Jack Tremonti's letter to Michael Preisfreund's agent in Amberhaven Ltd, offering to sell 500 million rubles on deposit in his account at Moscow's Promstrojbank.

ХИМБАНК

COMMERCIAL BANK OF CHEMICAL INDUSTRY OF RUSSIA

COMMERCIAL STOCKHOLDING BANK–"HIMBANK"

29, MJASNICKAJA STREET, 101851 MOSCOW, RUSSIAN FEDERATION

Issuing Office:-   OFFICE FOR INTERNATIONAL AFFAIRS
111 ALEXANDER STREET, ROCHESTER, N.Y. 14620-1105

Letter of Indemnity/Guarantee

Guarantee No. NB   US   Dollars
             Rochester, New York   of April 1993.

    As security for a credit which you will grant to   we Commercial Stockholding Bank "HIMBANK", Rochester, New York office, hereby irrevocably undertake to pay you on first demand, irrespective of the validity and the effects of the above-mentioned credit relationship and waiving all rights of objection and defences arising therefrom, any amount up to   million   hundred thousand dollars ($), INCLUDING PRINCIPAL, INTEREST AND OTHER CHARGES, in lawful currency of the United States of America. Upon receipt of your duly signed request for payment by duly encoded telex stating that the amount claimed has become due to you by the end of the term, 12 months and 5 days from the date of issuance, April 1993. Your claim will be considered as having been made once we are in possession of your written request for payment or the telex to this effect.

    The total amount of this indemnity will be reduced by any payment effected hereunder.

    Our indemnity is valid until   April 1994 and expires in full automatically if your claim has not been made on or before that date, regardless of such date being a banking day or not.

    This arrangement is governed by the laws of the United States of America.
    For and on behalf of COMMERCIAL STOCKHOLDING BANK "HIMBANK"
          MOSCOW, RUSSIAN FEDERATION.

....
authorised signature

....
authorised signature

STATE OF NEW YORK
COUNTY OF MONROE

before me personally came Terry John

The mysterious 'Himbank' operated by Russian and American mafiosi offers its phony credentials.

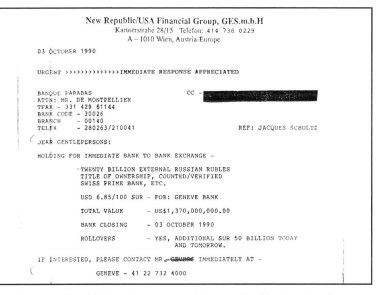

P5

in two or three addresses in
MOSCOW AND FROM EXPERIENCE I KNOW
how ALL BANKERS (LOVE TO) TALK NO MATTER
where they are in the WORLD — AND unilaterally
+ privately DECIDED to play A CATALYTICAL
ROLE to CRASH the Rouble — IT WAS
IN AUGUST THAT I SET UP the tRACKING
OF INTERNAL AND EXTERNAL SUPPLIES of
Roubles AND how the exchange RATES could
BE ARTIFICIALly MANIPULATED ON PAPER
IN SPITE OF the (all profiteers-) PREISFREUNDS WANTA'S
TREMONTI's — let them pReDICT if they
could, I WAS AFTER IVAN'S JUGULAR.
SOME of THOSE (STRANGE) pAGES of seemingly
UNINTERESTING NAUTICAL TERMS etc. coupled
with the FLOOD = other paperwork

Mr X explains his 'unilateral and private decision ... to crash the ruble' in a fax to the author.

New Republic/USA Financial Group, GES.m.b.H
Kärntnerstraße 28/15 Telefon: 414 738 0229
A – 1010 Wien, Austria-Europe

03 OCTOBER 1990

URGENT >>>>>>>>>>>>>IMMEDIATE RESPONSE APPRECIATED

```
BANQUE PARABAS                    CC – ████████████████
ATTN: MR. DE MONTPELLIER
TFAX  - 331 429 81144
BANK CODE - 30026
BRANCH    - 00140
TELEX     - 280263/210041              REF: JACQUES SCHULTZ
```

DEAR GENTLEPERSONS:

HOLDING FOR IMMEDIATE BANK TO BANK EXCHANGE –

    · TWENTY BILLION EXTERNAL RUSSIAN RUBLES
    TITLE OF OWNERSHIP, COUNTED/VERIFIED
    SWISS PRIME BANK, ETC.

    USD 6.85/100 SUR – FOB: GENEVE BANK

    TOTAL VALUE   – US$1,370,000,000.00

    BANK CLOSING   – 03 OCTOBER 1990

    ROLLOVERS   – YES, ADDITIONAL SUR 50 BILLION TODAY
                    AND TOMORROW.

IF INTERESTED, PLEASE CONTACT MR. GRUBER IMMEDIATELY AT –

    GENEVE – 41 22 732 4000

The mighty French bank Paribas appears to be buying 20 million Russian rubles from the American swindler Leo Wanta in 1990. The price, $1.3 billion, was about half the going rate on world money markets at the time.

Orlando Cediel Ospina-Vargas of Colombia, better known as 'Tony' Duran, photographed secretly during his stay in Rome in the autumn of 1992, to negotiate a top-level partnership between the Sicilian Mafia and Colombia's main cocaine cartels.
(Mario Proto)

Leo Wanta, the American snake-oil salesman who stormed world money markets to crash the ruble in 1990-91.

John Galatolo, proudly displaying his marlin on the island of Aruba, where he negotiated a historic deal on the part of the Sicilian Mafia with representatives of Colombia's Medellín cartel in 1987.
(Police Photo)

Salvatore 'Totò' Riina, the Sicilian Mafia's fearsome capo di tutti i capi, *photographed on the day of his capture after twenty-three years in hiding. The portrait on the wall above him is of General Carlo Alberto Dalla Chiesa, murdered by the Mafia in 1982.*
(Publifoto)

ПОСТАНОВЛЕНИЕ
ВЕРХОВНОГО СОВЕТА РСФСР

О результатах депутатского расследования
по фактам заключения соглашений между россий-
скими организациями и иностранными фирмами

The Russian Parliamentary report on the 140 billion ruble scam: front pages and signatures of Commission members for the final report dated February 27, 1991.

PAR LA PRÉSENTE NOUS FAISONS SAVOIR À TOUS QUE LE CITOYEN
DE LA RÉPUBLIQUE ITALIENNE MONSIEUR LE VICAIRE GÉNÉRAL

ROBERTO COPPOLA

EST NOMMÉ LE CONSUL ITINERANT CHARGÉ DE LA CHARITÉ DANS LE MONDE
DE LA RÉPUBLIQUE FÉDÉRALE SOCIALISTE SOVIÉTIQUE DE LA RUSSIE.

LE SOVIET SUPRÊME DE RSFSR PRIE DE LUI ACCORDER TOUTES AIDES
ET PROTECTION DANS SES ACTIVITÉS INTERNATIONALES AUX INTÉRÊTS DE LA
RÉPUBLIQUE FÉDÉRALE SOCIALISTE SOVIÉTIQUE DE LA RUSSIE.

LE NOMINATION PREND EFFET ET SERA VALABLE APRÈS SA SIGNATURE.

... DU SOVIET SUPRÊME
DE RSFSR   ELTSINE B.N.

LE MINISTRE DES AFFAIRES
ÉTRANGÈRES DE RSFSR   KOZYREV A.V.

MOSCOU, LE 10 OCTOBRE 1990

27 февраля 1991 г.

А. Починок
Д. Воронин
В. Вгучевский
А. Гуров
Д. Жигулин
Е. Кожокин
В. Сердюков
И. Смирнов

Diplomatic credentials for Roberto Cappola, according him 'all aid and protection in his international activities in the interests of the Federal Socialist Soviet Republic of Russia', signed by Boris Yeltsin and his Foreign Affairs Minister, Andrei Kozyrev, on October 10, 1990.

New Republic/USA Financial Group, GES.m.b.H
Karnerstrabe 28/15 Telefon: (414)738.0229
A – 1010 Wien, Austria-Europe

25 SEPTEMBER 1990

CONFIRMING

PREPARED FOR: MR. AVEL DE MILLER AND ASSOCIATES
STARL AG VADUZ
ATTN: MR. AXEL DE MILLER

IRREVOCABLE/CONFIRMING PURCHASE ORDER NO: SUR/90.EXT.04

WE, NEW REPUBLIC/USA FINANCIAL GROUP, GmbH, ARE READY, WILLING AND ABLE AS A USDOLLAR PROVIDER WITH GOOD, CLEAN, CLEAR AND LEGAL USDOLLARS TO EFFECT THE IMMEDIATE EXCHANGE(S) OF EXTERNAL RUSSIAN ROUBLES (SUR), WHICH ARE TO BE CLEAN, CLEAR, GOOD, LEGAL, BUNDLED, COUNTED, VERIFIED, PACKED AND STAMPED IN 100 DENOMINATION BANKNOTES BY A PRIME/FIRST CLASS BANK FOR THE AMOUNT OF ___100 BILLION___ SUR, WITH ROLLOVERS PLANNED UP TO MAXIMUM AVAILABILITY, UNTIL EITHER FUNDING IS EXHAUSTED.

COMMODITY : EXTERNAL RUSSIAN ROUBLES – CASH SUR NOTES
EXCHANGE(S) : TWENTY FIVE BILLION SUR PER DAILY EXCHANGE TRANCHE, CIF: ZURICH, SWITZERLAND.

EXCHANGE RATE : USDOLLARS SIX POINT SIX THREE PER 100 SUR
MODE OF EXCHANGE : LETTER OF CREDIT, SIGHT DRAFT AND/OR SWIFT WIRE TRANSFER AGAINST PRESENTATION OF THE FOLLOWING BANK DOCUMENTS:

        A. DEPOSIT CERTIFICATES
        B. VERIFYING CERTIFICATES
        C. REPATRIATION CERTIFICATES

        (ALL BANKING FEES/COSTS TO SUR PROVIDER ACCOUNT)

BANKING COORDINATES : TO BE EXCHANGED UPON SUR PROVIDER RWAD ACCEPTANC OF ABOVE-MENTIONED TERMS AND CONDITIONS THROUGH RELEASE OF ADDENDUM A.

DELIVERY : IMMEDIATELY VIA PRIME SWISS, AUSTRIAN, N.V., OR OTHER ACCEPTABLE BANKING INSTITUTIONS.

SUR ACCEPTANCE : SUR PROVIDER TO ISSUE RWAD IMMEDIATELY THROUGH TELECOPIER – (414) 738.7007 USA OPERATIONS, IN FAVOUR OF NEW REPUBLIC/USA FINANCIAL GROUP, GmbH

THANK YOU FOR YOUR RAPID RESPONSE TO THIS PENDING TRANSACTION.

FAITHFULLY YOURS,
FOR AND ON BEHALF OF NEW REPUBLIC/USA FINANCIAL GROUP, GmbH.

By: _____ Telecopiador – (414) 738.7007
L E WANTA, DIRECTEUR-GENERAL, WIEN

LEW/DV

NEW REP...
FINANCIE...
Ltd. Ges.n...

An obscure 'Starl AG Vaduz' in Lichtenstein appears to be supplying Leo Wanta with 100 billion 'clean, clear, good, legal, bundled, counted, verified, packed and stamped' Russian rubles, in cash, at 15 rubles to the dollar

NEW REPUBLIC / USA FINANCIAL GROUP, LTD.
2101 NORTH EDGEWOOD AVENUE
APPLETON, WI, USA 54914
TELE/FAX: (414) 738-7007

04 FEBRUARY 1991   REF/NIDETZKY GROUP

PREPARED FOR: CONFIRMATION - DO NOT DUPLICATE

EL-SIRAAT TRADING INTERNATIONAL (INC)[MANDATED AGENT]
IMPORT - EXPORT - COMM. REPS   ATTN: MR. FAISAL S. KHAN, ES
112 LAKEVIEW TERRACE, OAKLAND, NJ, USA 07436-0000
CONFIRMING IRREVOCABLE CORPORATE PURCHASE ORDER No. AU.910116.75(2X)

THIS DOCUMENT WILL CONFIRM THAT, NEW REPUBLIC/USA FINANCIAL GROUP, LTD.
GmbH, IS READY, WILLING AND ABLE TO BUY/SELL/EFFECT *2000* METRIC TONS
OF AU BULLION METAL, WITH ROLLOVERS UNDER GOOD LONDON DELIVERY (GLD), WITH
USDOLLAR FUNDING BASED ON DAY OF EXCHANGE - SECOND LMER FIXING, FOLLOWING
THE COMPLETION OF ASSAY AND VERIFICATION OF AU METAL;

COMMODITY   : AU BULLION IN 75 KG BARS, 999.5/1000 FINENESS
HALLMARK   : INTERNATIONALLY ACCEPTED HALLMARKS
QUANTITY   : ** 2000 ** METRIC TONNES, WITH ROLLOVERS
DELIVERY   : PER ACCEPTABLE LIFT SCHEDULE TO BE DETERMINED

USDOLLAR PRICING : GROSS DISCOUNT: 3.25 % NET DISCOUNT: 3.00 %

TRANSACTION CODE : AU/POL.91.SBC   SECURITY CODE: GEVERS/LEON

DOCUMENTATION   : CERTIFICATE OF ORIGIN   EXPORT LICENSES
                   CERTIFICATE OF OWNERSHIP   WAREHOUSE RECEIPTS
                   CERTIFICATE OF ASSAYER
                   TAX EXEMPTION CERTIFICATES
                   VERIFICATION OF FREE OF LIENS AND ENCUMBERANCES

LOCATION   : SECURITY VAULTS - KLOTEN, SWITZERLAND

PAYMENT TERMS   : TWO BANKING DAYS AFTER COMPLETION OF ASSAY AND THE
                   PRIME BANK DELIVERY OF DOCUMENTS;

NEW REPUBLIC/USA FINANCIAL GROUP, LTD GmbH, STANDS READY TO RECEIVE YOUR
PRIME BANK TESTED TELEX OF AU METAL AND ACCEPTABLE LIFT SCHEDULE, WHEREAS
OUR CLOSING BANK WILL CONFIRM USDOLLAR FUNDING. UPON AU SELLER GROUP
ACCEPTANCE VIA YOUR RWAD, PRINCIPALS TO EXCHANGE PRIME BANKING COORDINATES
TO FINALIZE THIS SPECIFIC AU TRANSACTION.

VALIDITY OF THIS METAL PURCHASE ORDER IS FOR FIVE (5) BANKING DAYS, UNLESS
AU METAL PROVIDER CONFIRMS READINESS AND AVAILABILITY TO OUR PRIME BANK
COORDINATES.

FAITHFULLY YOURS,
FOR AND ON BEHALF OF NEW REPUBLIC/USA FINANCIAL GROUP, LTD GmbH

By: _____   TELEFON: (414) 738 0229
    USA AUTHORIZED SIGNATORIE - L E WANTA

LEW/nv
                                     NEW REPUBLIC/USA
                                     FINANCIAL GROUP
                                     Ltd. Ges.m.b.H - AUSTRIA

*Leo Wanta announces that he is selling 2,000 tons of gold in February 1991.
An El-Siraat Trading International Corporation in Oakland, New Jersey,
is among his prospective clients.*

P R O C U R A   D E L L A   R E P U B B L I C A

PRESSO IL TRIBUNALE DI

C O M O

SEZIONE DI POLIZIA GIUDIZIARIA

SEGUITO PREGRESSA SEGNALAZIONE RISERVATA DEL 25.3.1992.

AL SIGNOR PROCURATORE
DELLA REPUBBLICA C/O
IL TRIBUNALE DI C O M O
Dr. Romano DOLCE Sost.

I sottoscritti ufficiali ed agenti di P.G.:

- Mar.Magg. MERLI   Gianpietro
- VBrig.   LAGIOIA Giovanni
- App.sc.   ERDAS   Antonio

Si evidenziano di seguito gli elementi informativi, ulteriormente
sviluppati, pervenuti per il tramite dei vari organi collaterali ufficiali
in ordine al traffico clandestino di materiale radioattivo ed altro che
verrebbe perpretato sistematicamente da una organizzazione internazionale
con ramificazioni anche in Italia.

Tali materiali (Plutonio, uranio, mercurio rosso ed armamenti di vario ge-
nere) verrebbero contrabbandati nel territorio nazionale (in transito) per
mezzo di intermediari.

La mente dell'organizzazione si identificherebbe nel tale Alexander Vikto
rovitch KUZIN, nato a Voronjez (ex URSS), il 15.07.1956 e residente a Vien
na 1° distretto, Brandstatte 3/16 e presso KOCH 80, Herlerstrasse 91/2, do
ve abita anche la moglie Nadezhda NIKOLAEVNA, nata il 16.05.1956.
Dal settembre 1991 domiciliato a Belgrado, via 29 Novembre 128.

Il KUZIN risulta essere in possesso dei seguenti passaporti:

- ordinario jugoslavo nr.CA831821 rilasciato dalle Autorità della Republi
  ca Serba il 20.9.1991;

- CK-I nr.493737, rilasciato dal Ministero degli Esteri dell'URSS il 26 mar
  zo 1990

Secondo il Ministero degli Interni dell'URSS, KUZIN, presidente della ditta
cooperative di Stato "BIOCOR", farebbe parte di una banda di criminali con
collegamenti in campo internazionale e serebbe coinvolto in truffe e rapine
commesse in Russia.

Avrebbe interesse (50%) nella ditta "KUZIN SYSTEMS" con sede a Vienna, 5000
Koch 80, Herlerstrasse 103-105 e a Colonia (Germania). Giunto a Vienna il

— segue —

Russia and East Europe found little more than tantalizing traces.

According to Criminalpol's Alessandro Pansa, they were 'probably not ready to invest millions of dollars in a wildly unstable Russian economy'. They were investing *fake* dollars, he said. This enabled them to pick up raw materials, real estate, factories and antiques without spending a dime.

More than a billion and a half counterfeit dollars in $100 bills (1.6 billion) were *confiscated* in Italy in the single year of 1992.[6] At least a *billion* more were adding to Russia's torments by the year's end.[7] Not all were Mafia-made, but forged $100 bills were one of the Mafia's biggest earners all over the ex-Soviet bloc, Dr Pansa told me – Poland, Hungary, Rumania, Czechoslovakia, Bulgaria.

Apart from counterfeit money, the Italians were doing scams: ruble swaps, food for precious metal swaps, credit card frauds, EC subsidy frauds, straight swindles. In Poland and Hungary, they were shipping girls into white slavery. In Rumania, they had a child adoption racket.[58]

Dr Pansa's men could ascertain only 200 such cases, plainly not the whole story. Nearly all the instruments needed to detect foreign criminals were lacking in these countries; the whole fallen Soviet empire was a perfect place for them to hide.

There were undoubtedly more of them in the ex-satellite states than the record showed.

'All kinds of criminals started to come here in 1992: that was the year the dam broke,' said Andrzej Kowezsko, head of Interpol in Poland:

This is their contact country, where they meet to discuss their business – Italians, Colombians, Turks, Russians.

They don't hurt Poles, so it's almost impossible to get them into court. For instance, the Russian mafia just stops Russian tourist buses at gunpoint and collects $5 a passenger, like checking tickets.

The Sicilian Mafia doesn't come to commit crimes. It's only interested in laundering money; we caught two of them when another one came up from Palermo to torch their place . . .

The Colombians see a whole new situation here – they can use Polish camels to move cocaine, instead of going the old Balkan route. It's not against Polish law to *possess* any amount of cocaine, so how do you catch the camels?

But the Colombians do money too . . . We cops in Poland

have no way to check the money's provenance. They can transfer it out of the country – you can get any bank documents you
want here if you pay enough – or they can invest it. God knows,
we can't trash investments. Now criminal interest in Poland is
growing. They're coming here to start producing synthetic drugs
themselves. We think the Italians or the Dutch, maybe both, are
getting into it. That's our nightmare.

If you're a foreigner and you buy a villa here, you're a noble-
man. You have flowers in your garden, you give candy to kids.
Then you open a little factory, you provide jobs, you pay taxes.
You say you're processing vegetables, and you're probably making
amphetamines; they have no smell. But how can we tell? We
cops get no information from the West saying you have dirty
hands.

We have no laws, we have no surveillance in hotels, we don't
have the mentality, the public doesn't *expect* us to deal with such
things. When we get around to looking, they'll be far, far ahead
of us.[59]

Czechoslovakia was in much the same predicament. 'We've been isolated, under glass. Now with open borders we get whatever the rest of
Europe gets: a wave of crime is advancing on us,' said Czechoslovakia's
police chief, Miroslav Opravil.

'They're all here: the Sicilians, the Camorra, the Colombians, the
Yakuza, the Yugoslavs, the Russian mafia, the Ukrainian mafia, the
Uzbekis, the Turkmenis, the Afghanis, the Chechen – a very dangerous mafia, the Chechen. They seem to have divided the territory;
they don't penetrate each other's turf,' he went on.[60]

Like the Chechen, the Sicilian Mafia and Camorra were buying real
estate, cafés and casinos in Prague, each carefully keeping off the
other's turf.

'Some very suspicious Italians have settled here. They bring in tax
and financial specialists to launder their money, and they're laundering plenty,' declared the head of the Czech financial police:

They're all doing it. The Medellín cartel tried to launder $300
million through Czech banks, and they got away with $100 mil-
lion. Our banks don't ask the origin of their money. This is a
paradise for them. We know of certain Italians who are using
straw men to buy their own banks in southern Bohemia: that's
the best place for washing.

We have no laws to stop them. Soon they'll start to influence
politicians. Then they'll block legislation. So we're racing to get
the laws. The question is who'll be quicker. I think they will.

As a new mafia hinterland grew discernible in the East, an old one
long and resolutely overlooked in the West began to emerge as well.

Around Christmas time in 1992, Belgian police came across a hud-
dle of wretched Africans from Burkina Faso waiting to be smuggled
into Italy. A ring of Camorristi had flown them to the Belgian capital
of Brussels, where they needed no entry visas. They were supposed to
go on to Naples by taxi, for $500 apiece.[61]

The Camorra was going to put them to work in its underground factories in Naples, turning out a fair share of the world's counterfeit
goods, worth an amazing $80 billion a year. (Apart from forged dollar
bills, the Camorra's products included fake Rolex watches, Vuitton
luggage, Scotch whisky and Chanel perfume, for which the bottles
were made in Italy and Spain, the labels in Holland, and the contents
in Mexico.)[62]

The Camorra and Mafia were both moving African illegals through
Belgium, where they did a considerable amount of business. Indeed, a
'Mafia milieu' had managed to 'penetrate and conceal itself in the
highest realms of Belgian industry and finance . . . including advanced
technology and armament,' warned an eminent judge in 1989.

The judge, Jean-François Godbille, got the brushoff from an incredulous Belgian parliament at the time. Three years later, however, he
was heading a national commission to combat a 'mafia des négriers',
running a colossal slave market in Belgium and northern France.

The ring worked out of a stupendous castle in Charleroi, owned and
expensively restored by an unemployed Sicilian labourer. The real
owner was Pasquale Cuntrera of Siculiana, Caracas and Aruba, whose
base in Belgium went back many years.[63]

From their castle in Charleroi, the Cuntreras' men were farming out
ten thousand black Africans to construction companies all across the
country. Seven people were murdered for nosing around, including a
young reporter for Charleroi's *Nouvelle Gazette*.[64] His killer simply
slipped back to Sicily; nobody of importance in the ring was ever
caught.

Brussels, seat of the European Community, turned out to be a drug
traffickers' haven also. Foreigners and citizens alike had a sacrosanct
right to privacy there: no phone taps, no bugs in the wall, no electronic
devices tracking a suspect van, and not many bank controls either.

Therefore, the Sicilian Mafia and Cali cartel were using Brussels as headquarters for a huge cocaine ring. French police got onto it when they seized 600 kilos of the ring's cocaine – a record haul – coming over the Spanish border at Perpignan, on the way to Milan.[65]

France was worse off, if anything. Though long occupied, the country was stunned to discover 'disquieting signs of a growing Mafia presence' in 1993. 'The Italian mafias' considered this a 'territory to colonize', a place to put money and men, reported a special parliamentary anti-Mafia commission.[66]

Don Michele Zaza, the ranking Camorra boss, incorrigible drug trafficker and longtime Italian fugitive, was 'the best example of their colonization efforts', the commission said.

'A scent of the Mafia' emanated from still bigger French holdings than Zaza's very considerable holdings, however. One, a development project for a golf course, hotel and 200 villas, was financed through 150 Dutch companies, largely controlled by shell companies in the Channel Islands.

Several other mega-investments were being made by a shady Italian millionaire named Giancarlo Casaccia, 'known to the Italian police' for illicit money dealings. Based in the principality of Monaco, Casaccia belonged to a financial consortium with thirty companies in France, Monaco, Luxembourg and Panama, specializing in real estate.

Through two intermediaries, he was investing on behalf of Carmine Alfieri, topmost Camorra boss, and Alfieri's number two, Pasquale Galasso, a *dollar* billionaire. (Galasso, arrested in Italy in 1992, confessed to thirty-two homicides and a working arrangement for shared payoffs with several Italian politicians of cabinet rank.)

Casaccia's projects included a thirty-storey tower in Beausoleil (Alpes-Maritime); an eighteen-hole golf course in Pierrevert (Alpes-de-Haute Provence); and a projected thirty-million-dollar residence complex around the golf green.

Even more ambitious was a joint project with the Mayoralty of Orange for 'the most important urbanization plan ever undertaken by the city': the restoration of its historic centre and a new satellite quarter giving on to the national autoroute, with apartment buildings, offices and a grand de luxe hotel.[67]

One of Casaccia's sub-companies, Transimmo, had paid 16 million francs (around $3 million) for 35,000 square metres of the land – nearly three times its market price (6 million francs).

Buying real estate for more than its worth was the classic mark of the money-washer. All the Italian mafias were investing heavily for this purpose in France, not just buying but building.

Sicilian mafiosi in particular were actually financing a third of all the new construction on the French Riviera: so the parliamentary commission learned from Judge Falcone. Full-page ads in the Italian press offered stupendous villas and high-rise condominiums on the Côte d'Azur for low, low prices.

Several other avenues were open for washing in or through France. Four-fifths of all casino receipts along the Côte d'Azur were of Italian origin, for instance.[68] Monaco, though subject to bank controls for French citizens, offered complete bank secrecy for anyone else. Shell companies of every description found it 'a particularly choice place to launder capital', the parliamentary commission said.

Best of all was the island of St Maartens, on the way to becoming the world's second Mafia state.

A Sicilian mafioso named Rosario Spadaro held the Dutch side, laundering for fellow Italians, Americans and Colombians. The proceeds were 'passing unhindered to Saint Martin' on the French side, and on into France itself. This capital was 'absolutely opaque', said Jacques de Larosière, governor of the Bank of France.

Like Germany, France was beginning to feel the Mafia's sinister powers of corruption – its ability to seduce and manipulate French middlemen, bankers and politicians, to contaminate whole economic areas, to pass as legitimate.

'France is not safe from the Mafia,' the parliamentary commission concluded. 'The Mafia is not folklore. The Mafia is a model of the future for organized crime. France has no immunity from Mafia-type organizations . . . There is no part of our territory or sector of our economy that could not interest [them].'

By a hair, in 1989, the American mafia had failed to lock into a peculiarly alluring sector of the French economy. A US corporation strongly suspected of mafia financing offered $178 million for the most advanced industrial incinerator in France, but got turned down.[69]

The Americans were not the only ones to know the value of garbage. Like New York's five families, many in Europe would kill for it. The Camorra was collecting a quarter of a billion dollars a year for keeping Naples clean, turning the city into Italy's toxic junkyard. Toxic waste in general was one of the fastest-growing earners in the crime business.

Apart from the money in it, however, garbage was a kind of statement for America's Cosa Nostra families, their way of staking out territory. They had rarely ventured across the Atlantic since the days of Lucky Luciano. Now they were joining the rest of the underworld in Europe.

The rest of the underworld had joined them in America long before.

7

In America

'This is gonna be a Cosa Nostra till I die. Be it an hour from now, or be it tonight, or a hundred years from now, when I'm in jail. It's gonna be Cosa Nostra.'[1] So John Gotti said, before a judge sent him up for life. The perceived wisdom today is that he was wrong, but the facts suggest that he may have been right.

Cosa Nostra's end, predicted regularly in America for half a century, *ought* to be near. Over a thousand of its members and associates have been indicted or imprisoned since the 1980s. Its entire governing commission has been convicted. The biological solution awaits its geriatric bosses. Practically all its top patriarchs are behind bars for good anyway, including the great Gotti himself.

Their younger successors are inexperienced, brash, incautiously greedy, several generations removed from the old Mafia culture and bereft of historical memory. Their discipline is poor. Their humus, the Italian-American community, is washing away into the mainstream of American life.

Their hold on the streets seems to be weakening, since they lease out rackets to others. Their nerve appears to be slipping, in that they kill less than some of their ceaselessly multiplying and recklessly violent rivals. On the other hand, they are killing each other off more persistently than they have done in decades.

'This is the twilight of the Mob. It's not dark yet, but the sun is going down,' one expert announced.

Yet for the FBI, Cosa Nostra is still 'the most serious organized crime problem in the United States'. The crime ring that has outlived every other in America since the 1890s is still recruiting, still creaming 20% off the top of all new construction in New York, still doing nearly everything it has always done, in the areas that have always been its strongholds.[2]

FBI field officers report that federal prosecutions have 'had little impact on Cosa Nostra's overall activity' in Detroit, 'no impact' in Los Angeles, 'little effect' in Chicago; that its activities 'do not appear to have diminished' in Miami and 'remain relatively unchanged' in Kansas City; that the Genovese family has 'a huge operation' in New Jersey, where its structure 'remains intact'.

Nationwide, the organization 'remains particularly strong in Chicago, New England, southern Florida, Las Vegas, Atlantic City and New York City,' the Bureau says.[3]

'In the universe of organized criminal groups, the racketeering activities of La Cosa Nostra are the most protracted and sustained, the most impacted and entrenched, the most expansive and profitable, the most corrosive and deleterious to legitimate sectors of society, the most resistant to enforcement efforts generally, and the most resilient to the aftermath of any single enforcement effort,' observes the FBI's New Jersey office.[4]

Second only to this seemingly unsinkable organization is its big brother from Sicily. An independent entity in America since the 1960s, Sicily's Cosa Nostra was supposed to have been finished there halfway through the 1980s, when its heroin network was cracked in New York's Pizza Connection case. Actually, it has been 'growing precipitously', says the head of the FBI's organized crime section, Jim Moody.[5]

It may become a graver menace than its American counterpart, warned Attorney-General William Barr in 1992. 'I've said this privately and I've said it at the cabinet table. We are facing a tremendous challenge from the Sicilian Mafia, one that could dwarf La Cosa Nostra here in the United States. We may be at the beginning of a more serious threat from organized crime than ever before,' he told a reporter for the *Legal Times*.[6]

There were clear signs by then that the Sicilian Mafia was rapidly colonizing the American underworld. Its men have been arriving legally; visas are no longer required for Italian nationals. Keeping away from big cities inhabited by the American Mob and knowledgeable cops, they have been fanning out over the countryside like KGB moles.

They settle into small towns, file for citizenship, go into business and win the community's respect. Their names and faces are unknown, and they have no rap sheets in America.

The harder the law bears down on the American mafia, the more Sicilian mafiosi arrive. The FBI thought there were a few hundred of them in the late 1980s. By 1991, it was speaking of 3,000, not counting members of the Camorra and 'Ndrangheta, 'noted with increasing frequency'. By the end of 1992, it was estimating 'between ten and twenty thousand members and associates'.[7]

That is roughly the size of the American mafia itself: 2,000 members, 20,000-odd associates. A second mafia as large as the first, accountable to Palermo, has calamitous implications for the United States.

These are the soldiers formed during Totò Riina's long and violent reign, veterans of Sicily's Great Mafia War, interlocked with the world's biggest crime syndicates, brutalized to a degree that frightens even their American cousins.

They are already drawing the American mafia into their planetary orbit – notably in the sack of Russia – and they can undoubtedly give it lessons in the art of wielding power.

'If you want your Cosa Nostra to be as successful as our Cosa Nostra, you oughtta use Sicilian methods, like killing judges and cops,' advised a prize Sicilian trafficker in New York.

Relations between the two mafias have always been mysterious, at times unfathomable. By mutual agreement, they have been separate and distinct for some forty years; neither can intrude on the other's sovereign territory. Actually, the Sicilians have occupied several of the Americans' exclusive enclaves since the 1960s, and poached all over their criminal preserves.

For the Americans, they are 'the zips', 'the geeps', 'the fuckin' siggies', secretive, predatory, resented and detested. John Gotti, then the highest boss in the land, had raged against them in an exchange with a couple of his soldiers recorded by the FBI:

1st soldier: They're opening up all over the fuckin' place, these zips, ain't they? There's three of them right on this avenue here, they all make money . . .

2nd soldier: If they run a game, you know, Johnny [Gotti] will go along with another game . . .

Gotti: They're not gonna play nothin' . . . I got four thousand guys I'll send from every neighbourhood, I'll put in there . . . Let 'em come ahead, let's see what they'll do.

1st soldier: They make like they don't understand, the mother-fuckers . . .

Gotti: They don't understand what they don't wanna understand . . . They go around with hundreds of thousands in their pockets, and you're going around with your hat in your hand . . .[8]

Yet the Sicilian Mafia's top emissary to the US was taken into New York's Gambino family with '5, 6, 7 of his crew' in the mid-1970s; a decade later, he was elevated to the rank of *capodecina* by John Gotti himself. 'You knew then that I made a mistake,' Gotti said to his *consigliere*, Sammy 'The Bull' Gravano, who so testified at Gotti's trial in 1992:

He's discussing the liaison guy from Italy to here who we believe might be a made member of our family and made in Italy and have one foot here and one foot in Italy, and he's doing business.
    John Gotti said: 'If it's true, if it's him, the liaison guy is getting whacked . . .'
    He meant: 'If the liaison guy is a made member with us and he has a foot in Italy and he's doing drugs, he's gonna get whacked' . . . The liaison guy is getting whacked because they don't belong to us. That's their crew . . .[9]

The liaison guy did not get whacked, however. Early in 1987, five different *capos* from New York's five mafia families sat down with him in the back room of the Café Giardino, his Brooklyn seat. John Gotti in person drew up in a limousine to call on him soon after. From then on, he was wintering with Gotti in Florida and seeing him in New York once a week.[10]

His name was John Gambino, eldest of the three Gambino brothers of Brooklyn and Cherry Hill, New Jersey, who had come over from Sicily in 1974. Though a distant relative of the late Carlo Gambino, boss of the most powerful family in America, he answered to the Cupola's innermost circle in Palermo.

Arrested in New York on the day that General Manuel Noriega of

Panama was arraigned in Miami for collusion with Colombian cocaine cartels, John Gambino got a bare mention in the press. But he had assuredly done more than the General to feed America's drug habit.

Tons of heroin had been shipped to him directly in Brooklyn since the 1970s, from Sicilian refineries 'transforming and selling heroin to the US silently, intensively and continuously,' wrote an Italian magistrate. Billions of narcodollars in need of washing had been entrusted to him, and through him to the Sicilian Mafia's banker in New York, Michele Sindona.[11]

In fact, John Gambino could not possibly be whacked, as Gotti discovered when the secrets of Cosa Nostra's previous top boss – the one Gotti got rid of, Paul Castellano – were revealed to him. John Gambino was the diamond point of the whole Sicilian Mafia heroin operation in the US, and guarantor of its longstanding arrangements with the Americans.

The deal, made at a summit meeting in Palermo's Grand Hotel Des Palmes in October 1957, allowed the Americans to divest themselves of the risks in dealing heroin while collecting a share of the profits.

The Sicilians took exclusive charge of import and wholesale distribution. The Americans got a rakeoff per kilo and announced that they were out of the drug business: officially, right after the Palermo summit, at their historic Appalachin congress in upstate New York.[12]

Whether or not this was an early sign of the Americans' decline, as some maintain, it marked the beginning of the Sicilians' ascendancy. Once installed in America, they could not be dislodged. Nor, for all their incursions, could they be molested.

They might be feared and disliked, but they were needed – are needed urgently today. American bosses habitually dodge their own ban on drugs by investing money in Sicilian deals. More and more of their soldiers are risking an in-house death sentence to work with Sicilian traffickers. Many families, running to flab, are in search of more backbone and muscle.

For an ageing organization tormented by the law and beset by new young rivals, the Sicilians have come to mean fresh blood and the saving strength of ancestral Mafia tradition. Compared to their American cousins, they are still the keepers of the ancient Mafia code, however they may have trashed it.

Thus, a growing number of Sicilians 'made' at home are getting made in the US as well. Several have become *capos* in American families. One has taken over a family altogether.

Spicy evidence to this effect dropped into the lap of FBI agents in

Medford, Massachusetts in the autumn of 1989. Twenty-one members of Boston's Patriarca family had gathered there on a Sunday to induct four new members.

A Bureau bug picked up every word, as a Patriarca captain administered the ritual oath *in Sicilian dialect*: 'Io, Carmen, voglio entrare in questa organizzazione . . .'

The oath-giver, a Sicilian Man of Honour named Biagio DiGiacomo, had to explain from time to time in strangled English: 'Put your hands out like this, Carmen, and when I read it to you, repeat after me and then go like this, boom, boom, boom,' he said, preparing to draw blood from Carmen's trigger finger, and he added: 'If I said you must kill a police informer, would you do that for me on behalf of our organization?'

'Yes, I would.'

'You would do that?'

'I would do that.'

'This thing of ours, we would be delighted to have you . . .'

Then DiGiacomo continued in Sicilian: 'I swear to enter this organization alive and leave it dead.' In English, he went on, that meant: 'We get in alive in this organization, and the only way we gonna get out is death, no matter what. It's no hope, no Jesus, no Madonna, nobody can help us, if we ever give up this secret to anybody . . . This thing that cannot be exposed . . .'[13]

The Patriarca family inducted several more Sicilians in 1992; bugged repeatedly and mercilessly by the FBI, it is plainly in need of their reviving presence. New York's Lucchese family has sworn in an unregenerate Sicilian drug trafficker, Enzo Napoli. The Philadelphia family, an exceptionally riotous lot, has actually come under a Sicilian's rule.

The Philadelphia family has dominated crime and politics in much of Pennsylvania for seventy-odd years. But it started to fly apart when its longtime boss, Angelo Bruno, was shot dead with a sawn-off shotgun in March 1980.

A month later, Bruno's *consigliere* was tortured, stabbed and shot to death. A few months afterwards, his chief loan shark was found stuffed into two green plastic garbage bags. At the year's end, his successor was blown up by a bomb packed with nails.[14]

The perpetrator, Nicodemo Scarfo, ordered the murders of nineteen more members after he took over: this out of forty in all, replaced by his own men. Ruling with a flamboyance and raw violence much like John Gotti's, Scarfo met much the same end. He was tried for criminal conspiracy and a continuing criminal enterprise – ten homicides, five attempted homicides, extortion, gambling, narcotics –and jailed for life.[15]

The fact that he left the Philadelphia family in shambles does not altogether explain why the highest echelons of America's Cosa Nostra sent in a Sicilian Man of Honour to replace him. The new boss, John Stanfa, once drove for Angelo Bruno, but he is still a 'zip'. Born and made in Sicily, he communicates regularly with Palermo's top bosses, and is part of their crowd in the US.[16]

Nevertheless, the Gambino family sent Stanfa down from New York; John Gotti backed him; and Cosa Nostra's national commission even authorized him to swear in a couple more Sicilians. Decisions like these are not casually made.

Philadelphia is where the American mafia is 'the *second* most serious problem, *after* the Sicilian Mafia,' says the FBI. Sicilian drug traffickers infest the city, indeed own the whole northern half of it. Angelo Bruno, Sicilian-born himself, turned over the north side long ago to John Gambino and his brothers in nearby Cherry Hill, New Jersey.[17]

It is in Philadelphia that the two mafias may decide to remarry, after nearly half a century apart: a union of imperial grandeur for the international underworld and a nightmare for American authorities.

There could hardly be much doubt about where such a marriage might lead. 'Them fucking zips ain't gonna back up to nobody . . . Those guys are looking to take over everything. You give them the fucking power . . . they'll bury you. They don't give a fuck. They don't care who's boss. They got no respect,' a Bonnano family captain observed some years ago.[18]

Invited to rejuvenate the American organization, the Sicilians may well end by running it. They will be on their way in if they can infuse a once-illustrious American family with fresh strength.

'A reorganization and perhaps a return to tradition is taking place in the Philadelphia family and others as well . . . What is developing may signal a new trend for the organization and operation of La Cosa Nostra,' says the authoritative Pennsylvania Crime Commission. 'If Stanfa is successful . . . we may see a powerful confederation of Sicilian Mafia members with the remaining family veterans. Cosa Nostra may emerge as far more powerful, effective and insulated from law enforcement. The metamorphosis in the Philadelphia family may represent the future of Cosa Nostra.'[19]

This was the Attorney General's bad dream: the emergence of a hydra-headed criminal monster in America that would certainly dwarf La Cosa Nostra as we know it.

Never again, the FBI vowed in 1991. The Mafia, as if designed by some diabolical hand, seemed impervious to everything the law could throw at it. The US could not let that happen again. Apart from redoubled efforts to eliminate the Mafia itself, the main thrust of FBI strategy now was to 'ensure that no other criminal organization can ever achieve a comparable level of power'.

Heartfelt agreement came from Assistant Attorney General Robert Mueller, testifying on the Hill. 'For most of the last thirty years we've played catch-up in eradicating what is still this country's most serious organized crime problem – La Cosa Nostra. We will not repeat that mistake. We cannot stand idly by while newer organized crime groups invade our society,' he told a Senate committee.[20]

But American society was invaded already, by the same forces advancing on Europe, working both continents as one. Though far ahead of others in trying to cope with them, US law enforcement agencies still cannot bridge what is known as the 'technology gap' between the crime syndicates' capabilities and their own.

Simply to deal with a thousand-odd organized gangs is overwhelming – Hispanics, Asians, West Indians, Mexicans, Afro-Americans, California's Crips and Bloods, motorbike gangs like the Pagans, the Bandidos, Hell's Angels.

These can be nationwide, disciplined, heavily armed and lethal. Jamaican Posses rampage through thirty-five states, pushing nearly half the crack sold in the country. Hell's Angels have thirty-five chapters in the US and as many again abroad, in Canada, Britain, Denmark, Germany, France, Brazil, New Zealand, Russia, Japan.[21]

But they are no potential Cosa Nostras. Most of them hire out to Cosa Nostra, or pay it tribute. Hell's Angels are its 'working partners', the FBI declares.

Cosa Nostra's Chicago family employs Mexicans, Puerto Ricans and Colombians. New York's families collect a tax from Cubans handling the numbers game in Harlem, not to speak of Russian crooks in Brighton Beach. The Philadelphia family collects a street tax from any criminal band trying to work there.

What worries Washington is an alarming invasion by Cosa Nostra's true peers – the Triads, the Yakuza and the Russian mafia, the largest organizations in the crime business.

The Triads have four times as many members and helpers as their American counterparts, the Yakuza five times as many, the Russians over a hundred times as many, more and more of whom are drifting into the United States.

Any one of the three in league with either of the mafias in the US would be a fright story, and they are all in league with both. Such concentrated criminal strength is beyond anything in American experience – in any country's experience, for that matter.

With a statesmanship yet to be achieved by the United Nations, these titans of the underworld have been sharing resources, personnel and protective cover for years, peaceably and to their mutual benefit.

They all 'pay tribute' (taxes) to the American Cosa Nostra, the FBI says. In exchange, they 'utilize Cosa Nostra connections to penetrate the country's law enforcement and judicial communities through long-established Cosa Nostra contacts.'[22]

The fact that Cosa Nostra gives them access to its private collection of bent judges and cops suggests extraordinary levels of complicity.

As far back as 1984, witnesses summoned by President Reagan's Commission on Organized Crime described some of their operational links. A compulsive Japanese gambler told how the Yakuza ran its high-stake games in New York, for instance:

Q: Were all of the people operating these games Japanese?
A: No, some of them Italian.
Q: How would the games run?
A: Different people sell drinks, but Italians were in the back room and approved play on credit.
Q: How was the credit collected?
A: If I pay in two, three weeks nothing happen, but if you took longer I would be visited by someone from the game, they say they hadn't seen me for a while and they hope to see me soon.
Q: The people who came, were they Japanese?
A: No, Italian-American.
Q: Did the Japanese carry weapons?
A: No.
Q: Did the Italian-Americans carry weapons?
A: Yes.[23]

A Chinese witness at the hearings told of ongoing collaboration between the Triads and the Sicilian Mafia in New York. First, the Sicilians had asked the man's Triad boss to open a letter of credit for them in Taiwan, covering the cost of a heroin shipment from there.

Then they gave him a suitcase full of cash to be laundered and delivered to Italy.

Finally they asked him to 'bring a letter over to Hong Kong' for 'a very wealthy Chinese gentleman wearing a very expensive gold Rolex watch', who provided them with a new heroin supply line. Back in New York, the witness got a classic Sicilian warning: 'He said that you know that I am very powerful in this country and I hope you don't betray me or be unfaithful to me.'[24]

Those were early days. The Triads had only a modest share of the heroin traffic then; the Yakuza were barely recognizable to the average law enforcer; and the Russian mafia was just getting started on multibillion-dollar scams which, 'for imagination and gall, rival anything La Cosa Nostra could ever have done', observes a harried California detective.

Today, the Triads are second only to the Mafia as a menace to American society, and they are the Mafia's best friends.

Those in Philadelphia's Chinatown buy their video poker machines from the Lucchese family in New York and the De Cavalcante family in New Jersey. Others pay percentage points on their gambling take to the family in Chicago, buy guns from New York's five families, import loan sharks from the Patriarca family for their Manhattan gambling dens.[25]

The more heroin they bring in, furthermore, the more they rely on their old Sicilian colleagues. Chinese traffickers are too exposed outside their community to distribute several tons a year – enough for the better part of half a million addicts. As usual, the Sicilians are moving it wholesale for them. 'Is the Sicilian Mob still doing what it always did in Brooklyn? Sure it is,' says the Brooklyn District Attorney's Special Assistant, Douglas Le Vien.

'People think it's the Triads because so much heroin comes from southeast Asia. But believe me, the Sicilians are still big in dope,' declares the FBI's Jim Moody. Many disparate Chinese are in the drug business, indeed in every kind of crime business, but it is the Triads who rule over America's Chinatowns.

More than a million and a half people live under their dominion: the largest Chinese population in the West, exceptionally conscientious and hardworking, exploited methodically and frightened into silence.

Those in charge are the cream of Triad society in Hong Kong and Taiwan. The Sun Yee On and Wo Hop To operate all over southeast

Asia. The 14K runs most of the Triads' European heroin trade from Amsterdam. The United Bamboo Gang has entered into a formal pact with the Yamaguchi-Gumi, leader of Yakuza society in Japan.[26]

Whether through fraternal Tongs or on their own, these are the top four in control of gambling, usury, prostitution and extortion in the Chinatowns of San Francisco, Los Angeles, Portland, Denver, Houston, Phoenix, Chicago, Boston, Philadelphia, Atlantic City and New York.[27]

Four out of five Chinese merchants pay them protection money on a sliding scale – $200 to $750 a week per restaurant table in San Francisco. A recalcitrant owner might lose his restaurant, or be beaten unconscious, or be sliced with a hundred cuts of a razor and hung on a meathook.

Law enforcement could never get far past the barriers of culture, language and fear in these Chinese settlements. But the Triads are on the loose now, 'expanding rapidly outside the Asian community . . . growing exponentially in sophistication and power', say federal authorities.[28]

Like the Sicilian Mafia, they are diversifying: laundering drug money, swindling insurance companies, defrauding banks, passing counterfeit currency, cleaning up with fake credit cards. (Triads in Hong Kong and Singapore make half the world's forged credit cards.)[29]

Virulent Asian street gangs under their influence – the Ghost Shadows, the Flying Dragons, Born to Kill – are burgling homes, terrorizing the inhabitants, threatening to slaughter the children, raping and occasionally murdering the women. 'It has happened in Washington, DC,' a shocked Senate Committee on Investigations was told by the FBI.[30]

Caught in this second game of catch-up, federal agents can see the enemy's troops multiplying before their eyes. For the Triads on the ground, America is the natural solution to the vexing problem of vacating Hong Kong. Before the Crown Colony reverts to China in 1997, therefore, they are racing to bring over money, fellow-members and a whole conscript army of illegal Chinese immigrants.

An astonishing $3.8 billion in currency was transferred from Hong Kong to the US in 1991 – up 540%. How much belonged to the Triads was impossible to say: a lot, the Senate committee thought.

A surge of illegal Chinese immigration started around that time. In the entire decade of the 1980s, Triad 'snakeheads' and associates had smuggled 108,975 Chinese illegals into the US. They were bringing in 80,000 a year by 1993.[31]

American agencies have identified at least sixty different routes of theirs by land, sea and air. Thirty-seven shiploads were on the high seas at once in 1991. Twenty-four carrying human cargo were intercepted off the coast of Manhattan over the following year, and at least as many again off San Francisco.

One syndicate bought six blocks of 200 tickets each for a European airline to get his customers as far as Central America, where a chartered 707 waited to make the final run.

At anywhere from $30,000 to $50,000 a head, the smugglers are grossing over $3 billion a year, not counting heroin picked up in Thailand on the way. This is practically found money, involving next to no risk; the US has granted refugee status to any Chinese requesting it since the 1989 uprising in Tiananmen Square.

'No one loses because we don't prosecute and we don't deport Chinese. All they have to do is get there, and they can stay forever,' says a US immigration officer in southeast Asia.[32]

Most passengers haven't a prayer of paying for their passage, especially coming from dirt-poor regions like Fujian. 'If you have $30,000 and live in Fujian Province, there is no reason to leave because you are one of the richest people there,' the immigration officer observes.

Those who fail to pay generally end up in brothels, sweatshops or the steel grip of a drug ring – expendable chattels, bonded slaves. Before getting there, they may be 'bound and handcuffed in some apartment, fed infrequently, beaten, tortured with claw hammers and lit cigarettes, and held until payment is made', a New York detective has testified.

'What if the full fee cannot be paid?' a *Time* reporter asked Big Boss Ma, a champion people-smuggler in Thailand. 'That is very dangerous business,' he replied, inasmuch as the debt 'is turned over to the Mafia in the US and Europe, or the Yakuza in Japan.'[33]

The Yakuza, or *Boryukudan*, have nothing like the Triads' ethnic hinterland in America, but they have an unnerving unseen *presence*. Their main pursuits in the US, as in Europe, are by definition the kind their interlocutors would rather not talk about: corporate blackmail and enormous capital investment.

Nobody knows how many billions of dollars they are washing through the US economy, how many of Japan's giant companies they are holding to ransom in New York or California, how many US companies may be falling victim to the provocative wiles of their *sokaiya*.

Investigators have enough evidence to believe that the Yakuza have a massive subterranean operation going in America. 'Insurmountable difficulties' lie in the way of proving it, says the Senate Sub-Committee on Investigations.

Tracing the source of Yakuza funds is next to impossible in Japan, which has total bank secrecy, and identifying Yakuza gangsters is scarcely easier. Since they have been known to sue the Japanese national police for releasing information to US officials, not much help comes from those quarters.[34]

They can no longer be spotted by their once distinctive markings either. Airport cops everywhere have learned to look for the elaborate body tattoos and missing finger joints that once gave them away. But the Japanese government is paying for cosmetic surgery now to conceal the one and replace the other, in hopes of persuading them to go straight and get a job.[35]

It is mostly through their cruder criminal ventures that American police are getting on to them – gambling, pornography, arms, drugs. Here, too, they might pass for the well-heeled Japanese tourists on whose backs they ride, if not for their ties to Cosa Nostra.

The Yakuza have been dealing with Cosa Nostra since the 1960s, when they first turned up as waiters, cooks and dishwashers in Hawaii, westernmost point of entry to the United States.

They are more than worthy partners. Compared to the Yakuza, says a US Airforce veteran who smuggled guns for them, 'the American mafia is kind of like, it is kind of funny to say but it is like a kid's game.'

The two have always traded in guns and dope. American guns sell for ten or fifteen times their cost in Japan, where they are severely banned. 'Ice', or crystal methamphetamine, the Yakuza's specialty, comes back in exchange, by way of Honolulu, where it is now the drug of choice. Increasingly, Yakuza traffickers are bringing in heroin and cocaine too.

But gambling is the real bond between them. Perennial favourite of the underworld, this is arguably the fastest way to take in cash, slip dirty money into the wash and trap clients into borrowing at outrageous interest rates: 1% a day, for a high-roller from Japan.

Japanese businessmen love to gamble in New York, Atlantic City or Las Vegas, where the Yakuza deliver them in luxury package tours, and the Mafia provides the facilities, supervises the play, bankrolls the losers and sends around the collectors.

Those who try sneaking back to Japan are merely putting off the day when a Yakuza hood comes along in Tokyo to make them pay up, on the Mafia's behalf.[36] (Recently a Brooklyn wiseguy forgot a suitcase containing $80,000 and a list of Japanese who owed in Las Vegas, with their phone numbers in Japan.)

Yakuza racketeers would have liked to buy Las Vegas, if the American mafia hadn't owned it. Short of that, their associates started by leasing a restaurant and spa in the city's Tropicana Hotel in the 1970s, then picked up two more hotels with casinos attached, then started on a $600 million resort project near Las Vegas.

They went bankrupt on that, but not for want of capital. Yakuza associates were investing as much or more in several similar projects at the time.

In 1991, for instance, the Yamaguchi-Gumi showed up on the tiny Pacific island of Tinian, off Saipan. Through a Tokyo-based front company, ASA Development and Investment Corporation, it proposed a $300 million project for a hotel and casino there: to develop tourism, the company said.

Tinian, an inconvenient five thousand miles or so from American shores, isn't even on the map. But it is a US trust territory, with all the resulting entitlements. 'The Yakuza think this is a great idea . . . This is their chance to get US passports and launder money,' said Frederic Gushin, director of Tinian's Casino Gambling Control Commission, who turned them down.[37]

Under a less vigilant authority, the Yamaguchi-Gumi might have bought the Pacific island, just as Sicilian Mafia families have bought Aruba. In fact, Yakuza associates have bought a sizeable chunk of Hawaii already, and a disquieting amount of choice real estate on the American mainland.

According to 'Mr. Bully', a confidential witness for the Senate committee, the Yakuza probably own 'close to fifty major properties in Hawaii', including several golf courses and the Turtle Bay Hilton. All are fronts for their money-laundering, he said.

'Mr Bully' explained how Yakuza associates used an intricate web of shell companies to buy the famous Pebble Beach Country Club in Monterey, California for $841 million in 1990.[38] Over half a billion dollars' worth of other Yakuza assets were traced by the Senate committee, in Hawaii, Nevada, Arizona, California and New York. These included a bundle of shares in Christie's auction house, owned by a Yamaguchi-Gumi associate known as 'The Snake'. Apart from buying into the company, he had invested $80 million in the works of Picasso, Van Gogh and other masters.[39]

The Senate committee took a year to uncover this much, a fraction of the Yakuza's camouflaged capital in America, beyond which came

the insurmountable difficulties. Any number of American businessmen might welcome their discreet offers of investment capital, no
questions asked – even the brother of the President of the United
States.

In 1991, the Kyodo News Service reported that Prescott Bush had
received a quarter of a million dollars as a consultant for a Japanese
company called West Tsusho. On his advice, and with his guarantee
for half the sum, the company had invested $5 million in two
American ventures: Quantum Access, a Houston-based computer soft-
ware firm; and Asset Management, a 'business development consulting
firm' employing Bush himself as senior adviser.

West Tsusho proved to be the overseas investment arm of Susumu
Ishii, number two boss of the Inagawa-Kai, one of the mightiest Yakuza
bosses extant. It was for questionable loans of $180 million to Ishii
that the world's largest brokerage, Nomura, very nearly crashed in
1991. Much of its money went into Susumu Ishii's investments in the
United States.[40]

There is no evidence that Bush knew this. But what of those who
do know and don't say – American companies eager for capital from
anywhere, or Japanese companies serving as Yakuza conduits in
America?

The Yakuzas' piratical *sokaiya* have been nosing around the
American scene since the 1970s.

A *sokaiya* famous for blackmailing a hundred companies in Japan
came close to capturing the City Bank of Honolulu in 1978. Several of
America's biggest corporations were approached or targeted over the
next few years: AT&T, IBM, General Motors, Dow Chemicals,
BankAmerica.[41]

The strongest pitch came from the star practitioners who raided
Paribas in France, the Rondan Doyukai.

In 1982, the Rondan Doyukai's boss showed up at a Chase
Manhattan Bank stockholders' meeting in New York. Presenting himself as 'a representative of your stockholders from Japan', he expressed
'sincere admiration for your high dividends', and bowed out. Chase
heard no more from him, perhaps because the *Wall Street Journal*
warned, '*The* Sokaiya *Are Coming!*' in front page headlines.[42]

Though America's blue chip corporations do not appear to have
been bothered since, the same cannot be said for Japan's blue chip corporations in America.

Leaders of Japan's hundred-billion-dollar-a-year trade with the US,
they have in effect been financing Yakuza expansion in America for

going on two decades. Describing their inaugural meeting with the *sokaiya* in Los Angeles in 1976, the authors of *Yakuza* wrote:

> According to police sources, fifty Japanese executives filed into one of the ballrooms of the Biltmore Hotel in downtown LA. They were the top-ranking officers of the largest Japanese corporations operating on the West Coast, and they had come to pay their respects to a group of visiting *sokaiya*.
>
> Police at the same time observed *sokaiya* Masato Yoshioka making a tour of Los Angeles to present himself at Japanese-owned banks, conglomerates and securities investment firms . . .
>
> Although the businesses were reluctant to talk about the incident, informants revealed that, as in Japan, it was cheaper to pay up than risk the consequences.[43]

Around the time of that *sokaiya* visit nearly a quarter of a century ago, a young US attorney called Michael Sterett warned, after coming upon the Yakuza in Honolulu: 'There are now shadow governments in the US and Japan that collect their own taxes, make their own rules and enforce their own laws. An alliance between the Yakuza and US organized crime means that drugs and guns and huge amounts of money will be moving across the world accountable to no one but the mobs themselves. It means an international shadow government.'[44]

He did not get much attention in those days. 'No one in Washington had ever built a career on chasing crime around the mid-Pacific,' the authors of *Yakuza* noted.

The Russian mafia's appearance on the American scene was not sudden, but long overlooked or underrated. A small number of Russian crooks were cheating tax collectors of around $3 billion a year in bootleg gasoline by the time they were caught at it in 1986.

Their leader, a true son of the Thieves' World named Marat Balagula, had made a fortune in Soviet Russia in the mafia of the Brezhnev era. He had left behind 'the charmed life of a high-flying black marketeer' in 1977 because 'he had read about capitalism and knew he could do well over here', a business associate told *Vanity Fair*.[45]

Like many others in his line of work, Balagula had got a visa as a persecuted Jewish refugee from Odessa, on the Black Sea. He really was Jewish, unlike a number of fellow-crooks getting in with forged papers to that effect – Chechen, for instance. He had served the

Nomenklatura much too well to be persecuted, however.

Before long, he became *consigliere* to Evsey Agron, reigning boss of the Organizatsiya in Brighton Beach, Brooklyn, known as Little-Odessa-by-the-Sea. Brighton Beach had nearly half of all the Russian emigrés in America: some 30,000 out of 70,000, due to double and more by the end of the decade. Most, like the boss of Brighton Beach himself, were there thanks to a 1974 US law favouring Soviet political refugees.

Agron, an ex-Soviet convict who carried around a cattle-prod to keep his subjects in line, had a hearty band of 500 thieves in the purest Russian sense.[46] Their income from shakedowns, arson, fencing, counterfeiting, burglary, armed robbery, gambling, prostitution, fraud, smuggling, drug running, arms running, contract-killing and so on was approaching $100 million a year by the mid-1980s.[47]

Russian gangs loosely associated with Agron's Organizatsiya were doing exactly the same in Los Angeles, San Francisco, Philadelphia, Chicago, Dallas, Miami, Boston, and a dozen other cities in America and Canada.[48]

Described by a senior FBI agent as 'very violence-prone', they were in fact the most brutal, remorseless and wholly frightening criminals that America had ever seen; and their ranks were growing fast as the tide of Russian immigrants mounted. Mingling with the newcomers were fresh forces from the Soviet underworld and its patrons in the professions, the military, the KGB.

Many were hardened criminals who had spent years in harsh Soviet prison camps, incurable troublemakers handpicked by the KGB to be dumped on the United States.

Others were Jewish reinforcements from the Ukrainian mafia, and their impostors, arriving with a ready-made international network. Before hitting the US, they had gone first to Tel Aviv, then to refugee camps in Vienna and Rome, where 'they made contacts with Italian Mafia people, who told them who to see in the US,' says the editor of New York's Russian-language newspaper *Novoye Russkoye Slavo*, Alex Grant.[49]

A Russian immigrant describing the pattern of one she had known in the old country told the Russian-speaking scholar Lydia Rosner:

> He was a thief there. When he left, the day after he left, they came to arrest him. But he had paid for documents to get out. He went to Israel and then to Italy. He was involved in narcotics there. My daughter had grown up with him and she found him

again here in New York. He was robbing again and he had diamonds and gold. He went back with them to Germany . . . He
got married and he travels the whole world . . .

For these criminals, as indeed for any new Russian immigrant, per-
ceptions of law and justice had been shaped in a lifetime under
totalitarian communist rule. All found the American justice system
'non threatening and inefficient', Rosner wrote. Criminals in particular found it laughably so.

American prisons held no fears for survivors of the Soviet gulag.
American courts presuming a defendant was innocent until proven
guilty were simply not serious. American cops who had to read you the
Miranda Act were 'Mickey Mouse', in Rosner's words. 'They feel we
are pussycats, and the United States is one big candy store,' said a New
York detective monitoring their network.[50]

This was the legacy inherited by Marat Balagula in 1985, when he
succeeded to the throne in Brighton Beach after Evsey Agron was
shot dead.

Balagula was not only more worldly and imaginative, but more lit-
erate: he had a graduate degree in economics, and he was not the
only one. 'John Gotti doesn't have college-educated people and
trained military officers like the Russian mafia does,' the FBI's Jim
Moody observed.

Balagula and his crowd had been working the gas tax scam for several years by then, with Cosa Nostra providing the cover. The deal had
been negotiated on Long Island in 1982, with a captain in the
Colombo family called Michael 'Sonny' Franzese and his associate,
Larry Iorizzo.

'The Italians thought the Russians were good guys, not too greedy,
reliable, innocent. So they made the agreement. The Russians gave
the Italians a rakeoff, and the Italians gave them security plus custody
of corrupted cops,' explains Alex Grant.

Specifically, the Russians were paying a 'family tax' to New York's
Gambino, Lucchese, Colombo and Genovese families – 2 cents out of
the 28 cents a gallon in federal and state gas taxes that they were
pocketing – in exchange for which they got Cosa Nostra's tolerance
and protection. 'The Mafia and the Soviet mob. It gives a new meaning to détente,' observed NBC's Tom Brokaw.

The gas tax scandal, as this ongoing scam has come to be called,
shows that not everything American is necessarily the biggest and
best. Though many like to think the American mafia dreamed up the

scheme, it clearly came as a surprise to John Gotti in 1986. 'I gotta do it right now! Right now I gotta do it!' he was heard to exclaim when told of it.[51]

Actually, a Russian 'petrol mafia' was already working a crude version in Baku, Azerbaijan when the Russians cut their deal in New York. 'The town pumps in Baku sold gas for unrecorded cash,' wrote Russian journalist Arkady Vaksberg.

In America, however, the Russians developed a much more sophisticated model, the most brilliant ever sprung on US revenue men, known as the daisy chain.

Simple in conception and dazzlingly intricate in execution, the scam rested on the fact that the law required gas taxes to be paid not at the wholesale terminal, but at the pump. The daisy chain consisted of numerous shell companies starting at the wholesale terminal – often in South America or Africa – passing the gas along from one to another in fake paper transactions until the trail was irretrievably lost.

The dummy company at the end of the line then sold the gas to retailers at a discount, with forged tax receipts. At the first sign of an approaching tax inspector, the dummy company folded its camp chair and moved on.

Nobody in America had ever invented such a faultless moneymaking scheme: 'A hell of a lot less risky than dealing in drugs and just as profitable,' a federal prosecutor observed.

Gas retailers faced with cut-rate competition were forced either to go along or go under. Even the giant Getty Oil went along. Countless others fell into line as the racket spread from New York to the rest of the east coast to the middle west to the west coast.

The federal government was losing a billion dollars a year and state governments across the country another two billion. Cosa Nostra's four families in New York were collecting over $40 million a year without lifting a finger. The Russians and their close Mafia confederates were sending hundreds of millions to the laundry in Panama, Austria and Russia. They were planning to buy up oil terminals all over Eastern Europe to assure a cheap and steady supply when the long arm of the law reached them.

Discovering the scam did not stop it. Balagula, picked up at Frankfurt airport in 1989 after visiting thirty-six countries as a fugitive, is doing time now. Sonny Franzese has done his, and Iorizzo is in and out of the Witness Protection programme. But the scheme is so profitable that it 'continues to flourish throughout the nation', law enforcement officials say.[52]

Despite over a hundred bootleg gas convictions, the Justice Department still has several hundred investigations under way from New York to Los Angeles, some dating back to 1983. 'We could be investigating this forever,' said the chief of a rackets bureau in upstate New York.

US authorities were slow to see something more than 'just a guy with a brilliant idea' behind the gas scam. As late as 1989, the Senate Subcommittee on Investigations did not include the Russian mafia on a list of 'non-traditional crime groups' that did include the Jamaican Posses and the Bloods and Crips.

By then the Organizatsiya was showing up in a multitude of counterfeit currency cases, forged icons and fake Fabergé antiques, fabricated credit cards (American Express) and bank cheques (Citibank), nationwide burglaries, jewellery heists, and a multitude of other scams including at least one more in the billion-dollar range. 'The Russians add a zero to anything that anyone else thinks of,' said an FBI special agent in New York.

Their billion-dollar scam in California was the largest health insurance fraud in US history. A fake medical clinic was used to front the operation in Los Angeles, luring patients to mobile 'diagnostic centers' by promising free checkups, persuading them to sign over their insurance claims, and billing insurance companies for from $8,000 to $10,000 per patient.

Some 1,400 insurance companies paid out on the phony claims. The companies were hurting so badly that health insurance premiums went up throughout the state of California.[53]

The small group pulling this off consisted of a Michael Shmushkevich from Brighton Beach along with his brother, wife and girlfriend, two doctors, a lawyer and five others. Shmushkevich alone was charged on 175 counts of mail fraud, money-laundering, racketeering and conspiracy, for which he faced 1,980 years in jail.

That was in 1991, by which time the Soviet Union was breaking up, and the Russian mafia had joined the planetary crime club.

The Organizatsiya in America, though still a loose association of crooks, was now hooked in solidly to the Sicilian and American mafias, the Colombian cocaine cartels and its own mother cell in the old country. Its ranks were swelling with thousands of new arrivals from liberated Russia, some of whom were 'probably younger than Marat, tougher than Marat, and smarter than Marat', said Marat Balagula s lawyer.'[54]

Numerous Chechen were among them, the embodiment of their

rising expectations. 'I want to send my son to Harvard and own a Rolls Royce,' one said.

By 1992, the FBI was setting up a federal task force devoted solely to the Russians. The DEA broke a Russian ring bringing in heroin from Poland for Sicilian mafiosi in New York: a 'small part of a growing Russian involvement in heroin smuggling and distribution', a spokesman declared.

The Immigration Service, Secret Service and Internal Revenue Service were all watching a two-way traffic between Brighton Beach and Moscow.

Contract-killers were flying in from Moscow, or St Petersburg or the Caucasus to do a quick and inexpensive turnaround job, for the Organizatsiya, or the American or Sicilian mafia, or even ordinary Russian emigrés. 'If you're a Russian shopowner, you don't go to the local mafia boss to complain any more: you just call Russia and ask them to send a hit-man,' said Alex Grant.

America's Russian criminals were returning to their homeland to work a whole new set of crooked deals, often in partnership with their American and Sicilian counterparts. 'They go to Moscow all the time,' said an investigator studying the Brighton Beach crowd.

Police were overwhelmed by such goings and comings in a closely sealed criminal society whose language and customs they did not understand. 'It was hard before, but this is ridiculous,' an agent tracking emigré crime observed.

By 1993, the Russian mafia's parent export-import companies in Berlin were known to have daughter companies in New York, Los Angeles and Miami; doubtless there were others, still unknown. 'These are storefront companies, moving Soviet raw materials and finding buyers across the United States. They have lists and will deliver,' the FBI's Jim Moody told me.

This was the key to an operation that had mystified the police of America and Europe since that momentous year, 1990, luring the entire international underworld to Moscow, culminating in the biggest swindle ever perpetrated anywhere, exposed in Russia but almost nowhere else in January 1991.

Part 4

The Great
Ruble Scam

8

The Buildup

As the winds of freedom swept across Soviet Russia in 1990, traces of an apparently senseless traffic in rubles appeared in America and all over Europe.

A 'solid European bank' offered an American investor a billion dollars' worth of rubles 'with official letters guaranteeing their re-entry into the Soviet market', reported Eugene Milosh, President of the American Association of Exporters and Importers. 'There are rubles out there trying to find a home; there's a lot of hanky-panky going on,' he declared.[1]

A trainload of rubles passed through Poland in transit for Belgium.[2] 'Large, suspicious transactions involving rubles' were reported by Belgian, German and Dutch police.[3] A TIR truck packed with rubles was tracked across half the continent by Italian and Belgian intelligence agents. 'The TIR was protected by KGB men. From Avignon to Marseilles to Turin we seized 2 million rubles, 2 million, and 300,000, but we never got the TIR,' the Italian agent in charge told me.[4]

The guardia di finanza (financial police) picked up a sample 200,000 rubles from a Palestinian in Rome, one Ibrahim Siyam, who said he was selling 10 million. (The guardia sent someone to the Soviet embassy to ask if the rubles were real, then fined Siyam for not declaring them.)[5]

In the spring of 1990, the guardia di finanza listened in on a deal actually made with, and in the office of, a director of the Banco

Lariano in the northern city of Como. One of the Italians present
bought $5 million worth of rubles in cash from another, to be delivered
through the bank. ('Not too many 50-ruble notes, because that would
mean wagonloads,' the buyer specified.)[6]

During the autumn of 1990, Italy's High Commission to Combat
the Mafia turned over 'informative' phone taps on the subject to a
judge in Palermo, as I learned later from the then High Commissioner,
Domenico Sica.

'A TIR truck stuffed with rubles was travelling around the area
from Bologna to Verona to Rimini,' he said. 'We couldn't count them;
how do you count a TIR-full of banknotes? But we knew that a
German and his Sicilian wife – a Ludovica Bahl from Catania – were
selling them in blocks, and the Soviet embassy was involved.'[7]

The High Commission's office had advised the Palermo judge that
'a vast criminal organization, dedicated mainly to illicit financial
activities on Italian territory and abroad' was working 'in collusion
with Mafia groups in Palermo, Catania and Trapani, laundering the
money of Mafia families [and] converting their capital into rubles
through Swiss banks.'[8]

Though the tip led eventually to a hot criminal case, the ruble side
of it was never fully explored. Nor was similar police information elsewhere.

In Bellinzona, Switzerland, that December, an undercover narcotics
agent was approached by a notorious Turkish heroin trafficker, Hamza
Turkeresin, trying to peddle rubles packed into a shipping container.

Turkeresin was the Milan pointman for the Turkish mafia's babas
(godfathers) in Istanbul, wanted in Switzerland for a 100-kilo heroin
shipment intercepted on the way to Italy. Constantly on the move
around Western Europe, he worked with Pablo Escobar's cocaine traffickers and, more closely, with the notorious Italian drug trafficker
Santo Pasquale Morabito.

Morabito, who had bought 70 billion rubles in cash, was looking to
turn a profit by re-converting them to hard currency.[9] On his behalf,
Turkeresin offered the Swiss undercover agent a sample 100,000. The
agent bought them and referred the case to Geneva.[10]

In Geneva some days later, Judge Jean-Pierre Trembley ordered the
arrest of five men representing a German fugitive, Andreas Behrens,
wanted for washing several million narcodollars through Canada for
Pablo Escobar.

Respectively a Colombian, a German and three Argentinian
money-changers, they had been meeting at the Hotel Century, trying

to broker a swap of Morabito's 70 billion rubles for $4.6 billion – fifteen times below Russia's then official commercial rate of 1 ruble for $1.20.[11]

Judge Trembley could not locate the rubles, reportedly in a container left at Brink's in Holland, with certificates of deposit in Germany's Deutsche Bank in Cologne. Whether or not the judge looked that far afield, an open question, he finally released the suspects. 'I just couldn't believe that anybody in his right mind would swap narcodollars for rubles that nobody can spend,' he said.[12]

Yet swaps were undoubtedly going on, as a baffled judge in Sicily discovered. In 1989, Palermo's San Lorenzo family had bought 500 million rubles, Judge Carmelo Carrara found: this when a single ruble still cost $1.20 at the commercial rate.[13]

The San Lorenzo family ranks high in the Mafia command. Its boss, Mariano Troia, was reportedly in line to become capo di tutti i capi after Totò Riina's arrest. The fact that he had bought half a billion rubles was beyond understanding in Sicily in 1989.

The intermediary in the deal turned out to be a German national named Ulrich Bahl, the man selling blocks of rubles around Bologna the following autumn. The maiden name of his wife Ludovica, from Catania, proved to be Morabito; Pasquale Morabito, the 'Ndrangheta boss brokering 70 billion rubles in the north, was her father.[14]

Thanks to the tip from High Commissioner Sica, Ulrich Bahl was spotted in Sicily again in December 1990. This time he was at the centre of a case pointing investigators beyond Italy to Germany, Austria, Switzerland, Holland, America, Bolivia, Panama, Yugoslavia, Hungary, Rumania, Bulgaria and Russia.

Police closed in first on a pizzeria in Palermo's Mafia-infested district of Santa Maria di Gesù, where three Men of Honour were printing $20 million worth of fake $100 bills with the aid of a MacIntosh computer.[15]

Two Germans were caught with $1.5 million in Freiburg, Germany over the next weeks. Three Sicilian mafiosi were arrested in Switzerland, where they were holding a German girl hostage until her father, one of the arrested Germans, paid up for the counterfeit bills. Ulrich Bahl, trying to hawk $2 million of the fake bills, was picked up by the US Secret Service in Phoenix, Arizona.

With his arrest, another ruble deal, this one for $40 million, fell through.

Bahl, allegedly in the helicopter business, was juggling prodigal sums in mysterious conferences with international bankers, moving at frenetic speed from one sumptuous hotel to another with a coterie of German 'counsellors', travelling by private plane to and from Palermo, Bologna, Milan, Miami, Vienna, Zurich, Munich, Amsterdam, Budapest, Bucharest, Sofia, Belgrade.

His main connections in Sicily were with Ciccio Madonia's family in Palermo and Nitto Santapaola's in Catania. On their behalf, he was trying to unload stolen, forged or irregular bank cheques, government bonds and illicit currencies amounting to 500 billion lire, close to half a billion dollars at the time.

A good share of this was in Bolivian travellers' cheques for 1,150,000,000 pesos – $220 million – a payment for moving cocaine.

Bahl had trouble with the Bolivian pesos, since the cheques were out of date, but did fairly well with the rest in Switzerland (Credit Suisse of Bern, Banca Svizzera Italiana of Zurich); Germany (West Bank of Hamburg, DSK and OSK Bank of Munich); and the United States (First Union Bank USA, Barnet Bank of Miami, American Express in New York).

Meanwhile, Bahl was brokering a major arms deal for his Sicilian connection, with a state factory in Yugoslavia. The initial shipment in what was to be a regular monthly supply included 100 Kalashnikovs, 200 Russian Tokarev pistols, 10 silencers, 100 grenades, night sights, bazookas and munitions.

All was ready for the passage through customs in Milan (a pushover by arrangement, the Sicilians said), when fighting broke out in Croatia and the deal collapsed.

During the same month of December 1990, the DEA's Rome office had advised police in Palermo that Bahl was on his way down with $40 million for the Madonia and Santapaola families, with which they were going to buy rubles.

The dollars were the washed proceeds of the Mafia's stolen cheques, wrote investigating magistrate Agostino Gristina. 'This capital, converted through Swiss banks into rubles and, successively, into certificates for *gold* rubles, was to be used to buy dollars, arms and drugs in Miami, Florida,' he said.[16]

The Soviet gold ruble was legal tender abroad, freely exchangeable at the official rate of $1.20 per ruble. The common ruble was selling for around six cents on the black market when Bahl came down with the dollars.[17]

Converting the common one to the gold one was tricky but certainly possible with connivance on the Russian side; Russian crooks were adept at this.

Thus, barring unforeseen complications – Bahl's premature arrest in this case – the Sicilian Mafia's leading families, their German confederates and, presumably, their Russian accomplices stood to turn $40 million into $480 million.

Judge Gristina had no idea of the gold ruble's possibilities in 1990, nor did any investigator I questioned in Italy or elsewhere in Western Europe even a year afterwards (nor did I).

Much the same puzzle faced a judge in Rimini, on Italy's Adriatic coast. Several months of wiretaps in late 1990 had led Judge Roberto Sapio to arrest a ring of fourteen money-washers, overheard as they discussed heavy transactions in lire, dollars, Swiss francs, deutschmarks, Algerian and Libyan dinars, and rubles.

They had exchanged 'masses of rubles – trainloads, billions', their leader admitted later to the judge. Among others, the Mafia's ubiquitous Santo Pasquale Morabito of Catania and Milan had sold a hundred million; a noted Sicilian mafioso called Tommy Marsala had bought half a billion for Lebanon's Druse chieftain Waled Jumblatt.[18]

The ring's leader was an elderly, suffocatingly pious fake 'monsignore' by the name of Roberto Coppola, with phony credentials from the Sovereign Military Order of Saint John of Jerusalem, Knights of Malta.

Over the previous year, he had collected eighteen *authentic* diplomatic passports as Ambassador Extraordinary or Plenipotentiary, endowing him with 'full powers' to 'spread charity in the world', or 'develop economic and financial activities' for his honorary homelands. As he said himself on a tapped phone, he was laundering politicians' secret funds.

('You understand, this money is from rakeoffs for Algerian politicians, and these politicians have to get the money back in francs or Italian lire or Algerian dinars . . . so they say they'll give a discount of 20%,' he explained to an associate.)[19]

Along with Algeria, Antigua, Bulgaria, Equatorial Guinea, Fiji, Gabon, Israel, Rumania and the Solomon Islands, 'Monsignore' Coppola had credentials from the Russian Republic, the Leningrad Region, and the Soviet Republics of Byelorussia and Georgia.

The Russian Republic's credentials had been signed by Boris Yeltsin and his Foreign Minister, Andrei Kozyrev, in October 1990. 'Listen to this! Twenty minutes ago I was named Ambassador of Russia!' Coppola exulted over his tapped phone. 'Congratulations,' said his interlocutor.[20]

Three months later, on January 28,1991, Coppola was passing on more exciting news to his associates. A phone intercept by police in Rimini caught the conversation, reported as follows to Judge Sapio: 'G. calls His Excellency [Coppola], who informs him that the Russian embassy is selling 2,000 tons of gold and there would be a 1% profit. He asks G. if he has the possibility of buying any. G. says yes, and they agree to phone each other the next morning.'

Two thousand tons of gold was worth $22 billion. Such quantities could hardly have hit a meticulously regulated world market without causing cosmic disturbance. Nor was so much likely to have been amassed abroad, still less sold, all at once. Nevertheless, a 'package' worth $12 billion was said to have moved out of the USSR by the spring of 1991, 'by-passing normal export channels', reported the Manchester *Guardian*.

The following September, Soviet economist Grigori Yavlinski told leaders of the G-7 meeting in Bangkok that his country's gold reserves, thought to be between 2,000 and 3,000 tons, were down to 240 tons. In November, Western analysts were shocked to learn that *all* the reserves in the Soviet Central Bank were missing. 'Not a gram of gold remains; the vaults are empty,' said Gosbank director Viktor Geraschenko.[21]

Who in the Rome embassy had asked Coppola to sell all the gold in the Soviet Treasury? In January 1991, the embassy still belonged to the central Soviet government. On the other hand, 'Monsignore' Coppola had credentials from the government of the USSR's Russian Republic, Therefore, the answer could point either way.

One way or the other, however, the missing gold was entwined with the scandal that rocked Russia in the same month of January, when the whole subterranean traffic in its currency culminated in the Great Ruble Scam.

9

The Deal

Criminal Case No. 18/5922–91 hit Russia with hurricane force in the winter of 1991, but soon subsided. It took an effort of will to believe that the Russian government had made a deal with a bunch of international crooks to swap all the rubles in circulation for black market dollars. The story looked preposterous. Politicians claimed it was a frameup; nobody went to jail for it; the foreign press largely ignored it.

But the story was true. Exposure was not the end of it, either. Negotiations were resumed and new deals were struck – are still being struck. The same crooks are running fabulous joint ventures in Moscow to this day.

The crooks were only part of the story. While they were in it for money, others were in it to manipulate the politics of a dying Soviet state.

In the end, the case that shook Russia turned out to be an enormous and almost indecipherable conspiracy, in which elements of the KGB, in collusion with the international underworld, set out deliberately to de-stabilize the Soviet Union's currency, almost certainly with the tacit consent if not active participation of the Western intelligence community.

What they did together, or helped greatly to do – some intentionally, some otherwise – perfectly reflected the teachings of John Maynard Keynes. 'There is no subtler, no surer means of overturning the existing basis of society than to debauch the currency. The process engages all the hidden forces of economic law on the side of destruction, and does it in a manner which not one man in a million is able to diagnose,' Keynes once wrote.

Though the criminal forces involved were only one of the hidden forces on the side of destruction, they opened the way to the ongoing and relentless sack of post-communist Russia. The magnitude of their operation is a measure of the great new spaces open to international crime with the end of the communist era, and of the apathy, or dangerous self-absorption, or diplomatic cowardice, allowing the spaces to grow.

The fact that scarcely anyone outside Russia has heard of the Great Ruble Scam may be explained partly by its seemingly unbelievable details, but partly too by Western reluctance to touch exquisitely sensitive political nerves.

The scandal involved the new as well as the old Nomenklatura – far more the new than the old, indeed. Western governments rejoicing in the collapse of the Evil Empire wanted to assume, and to all appearances did assume, that all the evils in an emerging democracy emanated from politicians identified with the fallen communist state. Not one was prepared to acknowledge indelicate evidence to the contrary.

The story broke in the first month of the year the Soviet Union died. Tensions were building toward the abortive coup of August 1991, foreshadowing the Union's death at the year's end. Mikhail Gorbachev was struggling to hold its fifteen republics together. Boris Yeltsin was straining to free his Russian Republic of the Kremlin's hold.

The secret agreements coming to light that winter had a lot to do with the implacable enmity growing between these two men.

On January 23, 1991, a British businessman named Paul Pearson was picked up at Moscow's Sheremetyevo airport. In his briefcase was a signed contract, endorsed by the government of the Russian Republic, involving a swap of 140 billion rubles for 7.8 billion dollars.

No wonder people disbelieved; 140 billion rubles was the sum of all Russian cash extant at the time, worth $224 billion at the commercial rate and around $10 billion on the black market by January 1991.

The deal seemed to make no sense for the Russians, and hardly more for their foreign interlocutors. 'Who in his right mind was prepared to part with a fortune in solid US dollars for bales of coloured paper?' asked a Western reporter much amused at the thought.[1]

Unamused, the Russian Republic's Supreme Soviet formed a

commission of inquiry headed by a staunch Yeltsin supporter, Alexander Pochinok, who said the commission 'should not cast doubt on the government's probity'. Simultaneously, the Soviet Union's Prosecutor-General appointed a famous and incorruptible investigator – Vladimir Kalinichenko, hero of the assault on the Uzbek mafia in the 1980s – to handle Criminal Case No. 18/5922–91.[2]

Despite the friction between their respective governments, both turned up more or less the same astonishing information on the Russian side.

Without outside help, however, and there wasn't much, they could learn little about the Western characters concerned, or the secret consortium in the background, or a covert traffic in rubles reaching from Poland, Germany, Belgium, Italy, Austria, Sweden and Switzerland to the United States, Turkey and Singapore.

Certainly they had no knowledge then of the international underworld's avid interest in the ruble, dating back a good year or more.[3]

Many of the missing facts fell into place for me in two years of exceptionally difficult investigation. They are not complete, but they are verifiable.

The final report of Russia's parliamentary commission, published on March 1, 1991, revealed not just the criminal designs of the foreign parties to the deal, but the alarming innocence of the first freely elected government in the Soviet Republic of Russia: Boris Yeltsin's, voted in the previous summer.[5]

Beginning in that summer of 1990, the report said, three obscure Western 'businessmen' in succession made nearly identical propositions to Yeltsin's government. All three, 'in close liaison', offered to buy 140 billion rubles or more for $7.8 billion and up.

All held out radiant if elusive prospects of feeding and clothing all Russia, by earmarking the dollars to bring in Western consumer goods. In exchange, they wanted permission to keep the rubles in Russian bank accounts, and government licences to buy raw materials with the rubles for export – duty-free, tax-free and under state protection.

The first to appear in August was a 'John Ross' of New York, who turned out to be Zubok Jan Semyenovich of Ukraine, twice convicted of theft there before heading for the US.

Owner of a small condom factory with six employees in New York, he presented himself as the president of 'New Technology and Production International'. By the time he was found out, he had signed a protocol of intent with Russia's then Prime Minister, Ivan Silaev, to the amount of 300 billion rubles for $50 billion.[6]

The deal included a state licence 'to buy and export raw materials, waste materials, precious metals, etc. without paying duties' – 480 billion dollars' worth, at the commercial rate.[7]

Next, in October, came a Leo Emil Wanta who, when asked for credentials, proffered a signed photograph of President Reagan and said he belonged to 'the President's Club' (meaning he had contributed $50,000 to a presidential campaign). His outfit was the 'New Republic Financial Group', incorporated in Appleton, Wisconsin, affiliated with a bankrupt company in Norway, and registered in Vienna, Austria with a declared capital of 500,000 schillings ($17,000).[8]

Received in the best Moscow circles, Wanta proposed a swap of $5 billion for 140 billion rubles – an outrageous 28 to the dollar, well under half its going black market rate – rising over a period of five years to $50 billion for 300 billion rubles (the 'John Ross' proposal).

This extravagant arrangement would have been beyond the means (and comprehension) of the biggest Western banks. Nevertheless, Prime Minister Silaev asked President Yeltsin for 'the necessary authority to sign the appropriate agreements'.

The 'foreign partner' (Wanta) would spend the dollars to import Western goods for 'an emergency saturation of the consumer market', the Prime Minister wrote to Yeltsin. In exchange, Wanta was 'requesting an immediate line of credit of 140 billion rubles for investing in the economy of the Federal Soviet Russian Republic and purchasing raw and other materials . . .

'I believe that it is possible to provide the credit indicated from the funds of the [Russian Federation's] state budget,' continued Silaev. It was 'feasible' to 'control and coordinate' the ruble funds through a joint venture allotting 25% of the shares to the Russian government and 75% to Wanta, he concluded.[9]

In other words, Leo Wanta would control both the dollars and the rubles.

Whether or not Yeltsin consented personally, his closest adviser, Gennady Burbulis, did so implicitly: the proposal was referred to him, and he did not object. In fact, the parliamentary commission found an agreement already drawn up by Silaev's cabinet, accepting Wanta's offer.[10]

The agreement fell through, or seemed to, when the US State Department warned that Wanta 'had major debts and some credit card problems'. ('I confronted him in November 1990 and he fled,' says the chief investigator, Kalinichenko.)[11]

Just as Wanta was falling from grace, a Colin Gibbins of Great Britain appeared. President of an unknown South-African based 'Dove Trading Company', he had talked his way into a signed 140 billion-ruble contract and an authorized Russian bank account when his partner, Paul Pearson, was stopped at the airport.

The signatory on the Russian side was an A.A. Sveridov, Regional deputy from Chelyabinsk, at the centre of Russia's military-industrial complex in the Ural Mountains. He signed on behalf of an improbable 'Ekho Manufacturing Ecological Company' and a dubious charity called 'Eternal Memory to Soldiers', fronting for a brand-new foundation named 'Revival of the Urals Countryside'.

According to the parliamentary commission, Sveridov 'never intended to revive the Urals', nor did he have any money. Russia's Deputy Prime Minister, Gennady Filshin, had arranged to provide the rubles from the stated budget.

Gibbins had faxed his proposal to Prime Minister Silaev, who consulted his Ministers of Trade, Foreign Economics and Foreign Affairs, and passed it on to Deputy Prime Minister Filshin, who gave his blessing to an arrangement just like Wanta's.

Gibbins, acting for an unnamed investment consortium, was to deposit $7.8 billion in a Swiss bank, while a credit line of 140 billion rubles would be opened for him in a Russian bank. Both accounts would be under Gibbins' control: he had this in writing.

The contract was flagrantly illegal: only the Soviet Central Bank could handle foreign currency transactions of any size. The commission found nine other violations of the law as well: enough to incur a death sentence for 'large-scale speculation' under Article 154 of Russia's still valid criminal code. (The death sentence was abolished at the end of that year.)[12]

Nonetheless, Deputy Prime Minister Filshin had directed Russia's Foreign Trade Ministry to 'render assistance and support for the contract', and instructed the Director of the Moscow Inter-Regional Commercial Bank to open the necessary ruble account (No. 713713). The documents for this last were 'an obvious forgery', the commission declared.[13]

Summoned to explain himself before parliament, Filshin claimed that the deal would not really cost Russia anything, since it was actually 'a version of the Marshall Plan'.

Gibbins was going to spend his dollars to 'saturate the Russian market' with 700,000 tons of meat, 300,000 tons of butter and other 'top quality' Western goods, Filshin asserted; and he was going to spend his rubles to 'invest and re-invest' in the Russian economy, thereby 'supplying the population with goods of primary necessity . . .

'This kills two birds with one stone: on the one hand consumer demand is satisfied, and on the other additional financial resources are poured into industry and agriculture,' Filshin maintained.[14]

In reality, Gibbins had expressed only a vague 'readiness' to spend his dollars on imported food supplies, and no readiness whatever to invest his rubles in industry and agriculture. He was just after the currency, he said under interrogation. 'One of his clients' had asked him in June 1990 to 'buy a great sum of Soviet rubles'.

'We planned to swap currencies in a straightforward credit transfer. A consortium of European and Canadian banks were involved. It is no different to arranging to buy travellers' cheques,' said another of his partners in Johannesburg, David Frye.[15]

It remained for the parliamentary commission to discover that Gibbins was a professional con man. Interpol had had an international arrest warrant out for him since 1984, when British customs discovered that he had smuggled the world's fastest video camera to the Soviet Union: the Imacom 790, ten million frames a second, capable of filming the heart of a nuclear explosion.[16] ('Nobody seemed to know a thing about Gibbins, so I thought I'd give Interpol a call,' says Alexander Gurov, then head of the Interior Ministry's Sixth Department and a commission member.)[17]

Yet the Russian government would not give up on the Gibbins proposition even after losing Gibbins. Here, the parliamentary commission must have flinched at what it found. For within five days of the con man's exposure in Moscow, Russia's Deputy Minister of Trade, Vladimir Kozlov, was meeting with the same 'businessmen' in Zurich, Switzerland.

The parliamentary commission knew only that the meeting was held, since Kozlov confirmed it. The details were given to me by British authorities tracking the fugitive Gibbins.

The talks started in Zurich's Hotel Savoy on January 28,1991 and lasted through early March, these sources said. Nine or ten Russians showed up with Minister Kozlov, presenting a 'fantastic' shopping list for the first billion-dollar instalment, including frozen chickens and Tampax: so said Colin Gibbins' partner, David Frye, who was there.[18]

Also attending was Gibbins' other partner, Paul Pearson, fresh from his brief detention at Sheremetyevo airport.

Others present included Gibbins' predecessor in the negotiations, Leo Wanta of the 'New Republic Financial Group'; two American confederates of Wanta's named Jack Tremonti and Martin Gulewicz; a Vladimir Rozenberg and an Igor Chernyafsky, described by a British newspaper as emanating 'a whiff of brimstone'; and a mysterious Omar Khan.[19]

Several more represented seemingly unknown trust companies: Golden Eagle of Zurich; Van Lynch of Knightsbridge, London; Eurofin of Geneva; and Balaton NV of Holland which, in a fax to Dove Trading that January, had 'reiterated that our funds are in place to effect this exchange with additional rollovers [repeat orders] of up to 500 billion rubles or more.'[20]

'All the buyers were shady,' David Frye told me.

The meeting was inconclusive. The Russian contingent was apparently unable to scrape up the rubles at that stage. The buyers seemed to be getting cold feet; and Leo Wanta, a dominant figure in the whole affair, seemed to be getting nowhere. To all appearances, he dropped out of the game.

Upon unravelling this much of the story, the parliamentary commission of inquiry delivered its devastating opinion. The Gibbins contract was 'a fraud . . . that could give rise to uncontrollable financial processes, and provide conditions for grave financial sabotage,' it said.

The unidentified 'buyer company' behind Gibbins 'could use its ruble account to make massive purchases of raw materials, recyclable products and fixed assets – the whole national wealth – at extremely low prices.'

'With privatization of state enterprises on the way, this could even result in the loss of the Republic's economic sovereignty,' the report concluded.[21]

The commission did not suggest any arrests (since the contract was never consummated), but recommended that Deputy Prime Minister Filshin be dismissed for 'incompetence, negligence, insincerity . . . and deliberately misleading the commission'. In a decree signed by President Boris Yeltsin, Russia's Supreme Soviet fired him.

The staggering swaps sanctioned by Yeltsin's government were not necessarily, or not only, for personal gain. This was government policy.

Russia's leaders were desperately pressed for dollars, and not just to feed and clothe their people: Boris Yeltsin's most passionate objective that winter was to build up a war chest, assert Russia's independence, fight free of Gorbachev's rankling authority and Soviet control.

Unlikely to get enough dollars through conventional channels, his ministers had turned to the other kind, sadly unaware of the sharks circling in the outside world. If some in his cabinet were undoubtedly on the take, others were mercilessly gulled.

Yeltsin in person had authorized such black market swaps, as the only practical way of luring foreign capital to his bankrupt country. His Prime Minister, Silaev, had actually issued a decree to 'promptly implement such government agreements with several foreign companies'.[22]

Silaev's decree provided explicitly that foreign firms bringing in Western food and goods in exchange for rubles were 'authorized to sell goods and services in the Russian Federation's territory without middlemen for rubles'; entitled to 'protection of [their] subsequent investments in industrial and trade projects'; and 'allowed to buy on licence, for Soviet money, and to export without paying duties, a strictly limited range of raw and other materials, waste products for recycling, products made of precious metals, etc.'[23]

Western businessmen usually had no such privileges.

Silaev's 'ideologist', former Deputy Prime Minister Filshin, conceded that he had 'spent a long time' formulating these plans.[24] In fact, he had begun negotiations almost directly after the Yeltsin government came to power in the summer of 1990. 'Gennady Filshin's programme of fantastic currency transfers was a substitute for all programmes and reforms of the Russian government, until it collapsed with a crash,' observed the *Independent*.[25] Far from being punished when caught out, Filshin was promoted directly after being fired, to the lucrative post of Foreign Trade Minister; from there he went on to head the Russian Trade Mission in Vienna, where he has remained.('We shall preserve Filshin for Russia,' Yeltsin had declared.)[26]

Once the deals came to light, however, a shocked public could scarcely believe the appalling sums and sleazy interlocutors. The idea that Russia's leaders could have signed the country away – and to such swindlers – seemed so incredible that many thought the KGB must have set them up.

Suspicions grew when, less than a week after the case was blown, the Soviet Union's then hardline Premier Valentin Pavlov ordered the recall of all 50- and 100-ruble notes, the largest in circulation at the time. Yeltsin's government was to blame because of the Gibbins deal, he said.

Pavlov denied that his order was meant to wipe out popular savings, though it very nearly did. He insisted that its primary purpose was to stem an uncontrollable flow of rubles to the West, and 'a river of dirty money' coming back by the winter of 1991.

The 140 billion-ruble deal was just one of several amounting to hundreds of billions more, he told the press. The Moscow Commercial Bank had offered to sell 20.5 billion rubles to the Bank of East Asia, for instance. A 'Spartan International Company' had ordered 100 billion rubles by mail.[27]

Predictably, the communist Premier spoke of an imperialist plot. Western banks were conspiring to dethrone Gorbachev and derail the Soviet economy, 'flooding the country with billions of rubles hitherto stashed abroad, triggering hyperinflation and a financial catastrophe,' Pavlov alleged.[28]

Western diplomats dismissed the charge as 'bilge' or 'xenophobic rubbish' – Britain's Foreign Minister called it 'manifestly dotty' – but Pavlov was not far wrong.

The flow of rubles out of Soviet Russia was unquestionably heavy enough to suggest a conspiracy, and a lot of it was moving through Western banks. It was moving through Russian banks also, however. Everybody with any rubles to speak of was racing to exchange them illicitly for hard currency, starting with those who had the most: communists on the way out, politicians on the way in, and the Russian mafia.

As one, they all turned to the same bunch of international con men.

A year after the Case of the 140 Billion Rubles was presumably closed, a providential hand led me to a man with personal knowledge of the whole affair. Rather, he came to me.

Mr X, a hearty American with a springy step, an easy smile and a forthright clear-eyed stare, was a private investment banker operating at the outer edges of the law in Europe. After reading an article of mine on the Case of the 140 Billion Rubles in the *Corriere della Sera*, he looked me up.[29]

Mr X had played a considerable part in the ruble scam, dealing with the major players. Whether through pride or a bad conscience – his motives grew somewhat clearer later on – he wanted to tell me how it had really worked.

There were four main characters besides himself, he said. One was a Finnish national operating out of Helsinki named Michael Preisfreund, for whom Mr X acted briefly as fiduciary banker. The others were Leo Emil Wanta and his two confederates, Jack Tremonti and Martin Gulewicz.

Preisfreund, 'six foot five and straight as an arrow', elegant in 'a wardrobe that smacked of Savile Row', was brilliant, handsome, charismatic, 'the perfect model of an East European James Bond', said Mr X. 'He was fluent in German, Swedish, French and Italian [and Finnish presumably] and passable in Spanish, Danish and English; and he was incredibly astute about Western economics and politics.'

Since the Preisfreund family had been suppliers to the Russian navy for two generations, Michael 'knew most of the powerful men in the old Russia, and had access to the highest levels of Russian governmental and military personnel,' Mr X explained.

Leo Emil Wanta, born in Appleton, Wisconsin, was a fifty-year-old, heavyset, jumped-up snake oil salesman, as Mr X described him. Starting out in the pinball machine business in Menomonee Falls, he had gone on to 'work credit cards and many, many other scams' for the Mafia's Gambino family in New York, says a senior FBI official.[30]

For the US Secret Service, where the files on him are a yard long, he is a 'flim-flam artist', imprisoned for money laundering and document forgery in Switzerland, deported to face tax fraud charges in the US, and wanted for 'aggravated credit card fraud' in Austria – this last going back to September 1990, just when he was moving in on the Russian government.[31]

An eclectic trader, Wanta's faxed offers to a worldwide clientele in the summer of 1990 included 1,000,000 atropine sulphate tablets from Germany; 10 million jute sandbags from Saudi Arabia; 20 million cartons a month of tax-free Marlboros from the Ukrainian capital of Kiev; and 2 million gas masks from the USSR 'while the supply lasts'.[32]

Apart from miscellaneous goods, Wanta was trading not just in rubles but in lire, yen, pesetas, deutschmarks, Swiss francs, pounds sterling and Singapore dollars for commissions up to 14%: the clear mark of a money-washer.

Jack Tremonti came from Detroit, which has an American mafia, a Sicilian Mafia and a Ukrainian mafia.[33] Whether a made man or a Mafioso wannabe or simply someone who moved in the circles of the heavily Sicilian Biondo family, he was 'a macho Mafia asshole – he's got the walk, he's got the talk,' said Mr X.

Tremonti had been convicted in 1976 on three counts of theft and inter-state shipment of stolen goods, by a Federal court in Grosse Point, Michigan. (The FBI referred him to the US attorney in Los Angeles for suspected money laundering late in 1991, but the charge was dropped.)

Martin Gulewicz, an ex-football player closely associated with Tremonti in Detroit, was 'pure rotten bad', in the view of Mr X. A federal court in Grosse Point had convicted him for drug trafficking in 1987.[34]

For the purposes of the ruble scam, Wanta worked through his 'New Republic Financial Group' and something called 'Anthem'. Tremonti was president of a 'Global Tactical Services' based in Duncan, Oklahama. Gulewicz was with Tremonti.

Preisfreund, like Mr X, worked prudently out of countries sanctioning such ruble traffic. He worked through a 'Transatlantik Foundation' in Lettstsrasse 37, Vaduz, Lichtenstein (where the lawyer he used was Saddam Hussein's legal adviser and money man, said Mr X).[35]

Preisfreund also had a subsidiary 'Consulting Liberty Company' based in Founex, Switzerland, and an 'Amberhaven Ltd' working on commission in Geneva, after being struck off the commercial register in London.

Together, these four and Mr X cut the black market price of the ruble in half within three or four months: from around ten to the dollar in May 1990 to eighteen to the dollar by the end of that summer.

Obviously they weren't the only ones in what became a colossal ruble traffic. The Soviet Communist Party alone is thought to have transferred the better part of its assets abroad through dozens of channels beginning that year.

Any number of other Russians were trying to swap rubles for hard currency also. 'We found out that 100,000 dummy accounts were used to export rubles through the banking system. As soon as our bankers saw these illegal accounts, they went crooked too,' says the Russian Prosecutor-General's Serious Crimes investigator, Boris Uvarov.[36]

But Mr X's group set out deliberately to manipulate the market from the start. What they did was not necessarily illegal. In fact at least Mr X and Mr Preisfreund were careful to stay within the law and only operated out of countries where such ruble transfers were legal. Michael Preisfreund started the run on the ruble in May 1990.

From Helsinki, Preisfreund began by offering blocks of rubles 'in manageable amounts, a few hundred million at a time', for discreet sale abroad. His faxed offers gave potential customers a choice: 'external rubles', meaning bank-to-bank transfers or cash shipped out of Russia with bank letters guaranteeing their re-entry; or 'internal rubles', meaning certified cheques or cash deposits in Russian banks such as Promstrojbank or Vnesekonombank.

'Michael told me that he had all the quantities of both internal and external rubles, and could provide any amount of ruble bank cheques that could be exchanged internally or externally, but *additionally* that he could obtain the Soviet Finance Minister's authority that the cheques would be honoured in Russian banks!' Mr X wrote in a long fax answering some of my questions.

At first Mr X thought Preisfreund was merely managing the old Nomenklatura's flight capital. The Soviet Union was crumbling. It would be plausible, therefore, for the KGB and its friends in the old regime to squirrel away hard currency for a rainy day, or perhaps a triumphant comeback eventually.[37]

But Preisfreund's offers were escalating rapidly. By July 1990, he was faxing customers in Geneva, Munich, London, Vienna and Hong Kong interested in a 'minimum of two billion Soviet rubles' up to 'twenty billion in five billion rollovers'.

His first big customer was Jack Tremonti. His second, for ten billion rubles, was Leo Wanta.[38] 'I'll take all the rubles you got,' Wanta said.

Like Wanta and Tremonti, Preisfreund was buying as well as selling. While this could have been 'pure currency speculation', it suggested that Preisfreund might in reality be 'attempting to manipulate world ruble prices', said Mr X. The proposition appealed to him strongly.

Mr X insists that what he did from then on was done strictly on his own, which is hard to believe. The ability of three or four seedy characters to mount such a planet-wide operation, their extraordinary impact on what was still a world superpower, their singular immunity from beginning to end, suggest the guiding hand of not just one but several intelligence agencies.

Every secret service has its own private agenda, usually incomprehensible to any but its adversaries in the game. Whether Eastern or Western, they all use criminals to serve their ends: in the drug trade, the arms trade, the laundering business, the manipulation of international politics. The KGB, for one, had a direct interest in this instance going well beyond the Colin Gibbons deal, as we will see in Chapter 11. Its purpose is still unclear. Possibly it wanted a cheap ruble to stave off Soviet Russia's radical reformers: create runaway inflation, stir popular unrest, force a tough repressive policy on Mikhail Gorbachev or force him out.

Or else, a deviate wing wanted a cheap ruble to buy up Russia's natural resources and make a pile of money – just as the Russian mafia and its international partners did.

Whatever the reasons, there are grounds to believe that the KGB did form an underground network abroad in the autumn of 1990, to 'develop commercial undertakings with broad possibilities for entering international markets'. Coded cables to that effect were discovered two years later. Judging from scandalous revelations in 1993, the old Nomenklatura invested billions of dollars in such ventures abroad.[39]

It is difficult to imagine that Western services, the CIA in particular, would be unaware of what was going on. The Soviet Union was collapsing, a fate ardently desired by the Western intelligence community for half a century. As John Maynard Keynes had taught, there was 'no subtler, no surer means' than debauching its currency to finish it off.

Somebody in some Western intelligence service must have read Keynes. Nevertheless, I have no evidence that Mr X was prompted or pushed. He is plainly proud of what he did, insists that it was not illegal – strictly speaking, it wasn't – and *wants* his role to be known, as he told me in a long written explanation.

His motive was patriotism, he wrote. Watching Michael Preisfreund in operation, he saw a chance to give the tottering Soviet regime a final shove:

> I knew there would be a possibility of a Western privately orchestrated economic Jihad that could help crush the communist ruling powers by destroying their unstable ruble. Unilaterally and privately, I decided to play a catalytic role to crash the ruble.
>
> [That summer] I set up the tracking of internal and external ruble supplies, and how the exchange rates could be artificially manipulated on paper, this *in spite of all racketeers* [his italics]: the Wantas, Tremontis. Let them profit, if they could; I was after Ivan's jugular.
>
> The flood of paperwork generated by the profiteers enabled me to implode the ruble whenever I could. Did I have any impact? Only history will be the judge.[40]

History would have a hard time judging who among the known players deserved how much of the credit or blame for what followed.

Their dealings were full of mysterious characters, obscure investment foundations and cryptic messages. Here are some samples of the faxes whizzing around the globe:

Preisfreund was looking to buy 500 million Soviet rubles to or through a Robert Hutschenraiter of Augsburg, Germany, and selling a billion up to 2.6 billion to a Franz Mikulits of Impex GMBH in Vienna.

Preisfreund's Consulting Liberty Corporation was offering to buy a billion rubles from a Comalco International via Anker Bank in Geneva.

Preisfreund's Transatlantik Foundation was buying a billion rubles from a Georg Horvath of Unitrade in Riemerling, Germany.

Preisfreund's Amberhaven was negotiating five billion rubles through the Atlalanos Ertekforgalmi Bank in Budapest; offering 700 million to a Van Moer, Santerre & Cie in Brussels; buying 50 million from a Faisal Finance in Istanbul via Impex in Vienna; buying 1.2 billion through a prominent Swiss lawyer in Chiasso named Francesco Campana, acting for if not with Jack Tremonti.

Leo Wanta was offering eight billion rubles to Volksbank in Bonn for $544 million – a 'first tranche', according to a fax from a bank officer; selling 9,630,000,000 rubles to a Noweka Co through the Regio Bank in Basel, Switzerland; selling or claiming to sell 30 billion to the French bank Paribas, of which 20 billion appeared to be confirmed by the bank's director-general for Foreign Relations, M. de Montpellier.

Wanta was looking to buy three billion in cash from a 'Sofidad' in Geneva (the 'French group', said Mr X); offering 'up to 3 billion internal rubles' from his account at the Metishe Bank in Moscow; selling 50 billion external rubles to a Corep-Gestion, Sari corporation (apparently through the good offices of 'the India Ministry et al'): and bidding for '100 billion clean, clear, good, legal, bundled, counted, verified, packed and stamped Russian Rubles' from a Starl AG in Vaduz, Lichtenstein.

(Apart from his Metishe Bank in Russia, Wanta was using accounts with Credito Italiano in Milan, Swiss Banking Corporation in Geneva, Anker Bank in Geneva, the Dutch Algemeine Spaar in Brussels, Zentralsparkasse und Kommerzialbank in Vienna, Creditanstalt Bankverein in Vienna and Citibank in Milan, New York and Los Angeles.)

Jack Tremonti had dozens of supposed buy/sell deals going with Wanta and Preisfreund as well as outsiders, including an offer of 'up to Ten Billion Internal Russian Ruble Bank Drafts' to a Basar Ltd/Presto AB in Istanbul and Stockholm.

(Basar Ltd was the Turkish group – 'very big, very serious', Mr X said. AB appeared to be the Avenue Banque on the Champs Elysées, where Wanta had another of his numerous bank accounts.)[41]

One of Tremonti's offers to Preisfreund's agent in Amberhaven Ltd, for half a billion rubles, came in an interesting letter from Sofia, Bulgaria. Tremonti had been 'up and down so many times on a Balkan Cargo Plane that my appearance now resembles a Basketball', he wrote, going on to say:

'*I am not* offering External White Checks or promissory notes. *I am* offering Internal White Checks. However, as any good smuggler can tell you "Nothing is impossible". Now: Let's you and I knock the flies off, and find solutions to this valid transaction. I believe we are all singing out of the same hymn book, but one of us is tone deaf.'[42]

Some of their transactions had to be genuine and legal, judging from estimates of the rubles draining out of Russia between the middle and end of 1990. 'Billions of Russian rubles were purchased by Westerners at most favourable prices,' said Leonid Fituni, president of Russia's Centre for Global and Strategic Studies, later. 'Tens of billions' was the estimate of the Soviet Central Bank.[43]

'I figured around 70 billion rubles were trading on the world market by late autumn of 1990,' Mr X told me. That would have been around half of the national currency in circulation.

Looking back, the deputy head of the Russian Interior Ministry's Sixth Department, Gennady Chebotarev, conceded this. 'We can agree with the figure of 70 or maybe 80 billion,' he said.[44]

On the other hand, the paper trail was full of phony transactions. These were never meant to be consummated and there is no evidence that the companies or individuals at the receiving end of these faxes were involved in the scam or knew of its nature. Many of the several hundred faxes I saw were purely invented buy/sell orders for astronomical figures – one of Wanta's was for 500 billion rubles – sent in icily professional prose, with occasional grammatical lapses. In fact, Mr X explained, Wanta and his confederates were working the fax and phone methodically to force the ruble into a free fall on world money markets, and Mr X was helping them. 'We were beating the ruble down with paperwork, proposing false deals at low, low prices,' he said.

('Leo: I desperately need phone, fax, computer links, etc. Please help soon, so we can slay the dragons!' he wrote to Wanta that fall.)

A 'ruble mania' ensued in the summer of 1990, wrote a reporter in Washington. 'The fax machine and international direct dialling combined with the age-old lure of instant wealth to create a global frenzy.'[45] The reporter thought it all came to nothing, and nobody else in Washington seemed to notice it.

Afterwards, if not beforehand, however, somebody somewhere in the West must have noticed this killer-attack on a disintegrating Soviet state, since it worked.

A non-convertible currency in an unstable country has few defences on the free market. In a blizzard of paper leaving a trail from

Seattle to Singapore, the Wanta crowd kept offering to buy or sell billions of rubles dirt cheap, until the price they had in mind – around 18 to the dollar – was accepted as the right one by the summer's end.

Then they went after all the rubles in Russia.

'John Ross' made the first pitch in August 1990, but Wanta was the central figure. Colin Gibbins, who horned in on the bargaining in Moscow, merely 'tried to steal the rubles', Wanta wrote to Mr X. 'He was just trying to do a mirror image of the New Republic Deal. New Republic offered real $ for rubles . . . NR are the only good guys.'[46]

As the whole troupe went for Ivan's jugular, Wanta kept saying he was on a crusade to 'rescue Boris' by plying Russia with food and consumer goods. 'What a laugh,' Mr X recalls. 'The real game was to rob the Soviet Treasury of all its currency and grab all the natural resources while the country was falling apart.'

Plainly the KGB knew but didn't tell, waiting to do exactly what Boris Yeltsin said it did – frame him. Colin Gibbins, who took the fall, had been smuggling hi-tech weapons for the KGB. According to Gibbins' partner, David Frye, the KGB actually sent him in to set up Yeltsin.[47]

Once he got a signed contract out of Yeltsin's cabinet, the KGB promptly tipped off the airport police to pick up his other partner, Paul Pearson, and then hustled Gibbins himself off to safety in South Africa. (Insistent British requests for his extradition since then have been denied.)

But Gibbins was almost irrelevant to the Case of the 140 Billion Rubles. So was Mr X, in the way that mattered most – the money. The one who mattered was Leo Wanta.

The Russian government never dropped Wanta.

Barely a week after the Gibbins deal was exposed in January 1991, Wanta sent a fax thanking Deputy Prime Minister Filshin 'for the invitation to work further on the documents'. Filshin helped him get a visa, despite the cloud over his head.[48]

Over the next months, he negotiated a government sanctioned food-for-petroleum swap for 50 billion rubles, by his own account.[49] The figure has not been confirmed, but the deal has.

The deal was completed in the last days of 1991, when there was no longer a good excuse for doing government business with an egregious crook: the Soviet Union had just perished, Russia was a free sovereign state, and Boris Yeltsin had no further need of a war chest.[50]

Nonetheless, Wanta was still running his government approved joint venture in Moscow when I went back there in the summer of

1992.[51] And he was in and out of Moscow the summer after that, by which time investigators of several countries were looking into his multifarious activities.

Italian investigators were interested in Wanta because he was thought to be among the suppliers of Russian weapons and nuclear materials to a ring of international traffickers, including members of the Italian Camorra. Several of the ring's couriers were caught that summer with samples of Cesium-133, first in Geneva, then in the northern Italian city of Vicenza.[52]

With the arrests in Vicenza, Italy's interest in Wanta was spreading to America. Apart from Cesium-133, the couriers picked up in Vicenza had brought in certificates of deposit amounting to $25 million, issued by the American subsidiary of the Commercial Bank of the Chemical Industry of Russia.

This was the mysterious 'Himbank' in vernacular English, with headquarters in Moscow and a branch in Rochester, New York. The Rochester branch, located in an empty back room and according to the FBI appears to be doing no legitimate business, was evidently a new laundry service devised by Russian and American mafiosi, including Jack Tremonti.[53]

Himbank's CDs, the first found anywhere, were going to be exchanged for narcodollars in Italy, to be redeemed for laundered money in Russia or the US, Italian invesigators believed. Evidently the two mafias were launching a portable washing-machine.[54]

Meanwhile Geneva's chief investigating magistrate, Judge Jean-Louis Crochet, had flown to Moscow to confer with Russian mafia-hunter Vladimir Kalinichenko about Wanta's murky currency dealings.

The two men were 'working to solve a money-laundering mystery which originated in Russia', revealed the president of the Russian Academy of Science's Centre for Global and Strategic Studies, Leonid Fituni, afterward: the seemingly forgotten 140 billion-ruble scam, in fact .[55]

It was while comparing notes on Leo Wanta that they came upon explosive indication of a possible connection between the Great Ruble Scam and Russia's missing gold.

In the very days when the 140 billion-ruble contract was signed – January 1991 – Leo Wanta had been storming the world market with faxed offers to sell 2,000 tons of gold.[56]

How much might be coming from Russia was not known. But the Extraordinary and Plenipotentiary Ambassador of the Russian

Republic in Rome, 'Monsignore' Roberto Coppola, was offering exactly 2,000 tons of gold at exactly the same time: January 1991.[57]

Interpol Moscow had noted Wanta's almost daily phone calls to Coppola from Moscow between that January and June – the same period when 2,000 tons of Soviet gold somehow disappeared. It had even queried Washington about the 'close contacts' between this pair of swindlers.[58]

(Indeed, Mr X told me, 'Roberto Coppola was the source for all the gold that Wanta was offering.')

Obviously the pair might have been pushing the gold for the Soviet Communist Party, in the best position to smuggle 2,000 tons out of the Central Bank's vaults and out of the country in 1991.

Nevertheless, the Wanta link was bound to suggest a different possibility. According to the Moscow daily *Kuranty*, Judge Crochet and Kalinichenko strongly suspected that the gold might have been pledged as security for the 140 billion-ruble swap, for lack of enough rubles to satisfy the Wanta crowd's faceless investors.[59]

Furthermore, they thought the investors were mostly criminals who saw Russia as a miraculous solution to the problem of their drug money. By then, police were 'pretty sure about the identity of some suspects', Judge Crochet told the press on returning to Geneva.[60] Indeed, Leo Wanta would be convicted and jailed in Switzerland for money laundering the following summer. Certainly the Swiss magistrate and his Russian colleague had learned enough to understand that this seemingly preposterous ruble scam was in fact the original model for the most fabulous money-washing machine ever invented.[61]

'International organized crime got into the whole gigantic fraud to launder narcodollars,' Kalinichenko declared.[62] Were these criminals in their right minds? Yes, indeed.

10

The Payoff

On November 16, 1991, Boris Yeltsin's chief of foreign relations, Valery Grishin, announced that the Russian government was 'closing the petroleum faucet'.

Planned oil exports for that year had been set at 61 million tons, but export licences had been issued for considerably more than twice as much (150 million tons). Domestic fuel supplies were running desperately short.

Therefore, all permits for exporting crude were suspended. 'We cannot permit sales of so much petroleum abroad; we are dramatically in need at home,' Grishin said.[1]

A month later, on December 20, 1991, Leo Wanta set up his food-for-petroleum joint venture in Moscow. A 'safe custody' bank account in dollars and rubles was opened jointly at the Status Credit Bank by Wanta and his partner in 'Asian-Europa Development Pte Ltd,' Kok Howe Kwong of Singapore.

Kok Howe Kwong had been Wanta's 'consultant' throughout the year when he was beating the ruble down on world money markets, and peddling Russian gold by the ton.

By the time the pair hit Moscow, Russia must have looked to them as a chocolate mountain might look to a wondering child.

Despite the government's new edict, Wanta appeared to have no trouble shipping out petroleum. Its price had gone up in the year since he'd made his 140 billion-ruble pitch. Even so, he could buy a ton for $26 in rubles and sell it for $140 in the West.[2]

Asian-Europa Development had a right to do this, so long as it promised to import Western goods in exchange. Under government guidelines, such phenomenal transactions were tax-free, duty-free and legal.

It was impossible to say how many other villains had similar privileges. During that same month of December, for instance, Russia's First Deputy Economics Minister signed new export licences for an unknown 'private charity' to ship out ten million tons of petroleum, and another ten million of petroleum products, at a potential *net* profit of around $2 billion. Though the faucet was supposed to be off, no harm came to him.[3]

Such was the Russian scene by the end of 1991 that nobody could tell if the private charity was Russian or foreign or both.

As early as the previous spring, the then Deputy Chief of Russia's Sixth Department to Combat Organized Crime, Gennady Chebotarev, had submitted this confidential report to Interpol's world headquarters in Lyon:

> Strong mafia groups, in association with business circles and various government establishments, are committing large-scale unlawful export-import transactions with foreign partners at the state's expense.
>
> Their activity usually involves raw materials. Using bribery and corruption of government officials, high quality materials are exported as 'waste'. Strategic raw materials are passed off as low-quality materials. Titanium is reworked and exported at scrap metal prices . . .
>
> The high price of non-ferrous and precious metals and alloys on the Western market has brought a dramatic increase in the export of such materials.
>
> Organized groups also engage in direct smuggling of Soviet currency through criminal avenues . . .[4]

That was in April 1991. A year later, Chebotarev told me of 'great sums going abroad through transactions with Sicilian and American mafias'. Raw materials were draining out of the country at a terrifying rate, he said: 'tons and tons a day, every day, every hour' of petroleum, nickel, cobalt, aluminum, roller steel, exported as 'scrap metals' or 'waste'.[5]

On the day I talked with Chebotarev, ten tons of copper pipe were stolen from a single enterprise. Reports were coming in of a military transport plane flying out from Chelyabinsk with 40 tons of copper, of gangs stealing close to a ton of cobalt from the Severonikel combine, stealing 67 tons of bronze in the Magadanskiy Oblast, stealing the rare earth metals tantalum and indium from the Yaroslavl radio plant – all for export.[6]

In a single two-day period, customs officers at one border crossing detained *and released* a ten-ton shipment of calcium carbide from Karaganda; 60 tons of fuel oil from Nizhegorod; two freight cars with 50 tons of benzene from Kirishi; and a railroad tanker of gasoline hitched to other freight cars loaded with sugar, paper, shampoo, rugs, children's clothing, rescue rafts, caterpillar tractors and an asphalt road-roller.[7]

Over just two months in 1992, a massive police operation called Operation Trawl *captured* $180 million worth of resources on their illegal way out of Russia: 18,700 tons of rare metals, 731,500 tons of oil, 65,000 cubic yards of timber, and a wide range of weapons including one Mi-8 helicopter, one armoured personnel carrier, 5,000 missiles and 10 million bullets.[8] Capturing this much was some indication of how much was getting away.

Above all, the petroleum faucet could not be closed, whatever the government's decrees.

'Oil. That is what bothers us most. We have had great losses in all strategic materials, but the oil matter is utterly catastrophic,' said the respected journalist Mikhail Gurtovoy, appointed that spring to head a special government commission fighting economic crime:

What has actually happened? The big Western companies who treasure their reputation were in no hurry to invest money, so they waited. But a swarm of scoundrels who very quickly found a common language with our oil generals came running . . .

All these joint ventures couldn't drill or develop anything, not that they ever planned to. One was supposed to drill a specific number of bore-holes and pump out 649,000 tons of oil. Not a single bore-hole was drilled, but they're contracting for the sale of 700,000 tons. What is this, a new invention – pumping oil out of undrilled bore-holes?[9]

Measures designed to deal with such illicit exports were consistently toothless. A parliamentary oversight committee had undertaken to 'open up quite a few black holes' in the autumn of 1991, but had no power to impose any form of punishment.[10]

The Department for the Struggle Against Corruption of the Ministry for Security (ex-KGB) could only impose 'administrative penalties' – this when 'the illegal issuance of export licences is the basic source of income for corrupt officials,' the department's director said.[11]

Government inspectors in Gurtovoy's own new anti-corruption commission could only monitor and report. They had no authority to investigate or make arrests; often, for lack of government funds, they were not even paid.[12]

In any event, Russia had no customs controls on its borders with the other ex-Soviet republics, no laws on procedures for confiscating contraband, and no laws to punish corruption.

Most of its lost resources are still crossing freely into the now sovereign Baltic states over unmanned frontiers, or 'transparent borders', as Yeltsin has called them. Thus Estonia, which has no copper, has become the world's leading copper exporter.[13]

On the very day the Russian government announced the drastic cut in oil exports, it issued a decree abolishing all requirements for registering foreign investments, all curbs on exporting or re-investing the profits, and all restrictions on foreigners wanting to open ruble bank accounts.[14]

A decree issued the previous spring already allowed companies to be formed with 100% foreign capital, permitting them to export and import without normal licences, exempt from taxes.[15]

These steps failed to lure many legitimate foreign investors, to whom Russia still looked too chancy, but obviously heightened its attractions for the other kind. The last restraints were falling away for representatives of Palermo's San Lorenzo and Madonia families, Catania's Santapaola family, Aruba's Cuntrera brothers, the 'Ndrangheta's Morabito family, the Colombian cartels, the whole array of operators like Leo Wanta.

Within a week of launching Asian-Europa Development, he was somehow involved in a 66-billion-ruble swindle through Russia's Central Bank: 36 billion on December 26, 1991, soon followed by another 30 billion.

The tireless mafia-hunter Kalinichenko discovered the scam, involving 'transfers'. Someone in the Central Bank agreed to give the swindlers an exchange rate of 100 rubles to the dollar, twice the going black market rate. They sold the rubles to American buyers at 50 to the dollar, and split the other 50 with a banker friend.[16]

The former KGB official who had been director of the Central Bank throughout the Great Ruble Scam, Georgy Matyukhin, resigned shortly afterwards 'for health reasons'.

Another transfer scam involved a joint venture calling itself DiP Sovgroup in Moscow and D&P Group Inc in California. Both were headed by a Ukrainian émigré named Alexander Dokiychuk, an old-time associate of Wanta's.[17]

During the very weeks of the above $66 billion ruble bank swindle, Dokiychuk's American D&P Group got a credit of $1 billion in rubles from the Russian Foreign Trade Bank, in exchange for a promise to bring in the equivalent in Western computers and food aid. The credit was endorsed by Vice Premier Gaidar in a directive 'On Attracting Preferential Credits from US Banks'.

As a deposit on the deal, the Russian Foreign Trade Bank advanced 9 billion rubles to Dokiychuk's DiP Sovgroup in Moscow.

No computers or food aid had arrived when the scandal broke three months later, whereupon Dokiychuk repaid the 9 billion rubles, without interest. Meanwhile he had converted the rubles to dollars and put the money out in short-term loans at Russia's current 40% interest. With inflation running to about 20% a month then, he could buy back the rubles at a third of what they had cost in the first place.[18]

Wanta was believed to be in on this deal, though his name did not come up, Kalinichenko told me. He and Dokiychuk were 'part of the same crowd', backed by an invisible army of foreign investors, working dollar-ruble 'transfer' deals ever since.

Some were straight swaps, with the Wanta crowd creaming 3% off the top. Others involved a Russian version of the loan-back: bank credits in rubles, pledged as security for an American bank loan in dollars, put out at high interest in rubles or simply made off with.

This last was a favourite for any number of swindlers. One Moscovite presented a document to a US bank showing he had an impossible 17 billion rubles in his Russian account. He got a $2 million loan from the US bank, and 'went off in an unknown direction', said an officer of the Sixth Department.[19]

Mostly, though, people like Leo Wanta were doing the big straight swaps. Like an underground clearing house, they were collecting the rubles from Russian enterprises, and rounding up foreign buyers.

'Hundreds of Russian firms chip in the rubles, to get hard currency that isn't taxed away by the government; without people like

Wanta, they'd be paying 30 cents on the dollar to the Central Bank. They're dying to do it; Wanta could line up a hundred billion rubles in a week,' Kalinichenko said when we met again in the summer of 1992:

> The dollars do bring goods into Russia – sold at Western prices – and the rubles don't even leave the country.
>
> But the point is that *the Western investors own the rubles*. They come and buy *anything* in rubles – petroleum, precious metals, mines, real estate, factories . . .
>
> This is American mafia money now, and Italian and Russian mafia money. Wanta and others like him work with Russian mafiosi abroad, with Sicilian mafiosi, with every kind of crook. They do swaps for Russian firms without documents: their guarantee is the mafia structure on the Russian side and the Western side . . .[20]

For all the colossal wealth they are draining out of Russia and everywhere in the ex-Soviet commonwealth, these consummate criminals are never caught. Indeed, the more they take, the more they appear to be protected – *cosseted* – at the highest government levels. Leo Wanta is an egregious example. But the one who towers above all others is Marc David Rich, the most notorious swindler in American history.

A fugitive since 1985, Rich faces a 325-year prison term in the US on 51 charges of racketeering, mail and wire fraud, tax evasion on a $100 million of unreported income, and trading with the enemy (Iran, during the hostage crisis). The FBI has offered a $750,000 reward for his capture.

These facts come from a report entitled 'They Went Thataway: The Strange Case of Marc Rich and Pincus Green', in which the House Committee on Government Operations reviewed his criminal history .[21]

Since Rich holds three foreign passports – Swiss, Spanish and Israeli – he roams the world at will. Much of his time was spent in Russia until recently.

An operator on Soviet territory since 1983, he was once obliged by an irate Special Commission to refund $20 million of 'surplus money' he had picked up in deals with the late Soviet government.[22]

As the Soviet regime was falling, he hooked into Istok, the joint venture founded by Russia's first ruble millionaire, Artjom Tarasov. Using Istok to wangle his supplies, Rich got 4 million tons of petroleum out to Western Europe in 1990, at a profit of around half a billion dollars.[23]

In 1993, his yearly turnover on ex-Soviet territory ran to $3 billion, up half a billion over the year before. Only a tenth of this went to Russia and the other ex-Soviet republics.[24]

Head of the second largest commodities firm in the world, Marc Rich & Co, he was Russia's largest provider of grain – 5 million tons a year – and largest raw materials exporter. His three huge joint ventures in Russia, for crude and refined petroleum, were touted as the nation's most 'capital-intensive' foreign investments. The largest, Nobel Oil, was unsurprisingly funded with half a million dollars (in dollars) and 30 billion rubles (in rubles).[25] All three were exempt from standard export duties on crude oil.

In a full-length TV film that he commissioned and paid for, Rich presented himself as 'a man whose every thought is for the good of Russia'.

Hogwash, said Moscow's Interpol chief Vasiliy Ignatov. Marc Rich was charging world prices for the grain he brought in, Ignatov explained. In exchange, he was shipping out not only a sea of petroleum, but four-fifths of Russia's exported aluminum (worth around $700 million), nine-tenths of its exported zinc, and quantities of nickel, ferro-alloys, carbon, copper and molybdenum.[26]

According to *Forbes* magazine, Rich had 'stunning contracts' with the former Soviet republics by 1992; his profits on Russian oil and aluminum alone were 'a factor of two to three higher than the average profits on the world market'. The Russians were 'losing about 30% on this trade', said the director of Britain's Lonrho.[27]

Similar stories were coming out of Ukraine and, more spectacularly, out of Kazakhstan, whose government accused the Balkhashmed factory there of selling cathode copper to Marc Rich & Co in massive quantity at far below 'universally recognized discounts' on the London market. The factory – Marc Rich's primary partner in Kazakhstan – was also accused of keeping 'concealed profits' in Marc Rich bank accounts all over Europe.[28]

Even as this came to light, Kazakhstan's President Nursultan Nazarbayev was cordially inviting Marc Rich to expand operations in Kazakhstan.[29]

In Moscow, meanwhile, Interpol's Red Alert warrant appeared briefly to be having some effect. 'The Russian government vowed to suspend its ties with Marc Rich & Co pending a thorough investigation,' the *Wall Street Journal* reported. This 'was never followed through', however, the paper said.[30]

With the warrant out, Rich took to running his Russian operations through 150 assistants on his payroll. A naturalized Swiss citizen, therefore unextraditable, he lived beyond the reach of both the FBI and Interpol in the tranquil town of Zug.

The Russian government was more generous than ever in his absence. On January 25, 1992, the Ministries of the Economy and of Fuel and Power agreed jointly to give him export permits for 2,616,000 tons of heating oil and 1,530,000 tons of diesel fuel for the year 1992.[31]

Did Russia's governing politicians know who they were favouring in the person of Marc David Rich? 'Sure they did,' says *Izvestiya*; the KGB's dossier on him went back a decade. Yet he led the lengthening list of criminals who continue to ransack Russia systematically, often in direct collaboration with the politicians who run it.

Why is the Russian government giving away the resources it owns to a bunch of proven crooks? The likely answer, known the world over as the payoff, would be no more unusual here than anywhere if not for the staggering size of the sums.

Early in 1993, Russia's Vice-President Alexander Rutskoi disclosed that the illicit flow of raw materials abroad in the single year of 1992 had amounted to $17 billion. Though Rutskoi was then on the way to becoming Boris Yeltsin's intractable enemy, and was himself perhaps no better than he should be, his estimate was accepted by all of Russia's top leaders at the time.

'It would be enough to get that money back; we wouldn't have to ask for foreign financial aid,' he said. Actually, it was more than enough: the world's seven most industrialized countries, the G-7, had pledged only $13 billion of aid for the year 1993.[32]

Instead of giving any money back, Italian crime groups were flooding Russia with counterfeit dollars that winter, forged well enough to pass almost anywhere, used to finance their purchases of privatized enterprises, real estate, petroleum, titanium, uranium, plutonium, missiles, Migs.[33]

The forgeries had come forcibly to police attention late in December 1992, when Moscow police captured four Italian 'tourists' after a shootout in the centre of town. They were not only bringing in $1,200,000 in forged $100 bills to buy arms – including a missile ramp – but preparing to fence two stolen Italian certificates of deposit for a million dollars each. Pledged as security for a loan from a Russian bank, these could have stripped the bank of around two billion rubles at the end of 1992.[34]

In the same month of December, Russia's Ministry of Security cracked an international ring preparing to pump in another $11 million of fake $100 bills. One in every ten US dollars circulating in Russia was counterfeit by then, the Ministry calculated: one billion in an estimated ten billion.[35]

That alone could be enough to devastate the Russian economy, if it weren't so blasted already.

Nothing in history compares to this cancer consuming the largest country in the world. Devoured by criminal predators and rampant corruption from within and without, Russia seems helpless to save itself. Certainly the West has not done much to save it.

From a position of averting their eyes and hoping this would all go away, Western leaders are shifting to one of open resignation.

'There's no point in handing over even $5 billion if it is merely going to end up in the Swiss bank accounts of [Russia's] ruling elite,' remarked a senior Western official at the G-7 meeting in March 1993. Britain's Foreign Secretary, Douglas Hurd, warned at the same meeting against 'putting huge sums of money into a pocket with holes in it'.[36]

Rather than write Russia off for its sins, Western governments might consider how they have failed it by refusing to notice, still less address, the worst of its numberless afflictions.

This sickness cannot be contained by quarantine. For every Leo Wanta whose operations may come to light, and he is still operating freely, there are hundreds, perhaps thousands of others. Some may be loners, but the Sicilian and American mafias are there, the Colombian cartels are there, indeed all the big crime syndicates are there.

The capital they are amassing is clean when it leaves the great laundry that Russia has become: billions and billions of untraceable dollars infecting the rest of the world, used to fortify criminal power around the planet, finance the drug trade, invest in money markets, stock markets, commodity markets, real estate, tourism, transport and every kind of legitimate enterprise.

Yet what is happening in and to Russia is 'not a priority' for Western police, a foremost European police chief admitted to me halfway through 1993. Apart from Germany's BKA, no agency I have questioned in the West keeps a close watching brief on the crime scene there or anywhere in the ex-Soviet bloc.

No Western agency has a workable system for exchanging police information with Russia or the rest of the ex-Soviet bloc. No Western country has an extradition treaty with the Russian Republic, in the absence of which the whole international underworld can shelter on its territory, while its most dangerous native criminals can and do find sanctuary anywhere abroad.

No Western government has made financial help to Russia contingent on the passage of laws to make law enforcement feasible – much simpler than complying with Western demands for a brisk transition to capitalism.

None has acknowledged the manifest collusion between a criminal force growing exponentially and politicians at the highest levels of government.

Several of the most powerful men surrounding President Yeltsin came under formal judicial investigation in Russia itself in the summer of 1993. Breaking the news to the Russian parliament that June, Assistant Prosecutor-General Nikolaj Makarov named Yeltsin's grey eminence, Gennady Burbulis; Vice-Premier Vladimir Shumeiko; Vice-Premier Alexandr Shokhin; former Foreign Trade Minister Piotr Aven; and the supreme Chief of Information, Mikhail Poltoranin. All were accused of 'illicit economic dealings with American and European companies for personal gain'.[37]

Even then, no Western government cared to confront President Yeltsin with the fact that his ministers continued to give away more than they were asking the West for: and this to organized criminals, the West's own mortal enemies.

Doubtless Western diplomats have kept silent for fear of giving aid and comfort to Russia's unregenerate communists. In the event, they have denied aid and comfort to the diminishing few still trying to save Russia from the mafias that are now 'the country's greatest single problem', in Yeltsin's words.[38]

11

The Spinoff

Mr Kalashnikov, a big attraction at an international arms fair in Abu Dhabi in the winter of 1993, told reporters that he dreamed of inventing a new gun that wouldn't kill people.[1] This was not exactly the hard sell his country needed.

Russia was trying desperately to fill the black hole down which billions of dollars had disappeared by that winter. Therefore it was storming the market with some of the world's most advanced weaponry – the deadlier, the better.

Why not? All arms-producing countries are mean fighters in the world's most lucrative trade. Solely in the Middle East, arms contracts amounting to $428 billion were signed between 1991 and 1993, and that was an old market.[2] The collapse of the Soviet Union has been opening new markets all over the map.

Even Slovenia, supposedly no part of the war tearing Yugoslavia apart after the fall, was caught storing a hundred tons of weapons secretly in the summer of 1993. Eleven containers presumed to be packed with blankets for Yugoslav refugees were actually packed with 40,000 88mm mortars, 10,900 automatic guns and nearly a million cartridges.[3]

The discovery that these were Russian-made didn't mean much in itself. The provenance might have been Czechoslovakia, Poland, Belgium, Sweden, Italy, Britain, America. Anybody in the arms trade might turn up in any war-zone.

But Russia and its fellow ex-Soviet republics are not just in the business of selling arms like everybody else. They own one of the two largest conventional and nuclear arsenals on earth, and, except for the most apocalyptic of atomic weapons, it is out of control.

All the familiar evils of the arms trade are compounded by the anguishing frailty of these governments, the appalling corruption pervading them, the misery weighing down their people, the undiminished force and indecipherable designs of the KGB, the regnant Russian mafia, and its formidable confederates in the international underworld.

Despite Russia's reassuring words to the West, its military arsenals can almost literally be sacked at will.

The Russian government 'exercises no control whatsoever' over domestic arms sales, meaning any sales not directly exported from former Soviet territory, said the deputy chairman of Russia's Military-Industrial Commission, Vladimir Lopatin, in 1992.[4]

Factory owners, free to sell for their personal profit, are selling the latest Soviet tanks, rocket launchers and tactical missiles to local armies, militia groups, front companies and any other buyers flocking to the domestic market, Lopatin went on.

(Holland and Yemen had just bought a thousand T55 tanks directly from the factory through Russian front companies at the time, reported *Commersant*. The tanks were being sold by weight: $100,000 a ton.)

'The head of a military academy recently bought shares in a military factory by selling some of the buildings of his academy, even though these buildings did not belong to him. And we have dozens of cases like this,' Lopatin declared.

With this built-in incentive to increase military production rather than reconvert, military production did in fact increase. Russia's arms industry spent double the fifty billion rubles allocated to it in the first quarter of 1992, he revealed.

Supposedly the lack of control applies only to conventional weapons, but the borderline is dangerously indistinct. There are no controls on exporting the *critical components* of nuclear weapons either, if they can be used in legitimate consumer goods as well.

Thousands of factories in the ex-USSR turn out such dual-use components for ballistic missiles, chemical warfare agents and nuclear weapons. Numberless Soviet technicians who know how to put them together are migrating to countries offering fabulous salaries.

Since these factories don't make complete weapons systems, they don't come under the rules for strategic armament sales and exports. 'We would have to have people in each and every factory to know what they are doing. This is beyond our means,' Lopatin said.

Such critical components are haemorrhaging out of Russia today. 'The crème de la crème of Soviet military technology is up for grabs,' a senior Pentagon official said late in 1991.[5] Nothing had changed, save for the worse, when the deputy chairman of Russia's Military-Industrial Commission spoke out in 1992.

Unless Russia imposes strict controls on dual-use exports, half a dozen Third World countries could acquire bombs 'made in the FSU' (former Soviet Union) within a few years, Lopatin warned.[6]

He did not add, though he might have, that it is not impossible – far from it – for the bombs to be acquired ready-made.

Some of the worst nuclear fright stories coming out of Russia aren't true, starting with the one about the terrorists' ultimate weapon.

'The pocket atom bomb is a reality,' reported Britain's *Daily Mirror* in May 1993. Russia had developed a nuclear ball the size of a grapefruit, fitting into a briefcase and useable in any common rocket-launcher, the paper declared.

Two TV reporters chasing the story for Channel Four had come upon the secret ingredient, an amalgam of mercury, oxygen and antimony called red mercury. American scientists were said to have developed the powder, which Russians had transformed into a heavy liquid capable of provoking nuclear fission in a tiny particle of plutonium.

American nuclear researchers at Los Alamos reportedly refused to discuss it, but the director of a Russian company authorized to sell it 'to friendly nations' didn't mind. 'The world is in great danger,' he advised the reporters. Nuclear bombs 'the size of a biro' could be made with red mercury. 'Eighty micro-bombs could wipe out Moscow,' he told them.[7]

Red mercury was selling for up to $375,000 a kilo on the black market when this story appeared. A Russian-US joint venture called Alkor Technologies Inc, formed in St Petersburg solely to produce it, claimed to be raking in a billion dollars a year.[8]

The product seemed to be worth every cent. Apart from provoking nuclear fission in plutonium, red mercury was presented as a remarkably versatile substance used to make microchips for high-tech computers, fabricate banknotes, improve aerial radar, produce intelligent bombs, increase the precision of missile guidance systems, cool off atomic reactors, and 'revitalize atomic warheads impoverished by disuse'.[9]

Hundreds of salesmen were crisscrossing east and west Europe and America with ten-gram samples. One was a notorious rightwing Italian terrorist named Marco Affatigato, working out of an impressive office in Valence, France that offered 'Diverse Services for Enterprises'. (He claimed to have an official licence from Russia and Ukraine.)

Buyers were lining up from Libya, Nigeria, Saudi Arabia, Syria, Lebanon, South Africa, Argentina, Pakistan, India, Germany, Canada and the United States.

Police and intelligence services everywhere had been braced for just this kind of traffic since the fall of the Soviet Union. Traffickers moving red mercury were sighted in all directions. The Czechoslovak Interior Ministry mounted a sizeable paramilitary operation at Ostrava airport in 1991 to intercept a $20 million shipment from Russia, which failed to arrive.[10]

Similar raids followed in Hungary, Bulgaria, Poland and Italy over the next year. Half a dozen red mercury salesmen picked up in Italy provided hair-raising descriptions of their product.

At the height of an international police alert, Russian Vice-Premier Aleksandr Rutskoi dropped his own bomb in Moscow. Charged with investigating corruption – a job he lost soon after – he accused Boris Yeltsin's grey eminence, Gennady Burbulis, of a gigantic scam.

Burbulis had given an exclusive licence for the export of red mercury to a small company in his home town of Sverdlovsk, Rutskoi alleged; and the company had made $3 billion on it.

'How is it possible that a little Siberian company with a capital of 30,000 rubles can be authorized to export ten tons of red mercury bringing $300,000 a kilo on the international market? And why did this need a secret directive?' he demanded.

And he answered: 'Because this is a pure fraud, designed to carry out an international financial scheme. Because red mercury does not exist. Because it's all a trick to cover exports of platinum, beryllium, osmium, uranium, plutonium . . .'[11]

To call it merely a fraud was to belittle the gifted minds behind this monumental hoax.

'If perception is reality, then red mercury definitely exists . . . [But] it serves absolutely no known industrial purpose,' a British expert told A. Craig Copetas, a writer in hot pursuit.[12]

Indeed, there is no such thing as radioactive red mercury. Something combining antimony and mercury might once have been tried in a Russian experimental plutonium breeder that didn't work; even this is a guess, by the only expert to venture that far.[13]

What the salesmen push is likely to be a mix of ordinary if toxic minerals, or plain water tinted cherry-red, or common silver mercury in a glass tube painted red (with nail polish, in one instance).

It may be mildly radiated if extracted from a breeding reactor, or treated to show traces of radioactivity in a laboratory within three days – its shelf-life, the time-limit unfailingly set for testing.

Sometimes it is presented as a camouflage liquid for minute quantities of the real radioactive element: a deadly substance labelled 'Trans-uranium', or 'Lawrencium 103'.

'Lawrencium is a heavy element that does not exist in nature,' I was told by an atomic expert at Italy's Alternative Energy Institute. 'No isotope in the range of Lawrencium 103 has been identified. Ten isotopes in all have been identified in the range of Lawrencium 253 to 262; one has a half-life of 3.6 hours, the other of 40 minutes.' Neither has any practical use, he stated flatly.[14]

The Russian analyst at the US Bureau of Mines in Washington guffaws when the subject is mentioned. So do colleagues at the International Atomic Energy Agency in Vienna, where hardly a day passes without a phone call inquiring about it. British customs agents say they've been hearing of red mercury for ten years but never seen it.[15]

Nevertheless, the traffic in red mercury is real and intense, masking an underground traffic in platinum, beryllium, deuterium, scandium, cesium, strontium, uranium, plutonium: the true fright story.

Perhaps the most frightening part of the story is the public's ignorance of its dimensions. A solid wall of secret agents – good guys and bad guys, Eastern, Western, Southern and Northern – blocks the view.

Secret agents have always been entangled in the arms traffic, traditionally their murkiest domain. The power it signifies and the money in it draw them irresistibly, for whatever enigmatic objectives: political, operational, frequently venal. Adversaries in their private wars, they are often allies in frustrating the police and the courts.

Here they can count on the discretion or collusion of potent politicians and party financiers, corrupt public servants, bankers who are all business and diplomats piloting their ships of state through tricky international waters.

This was bad enough when they were merely dealing with conventional weapons. Today, however, secret agents of every variety are active and prominent players in the nuclear arms traffic, aside from and often in connivance with its con men and crooks.

Therefore, it is extremely difficult to uncover the truth about nuclear leakage from Russia. The dimensions of this terrifying traffic are systematically obscured. Countless cases end with the rumour squelched, the fake reassuringly exposed, the con man bared, the fellow who got away. Reporters trying to sort the facts from the cover-ups are forever at the risk of being misled. Clear instances of nuclear materials actually found and impounded are still rare.

But there are such instances.

The evidence has been accumulating since October 1991, when a Swiss national and three accomplices were picked up with 0.3 milligrams of plutonium in Como, on Italy's Swiss border. Even this minuscule sample was three hundred times more than enough to cause cancer.

The Swiss national was turned over to Judge Romano Dolce, destined to become the first Western magistrate tracking the seepage of Russian nuclear materials.

Short, slight, energetic, inquisitive and determined, Judge Dolce is still threading his way among unfathomable and all but insurmountable obstacles.

His hunt began when, after interrogating his Swiss arrestee, he informed Swiss police of an imminent deal for 29 kilos of Russian uranium. Six traffickers of various nationality were arrested in Zurich with 100 grams on them; the remaining 28.9 kilos turned up in a parked car in the centre of town.[16]

The uranium proved to be 'proletarian', not enriched. Since Switzerland has no law on trafficking in nuclear materials anyway, the six were released.

Actually, 'proletarian' uranium was a standard item hawked among others less innocuous by the extraordinary organization Judge Dolce came upon that winter.

The Judge had first heard of it not from his Swiss arrestee, but from a Swedish businessman who had dropped in previously, uninvited. The stranger, Jorgen Quist Nielsen, was a freelance trader marginally involved in what he now knew to be a huge clandestine traffic in red mercury, uranium and plutonium. 'When I realized how dangerous the whole thing was, I decided to come to you,' he told the Judge.

Nielsen had been referred to a certain Aleksandr Kuzin in Vienna as someone who could sell Russian gold to the government of Kuwait. When they met, however, Kuzin asked him to find customers for red mercury instead. One thing soon led to another, he said:

> Kuzin confided to me that red mercury, plutonium and uranium were coming to him from Russia, from generals and colonels in the army who were exporting it illegally and making a lot of money.
>
> I was introduced to Italians who were buying red mercury. One was Marco Affatigato, in Valence. Another was a 'Mr Corrado', the director of Olivetti in Stockholm [Mr Corrado's connection to Olivetti has not been established], who proposed that I should go to Moscow to meet somebody in the KGB, who would fly me to a contact in Kiev, where they make nuclear material . . .
>
> Naturally I played along, but I had no intention of getting into such a risky business . . .[17]

Jorgen Quist Nielsen's testimony led police to four of Kuzin's agents, arriving in Milan from Budapest with two kilos of what passed for red mercury, a small quantity of strategic scandium and five kilos of plutonium: this last discussed at length on their tapped phones. They had just given the plutonium to a Libyan agent when they were caught.

The Libyan got away – the plutonium went to Libya, Judge Dolce has reason to believe – and, as in Switzerland, the four arrested traffickers were soon released. Incredibly, Italy has no law on trafficking in nuclear materials either. 'I had to dust off a law on "aggravated contraband" to hold them at all,' the judge told me.[18]

By holding them briefly, however, he got another and much more important informant.

Dezider Ostrogonac, a Viennese electronics engineer, was administrative officer for three of Kuzin's front companies, in Vienna, Budapest and Prague. A firsthand witness, he described a huge multifaceted network covering the continent.

Ostrogonac's testimony led to the arrest of thirty traffickers all over Europe, including Marco Affatigato in Valence and 'Corrado' in Stockholm (who fled to Moscow, after being freed with the rest of them).

All worked for Aleksandr Kuzin, a former KGB colonel, Ostrogonac said. He named nine other KGB agents in the network, and five

Russian military officers working directly with Kuzin in Vienna, including a certain 'Kizow', son-in-law of former Moscow Mayor Gavril Popov.[19]

This was an official Soviet operation, Ostrogonac insisted:

> I repeat that the true sellers of red mercury, radioactive and fissile material are agents of the KGB, officers of the Red Army and high officials of the Russian government . . .
>
> I want to make it clear that the clandestine traffic of Soviet armament spreading over Europe for some years – machine guns, fighter aircraft, tanks, red mercury, scandium, radioactive and strategic materials, as well as nuclear warheads and nuclear technology – is all part of a criminal design desired and supported by the Soviet state apparatus.
>
> I can say with absolute certainty that this traffic depends on the complicity and decisive participation of the ex-Soviet republics. The transfer of materials is between state and state, and those managing the traffic are state functionaries.
>
> A traffic involving the entire territory of Europe cannot proliferate without the government's knowledge and consent, to bring in indispensable hard currency – especially dollars – for its disastrous economy. Like hundreds and hundreds of other traders or intermediaries of every race and provenance, my role is to tempt buyers with offers of dazzling profits. When a client is hooked, the KGB demands bank proof that he's solvent. The bank's confirmation goes to Russia by way of its embassies or consulates in Malmö, Sweden, or Berne, Switzerland, or Vienna. When Russian officials send their approval, the material moves on to Iraq, Iran, Israel, Syria, Lebanon, Libya, South Africa, Saudi Arabia, Pakistan, Argentina, India . . .

Ostrogonac plainly believed in the strategic uses of red mercury, as did several other informants who came along. This was the beauty of the scam. With a single superbly constructed lie, red mercury could be sold at a fabulous price in its own right, while serving as bait, or cover, for those interested in the genuine radioactive article.

The dealings of Kuzin's network have led investigators far beyond the confines of Como's courthouse by now. This is what they had learned through arrests, seizures, phone intercepts and undercover agents by the autumn of 1993:

The Kuzin network operated out of luxurious offices in St

Stephansplatz, the most elegant square in Vienna. Its director, Aleksandr Victorovich Kuzin, was undoubtedly a KGB colonel, rogue or otherwise.

Russia's Interior Ministry described him as the President of a crooked state cooperative called BIOCOR, tied to 'a band of criminals with international ties, involved in theft and fraud.' Though the Russian government might disown him, however, it didn't get in his way. On the contrary, a KGB colonel known only as 'Boris' was stationed in his Vienna headquarters, collecting a percentage on sales 'for the friends'.[20]

Kuzin Group International, his parent company, claimed to be a holding company representing 57 firms in the West and 300 'branches and agencies inside the USSR', with a global turnover of $4.3 billion.

Its prospectus, issued in 1991, stated that it employed 46,000 people in the West and 120,000 in the ex-Soviet Union, engaged in 'trade of every kind from petrochemicals and fertilizers to computers, sophisticated electronics, diagnostic medical equipment, pharmaceuticals, construction, and many other fields'.[21]

Not only did Kuzin-International 'maintain very close relations with the USSR', but it claimed 'an active role in the process of converting the Soviet military industry to civilian production'.

Kuzin-International had a branch called Kuzin-Italia in the northeastern Italian city of Udine, near the Yugoslav border. As registered in Udine's Chamber of Commerce, Kuzin-Italia had no employees, but was nevertheless trading in 'ferrous metals, plastics, chemicals for industry and agriculture, textiles, food and agricultural products, building materials and exports of fresh meat'.[22]

Colonel Kuzin had another company in Vienna called Impex, with a branch on the Italian-Swiss border. Impex is a foreign subsidiary of what used to be called Kintex, Bulgaria's state-owned company trading in arms and drugs since 1968.

Kuzin-International also had a 'daughter-company' based in Vienna called Kuzin Unitrade. This one had its own branch in Udine; a Sovitrade in Italy's Adriatic port of Trieste; and Unitrade branches in the German cities of Munich and Cologne.

Unitrade was described in the prospectus as primarily 'directed toward the Soviet market, especially Russia's, for every kind of trade'. In reality, it specialized in a two-way trade, selling Russian rubles and arms in the West and re-investing the proceeds in Russian factories and raw materials.[23]

This was where the path of former KGB Colonel Aleksandr Kuzin intersected with Leo Wanta's, Jack Tremonti's and Michael Preisfreund's.

Kuzin-International itself opened for business in Vienna on May 6, 1990, the very month and year when Preisfreund got started in Helsinki on the great ruble scam. Kuzin-Unitrade was formed the same month.

The Italian terrorist Marco Affatigato opened his office in Valence that month, to sell not just red mercury but rubles as well, in blocks of five and ten billion.[24] Leo Wanta and Colonel Kuzin were both offering 2 million Soviet gas masks in the same weeks. AB Invest's client (the 'Turkish group') bought 10 billion rubles from Preisfreund's confederates then, and 544 kilos of red mercury from Colonel Kuzin afterwards (for $174,124,800).

Two of Colonel Kuzin's operatives had ruble transactions with Preisfreund and his crowd in the same week that summer. One was Franz Mikulitz of Impex-Vienna, among the four men arrested in Como for flogging Kuzin's plutonium; the other was Georg Horvath, who heads Kuzin's Unitrade in Munich. On July 4, 1990, Mikulitz bought a billion rubles from Preisfreund; four days later, Horvath sold a billion rubles to Preisfreund.[25]

Apparently Colonel Kuzin had a hand in the hanky panky that brought the ruble crashing down. Indeed, swapping rubles and laundering other currencies were constants in his multifarious activities.

Like the others in the ruble scam, he worked with crooks: the Jewish mafia in Ukraine, the Russian mafia in general, its subalterns in ex-Yugoslavia and throughout Eastern Europe, the Triads, the Yakuza, the Camorra, the 'Ndrangheta, the Mafia. 'The Sicilians do a lot of his currency deals; they have the money,' Judge Dolce told me. They also take a lot of his arms, 'buying partly for themselves and selling the rest,' the Judge said.[26]

The arms were what set Colonel Kuzin apart as a singular menace. In addition to conventional weapons from everywhere in Eastern Europe – Kalashnikovs, mortars, tanks, helicopters, plastic explosives, missiles – the Kuzin network was selling 'sizeable quantities of extremely potent radioactive material to Middle Eastern and North African countries', said a confidential Italian police report.[27]

These supplies usually travelled west through Rumania, Bulgaria and ex-Yugoslavia to the port of Trieste; through Hungary into Austria; and through the Baltic states to a 'Mr Lindberg' in Finland.

Informants spoke of storage depots for nuclear materials in Chiasso and in Traiskierchen, Austria. Conventional weapons were said to be stored in Trieste, Budapest, the Croatian capital of Zagreb and, above all, the Czech town of Slušovice, seat of what outraged Czechs call 'the communist mafia'.

The Slušovice arsenal sounded like pure fiction, as Engineer Ostrogonac described it to Judge Dolce. This is what he said:

> The largest store of Russian and Czech arms is under a mountain about 12 kilometres from Slušovice. This was an old mine; now it is restored and guarded.
>
> Here there are or were anti-tank missiles, land-to-air missiles, Czech-made Skorpions similar to Israeli Uzis, 200,000 Kalashnikovs with ammunition . . . [and] about 200 new Russian tanks and 30 old ones, the last time I heard . . .
>
> Slušovice is owned by a Czech cooperative with around 6,000 workers. They have companies all over the world, hotels, computers, farms, food processing, in Egypt, Austria, USA, Germany, Luxembourg.
>
> These gentlemen of Slušovice are so powerful that the President of Czechoslovakia can't touch them. They have their own police force, 'Cubpol', named for their own president, Engineer Cuba. All the big spies and secret agents [of the old regime] work for them.
>
> They sell food to Russia, so naturally they're Number One in Russia . . .[28]

I might have been sceptical of this account, if I hadn't heard about Slušovice myself; it was the scandal of the day when I visited Prague in the autumn of 1991.

The Slušovice cooperative had been the communist regime's horn of plenty. It did have 6,000 employees and companies all over the world. Apart from dominating Czech agriculture, it owned food processing and bottling plants, hotels, factories, department stores, even horse racing. It had its own security service, ran its own fleet of trucks, built its own roads.

When the communist regime collapsed, the co-op's top managers forced the whole enterprise into bankruptcy, put its funds into their personal bank accounts, and sold its assets for pennies to the private company they hastened to form.

Czechoslovakia's post-communist government did seem unable to lay a finger on them. The chief investigator on their trail, a Captain Zak, had just fled to Switzerland, he said for his life, some said with a ten-million-dollar share of the loot when I got to Prague. Half a dozen responsible Czech sources told me that the renovated Slušovice company was shot through with members of the fallen Nomenklatura and ex-agents of the STB, their secret police.[29]

The part of this traffic having to do with nuclear materials was not only full of hopeful liars, but of secret agents bumping into each other from every direction. Consequently, there was much confusion about offers flooding the Western market by the autumn of 1993.

'We are getting propositions from Vienna on a daily basis – osmium, cesium-133, scandium; Vienna is the centre for this sensitive business,' said a German dealer in precious metals. 'Yesterday our undercover was offered 40 kilos of plutonium and 30 kilos of enriched uranium,' Judge Dolce said on my last visit to Como. Only six kilos of enriched uranium would have been enough for an atom bomb the size of Nagasaki's.

Nothing on that order had been found up to then; only eight kilos had been confiscated worldwide, by the American, British, French, Italian and German services combined.[30] Nevertheless, the material was unmistakably out there.

Kyrgizstan, a Central Asian republic known mostly for its fruit exports, had actually announced its plans to sell weapons-grade uranium on the world market; it is among the largest producers in the former USSR.[31] Plutonium was showing up in several places, along with every kind of radioactive material.

The first sizeable seizures suggested a lunatic nonchalance in the traffickers' ranks.

In January 1992, Austrian police found 2.8 kilos of plutonium-239 hidden simply in a large metal screw, left in a safety deposit box in central Vienna. 'It is true; we have found a sample of plutonium,' said the department head of the state police. The sample was identical to the much smaller one found in Como a year earlier; the trafficker in charge worked for Kuzin.[32]

The following October, a German fire brigade in protective clothing opened a luggage locker in Frankfurt's main railway station, and found a simple metal tube containing 20 grams of strontium-90. As much again of cesium-137 in a similar tube – this one wrapped in a plastic bag – turned up in the boot of a BMW parked in front of an airport hotel.[33]

These two materials, by-products of nuclear power plants, are among the most volatile and lethal radioactive substances known to man. 'The mere thought that cesium was stored largely unprotected in a car makes my hair stand on end,' a German nuclear physicist said.

The tip had come from a Swiss doctor, who had treated a Polish traveller for severe radiation sickness. Two other Poles ended up in a special German hospital. All had driven over the border from Poland with the material in their car. One had carried two phials of the cesium in his breast pocket.

Samples of cesium-137 and 133, carried just as casually, have been seized several times since then: in Zurich, in Geneva, in the northern Italian city of Vicenza (where the bearer of the cesium was also carrying Himbank's certificates of deposit for $25 million).[34]

Only days after the seizure of cesium in Frankfurt, on October 16, 1992, police in Munich impounded 2.2 kilos of uranium in a parking lot: 'highly enriched' this time, according to Munich's customs chief, and just as carelessly wrapped.[35]

The next March, a team of carabinieri in Turin found 3.2 grams of plutonium-239 – ten times more than the Como sample – packed in yet another plain metal tube. It had been stored under the roof of an apartment house for ten months.

This last was not a casual find. The plutonium belonged to an ex-agent of the Bulgarian secret police who lived in the building; Italian detectives had been tracking him since the previous June.

The Bulgarian agent had been spotted originally in the same north-eastern Italian corridor favoured by Colonel Kuzin, and he had the same sources. The traffic in his case was verified by hundreds of phone intercepts, faxes, letters from Italian companies and banks, state documents from the ex-Soviet republics and Bulgaria.

The sample under his roof involved a deal for 62.3 kilos of plutonium-239.[36] This was too frightening to be hushed up, papered over or waved away. The full implications – for the world, not just for Italy – were put to the public by an Italian magistrate who could not be silenced or ignored.

'The collapse of the Warsaw Pact and consequent relaxation of controls over nuclear arsenals have opened dramatic scenarios,' warned Judge Pierluigi Vigna of Florence, heading what was now a nationwide investigation into the international arms traffic. 'We know that Soviet radioactive material is reaching countries interested in making nuclear weapons. There is a very immediate and substantial danger that nuclear, chemical and bacteriological arms are ending up in the hands of governments without scruples.'

And he added a concomitant warning. 'In Eastern Europe,

convulsed by the fall of the Soviet empire, the Mafia and other organized crime groups are running an enormous clandestine arms traffic.
These criminal organizations have formed organic ties and reached
worldwide dimensions. They are increasingly militarized, sophisticated
and aggressive. Extremely potent weapons are at their disposal. There
is a present and tangible danger that nuclear, chemical and bacteriological arms may be coming into their possession,' he said.[37]

Part 5

The Problem of the Solution

12

Getting the Money

'What bothers us most is when you take our money away. We'd rather stay in jail and keep the money than be free without the money: that's the main thing,' a ranking *pentito* explained to Italy's parliamentary Anti-Mafia Commission.[1]

There in a few words is the problem and the solution, in reverse order. Money is the reason for the big crime syndicates' existence and, like Samson's hair, the source of their strength. Taking it away is the solution, therefore. Finding it is the problem.

Many countries have passed seemingly stringent laws by now to trap criminal money as it flows through the laundry. With few exceptions, the United States and Australia most notably, the laws don't work. Even those that do are barely skimming the surface.

Except for Italy – and this not until 1993 – no country has managed so far to seize more than what these syndicates would consider petty cash.[2] The Pizza Connection investigation, which took five years, managed to trace only $60 million of the $1.6 billion known to have been laundered.[3]

The DEA, which leads the world in this field, doubts that it is getting more than 5% of the Colombians' cocaine money. France has made only thirteen laundering cases since its strict law was passed in 1990. Altogether they amounted to about 100 million francs ($20 million), an 'efficacy rate of 1%', says a French Senate commission.[4]

A few stark facts suggest the difficulties in the way of doing better.

One thousand five hundred billion dollars a year, a quarter of all the money circulating around the planet, is illicit 'grey' money in need of laundering, whatever its provenance – graft, shady business, tax dodging, arms trading, drugs and other criminal revenue.[5]

A thousand billion dollars a *day*, licit and illicit, moves in and out of the United States alone by electronic wire-transfer.

A hundred billion dollars a year changes hands in the American drug trade, and five hundred billion worldwide.

Any amount of dollars – even a thousand billion, theoretically – can be wrapped in paper parcels and sent through the mail with an acceptably low risk of detection. This is widely done nowadays.[6]

Any amount can be run through automatic money machines or street-corner exchange bureaux: a billion pounds sterling passed through just three of these in Amsterdam in 1992.[7]

Any amount can be sent from anywhere to anywhere else through an American Express moneygram. There is no limit on the sum, and no possibility of detection, since no identification or bank account is required for the sender or receiver. All they need is their own code word.

The moneygram costs more than the postal service: $150 for every $5,000, which amounts to 3%. American Express thought such a costly service would make no sense for money launderers, but 3% is ludicrous for Colombian cartels ready to pay 25%.[8]

Any amount can be wire-transferred bank-to-bank around the world once it gets past a single bank, 'layered' through perhaps one or two hundred others until it vanishes for good.

Getting past the first bank is the only hard part, and is getting harder in a number of countries. Whenever a country stiffens up, however, launderers merely move on. The list of places for them to go keeps lengthening; the competition for their custom is fierce.

Starting with the letter 'A' is the Sicilian Mafia's state of Aruba, whose banking centre has come to full flower since independence from the Dutch Antilles in 1986. Apart from impenetrable bank secrecy, Aruba has a model law for the establishment of shell companies, called Aruban Exempt Corporations (AECs). The AECs are not only exempt from taxes, but can be formed with only $5,000 in capital, and controlled through anonymous bearer shares.[9]

Another prime 'A' country is Austria, Switzerland's successor as Western Europe's number one laundry state.

Despite its lingering reputation as the whitest of washers, Switzerland no longer offers perfect protection for suspect funds. On the contrary, it was the first state to sign a mutual assistance treaty with the US in 1977; and it has had rather stiff controls since 1989, when it outlawed the laundering of money that stems from a crime.[10]

Austria has done nothing of the sort. Bank secrecy is guaranteed by the Austrian constitution, and zealously enforced. Consequently there are 49 million bank accounts in the country, seven for every man, woman and child. Nine out of ten are secret numbered accounts.[11]

Austrian banks have no shame. In the autumn of 1992, when laundering had become an acute international concern, they were soliciting questionable Italian patronage openly. 'Austria is the country with the best bank secrecy in the world protecting our clients,' wrote the Bank für Tirol und Vorarlberg in Lienz to potential Italian customers, an easy eighteen miles across an open border.[12]

Anyone in Western Europe has free entry through Germany to the Austrian enclave of Oberstdorf, in the valley of Kleinwalsertal, accessible only by way of southern Bavaria. Cash can move there by car or truck from anywhere in Western Europe without passing a checkpoint. 'You can come to the bank, show just the outside of your passport, and open an account,' says the BKA's Jurgen Maurer.

Germany itself was a scarlet sinner until September 1992, when it finally made laundering a crime. Like the others in Western Europe, however, its new law is not only full of holes but in no way affects German bank subsidiaries abroad – in the fiscal paradise of Lichtenstein or Luxembourg, for example, both with wide-open borders.

Twenty-three German banks have subsidiaries in Luxembourg (pop: 359,030), among a record 213 of various nationalities. Thirty billion deutschmarks were transferred to the German banks' Luxembourg branches in the last days before January 1, 1993, birthday of the EC's single market.[13]

Thirty-four brand new banks of varied nationality had opened for business in Luxembourg over the previous year. Many consist of one room, four telexes, a fax and a couple of personal computers, all that is needed for certain discreet operations.

The affluent Grand Duchy of Luxembourg has been leaned on so hard and long that it promised to go straight in 1989. Its law against laundering was 'in line with those existing elsewhere', asserted its Monetary Institute, and carried penalties of up to five years in jail.

According to the same French Senate commission, however, Luxembourg's system is still 'meant to attract capital like an offshore bank' operating inland – worse, inside the EC.

A charter member of the EC, it still 'passionately defends its bank secrecy', 'closes its eyes' to dubious practices, and 'participates in an automatic laundering system of illicit international drug profits on a grand scale,' the commission maintains.[14]

Actually, Luxembourg *tightened* its bank secrecy when it made laundering a crime, imposing a *duty* of confidentiality on banks and their employees. Indeed its law came close to farce in the case of Frank Jurado, the Cali cartel's Harvard professor caught there by the DEA on his way to Moscow.

In January 1993, Jurado came before a Luxembourg appeals court on charges of laundering $32 million. The court upheld his conviction for laundering the money, but refused to confiscate it on the grounds that it did not belong to him.

The $32 million had to be returned to the rightful owners, the judge said. The owners were the wife and mother-in-law of Jurado's employer, José Santacruz Londono, who heads the Cali cartel. The only money confiscated was Jurado's salary: $30,000[15] (Embarrassment caused Luxembourg to tighten its laws again after this.)

Frank Jurado had been washing freely in another fiscal paradise inside the EC, the Principality of Monaco on the French Riviera. He had various accounts amounting to $55 million at the Industrial Bank of Monaco in Monte Carlo, under names like Buma, Bufa and Bula.

The Industrial Bank, owned by Her Most Serene Highness Princess Isabelle de Bourbon-Parma, was closed down after several similar cases came to light.[16] Its depositors could find any number of safer havens elsewhere, however.

Officially, there are some twenty-five 'fiscally tolerant states' or regions, such as the Channel Islands, the Caymans, the Seychelles, Malta, Andorra, Uruguay, Hong Kong and Vanuatu.

Unofficially, the entire ex-Soviet bloc is near or at the top of a much lengthier list.[17] Japan is extremely tolerant fiscally, for instance. So are Ireland and Belgium. Furthermore, fiscally tolerant *banks* can be found everywhere.

The United States may have the most, because it is so big and rich. But the small province of Trapani in western Sicily, among Italy's poorest, has 142 banks or bank branches largely in that category. Trapani has 102 finance companies besides – Italy has 28,000 – and these are ideal for laundering. Much easier to set up than a chartered bank and more slippery to watch, finance companies will often accept dubious cash simply as security for a loan.

That gets the cash into the banking system, the hard part. The loan, never repaid, becomes legitimate capital, invested through a dummy corporation in a legal enterprise: a Yakuza golf course in America, a Triad residence complex outside Paris, a high-rise condominium for Don Michele Zaza on the Côte d'Azur.

This method is known as the loanback, and it is very nearly foolproof. French authorities believe it may be largely responsible for the fact that French banks are in hock for unrecuperable office-building loans they have issued to the amount of 500 billion francs – $100 billion.[18]

Obviously the best system of all is to buy a bank outright, as American and Sicilian mafiosi did in Sverdlovsk. Buying one can be surprisingly easy and is not necessarily expensive.

An American company in the business of selling offshore banks in 1991 offered 'a fully chartered Private International Bank in the Caribbean . . . plus a Management Subsidiary Corporation in the Bahamas . . . plus connection with a professional Bahamas Management Service – all for $9,900'.[19]

The *International Herald Tribune* carries regular ads like this one: 'Merchant Bank for sale. No assets or liabilities. No transfer or qualification requirements. Class A license. Bearer shares. US $10,000.'

Side by side with such ads are others offering 'Second Residence Incognito', 'Second Travel Documents, Any Country', 'Right of Abode' or 'Citizenship' in 'Various Countries', together with 'ID and driving license'.

The operational possibilities here may be gathered from an ad in Moscow's financial weekly, *Commersant*, offering dual citizenship to Russian nationals in the Caribbean mini-state of Belize for $320,000: no residence required or questions asked.[20]

As a former colony in British Honduras, Belize has 'privileged', meaning free, entry to the British Commonwealth, the European Free Trade Area and the European Community. Thus, a Russian who buys Belize citizenship can not only bank there but travel without visas to Denmark, Norway, Sweden, Finland, Germany, Ireland, Malta, Australia, Canada, Cyprus, Hong Kong and Singapore.

There are underground laundries that don't even need a Belize, or American Express moneygrams, or a fiscally tolerant bank. Enormous sums are transferred from one end of the map to the other through Asia's ancient *hawala* system, on the strength of a phone call, a designated playing card, a fax.

A brief message from London produces cash or gold in Lahore or Bombay without going through the monetary system at all. Asian immigrants send remittances to their families this way; Asian drug traffickers wash through the same channels. Together they move between ten and twenty billion dollars a year, relying entirely on trust.[21]

In the days when organizations like the Sicilian Mafia were just beginning to make big money, they could leave it in the hands of a single bent banker.

During the 1970s, Sicily's old-guard bosses chose Don Michele Sindona, the most renowned international banker-crook of our time. After killing off the old guard at the start of the 80s, Totò Riina and his close associates used Sindona's ex-partner and fellow-crook, Roberto Calvi.

Both men ruined thousands of depositors and investors before they went under. The crash of Sindona's Franklin Bank in New York was the biggest on record in America, entailing a loss of $40 million; the crash of Calvi's Banco Ambrosiano in Milan was the biggest in Western history, entailing a loss of nearly $2 billion.

Each of them did as much as any single bent banker could do for the Mafia, the Vatican, the Masonic lodge P2 and Italy's political elite. But both tried to take the Mafia's money away, and came to a bad end.

By the late 1970s, Sicilian traffickers were clearing around $1 billion yearly in America, largely consigned to Sindona for laundering and investment. Unfortunately he lost it on his way to jail in 1979, the year he went bankrupt.

It is likely, though not certain, that the Sicilians got their money back that summer.

While free on bail awaiting trial in New York, Sindona was rigged out in a wig, a false beard, dark glasses and yellow chicken skin pasted to his cheeks, and smuggled to Palermo.

The organizer was Sindona's close friend and financial client, John Gambino of Brooklyn and Cherry Hill, the Sicilian Mafia's liaison with its cousins in America. A covered Masonic lodge connected to Licio Gelli's P2 took care of logistics.[22]

Sindona was not kidnapped by communist terrorists, as the press was told then, nor was he in Sicily to organize a separatist uprising, as he claimed later; he was the Mafia's prisoner. 'He went broke in the US and cheated a lot of people, so it was necessary to fake a kidnapping,' explained the Mafia's reigning prince at the time to a confidant.[23]

After a month under close guard in Palermo, Sindona arranged to give his kidnappers 'compromising documents involving authoritative figures in the Italian political and financial world', said Judge Falcone later.[24] In fact, he offered them the wherewithal to shake down five hundred of Italy's leading businessmen and politicians, his former clients. None has come forward to say if the shakedown happened or not.

The Billion-Dollar Blackmail Scam, as this came to be known, was Sindona's last service to the Mafia. Shipped back to New York, he was sentenced to twenty-five years, and a life sentence on top of that in Italy, where he died of strychnine poisoning the day after his trial. Whether he took or was given the strychnine, he had been squeezed dry and tossed away.[25]

Roberto Calvi, working for the Mafia's winning families, might have hoped for a kinder fate. Yet he ended up hanging from a girder under London's Blackfriars' Bridge.[26]

Calvi's life was so full of mystery towards the last that any of a dozen theories might have accounted for his death. The least likely was suicide, the British coroner's verdict. But as Britain's Foreign Secretary Douglas Hurd admitted when the case was re-opened, Scotland Yard was 'moving prudently in an investigation considered very dangerous for the judges, the police, their families, everybody helping in some way to collect evidence of the murderer's guilt.'[27]

The mystery was kicked back and forth between London and Rome for ten years. The evidence of guilt came in 1992, from the most credible of all Mafia defectors, Francesco Mannino Mannoia.

Calvi was strangled by the Mafia's heroin traffic manager in London, Francesco Di Carlo, he said. The orders had come from the Mafia's treasurer and ambassador to Rome, Pippo Calò. [28]

Like Sindona, Calvi had been embezzling on a monumental scale for years with his fellow-Mason in the P2, Licio Gelli. By 1981, he was navigating in such troubled waters that he asked for a contact with the Mafia, to make a pot of money and get out of his financial predicament.[29]

Gelli was handling a pot of the Mafia's money already, for the inner Corleonese circle: Totò Riina, 'Ciccio' Madonia and Pippo Calò. The money was passed on to Calvi, who lost it in the quicksands of his doomed financial ventures.

Once again, the Mafia got its money back, partly at least. 'Before having Calvi knocked off, Calò and Gelli managed to recuperate tens of billions of lire,' testified the *pentito* Mannino Mannoia. 'What matters more, Calò got a weight off his chest – the thought that Calvi had proved to be untrustworthy.'

The Mafia's representative in London took the weight off Calò's chest in person, according to Mannino Mannoia. 'It takes at least three men to strangle a man,' he said. 'But I never doubted that Francesco Di Carlo had his own hands around Calvi's throat. It is not admissible in Cosa Nostra for a Man of Honour to delegate such an order.'[30]

The Banco Ambrosiano, Italy's largest private bank, had been looted to the last cent when a Mafia envoy escorted Calvi on his frantic flight to London and imminent death. 'Never forget that an entire organization of friends is working for you, an organization ten times bigger than the Christian Democratic Party,' the envoy had assured him.[31]

Whatever the role of other sinister forces, the Mafia clearly had a hold all of its own on Calvi. Almost certainly its ruling bosses owned part if not all of the half a billion dollars that could not be accounted for after he was gone (not counting the billion and a half he is known to have stolen).[32] Certainly they had gained a murderous grip not just on the banker but on his bank.

Nobody had realized how deeply the Banco Ambrosiano was immersed in the financial affairs of the Mafia and the whole international underworld.

Combing through Calvi's tangled accounts, for example, investigators came upon one of his biggest money laundries, in Miami. Hundreds of millions of narcodollars had moved out of there, passing through a dizzying succession of foreign banks before ending up at the Banco Ambrosiano Overseas in the Bahaman capital of Nassau.

Returning to the US in the form of Panamanian investments, the washed dollars were redistributed to international accounts in Nigeria, Venezuela, Luxembourg, Argentina, Egypt, Peru, Belgium, France, Brazil, Uruguay, England, Greece, Switzerland and Spain (to name some).

In an endless wilderness of ghost companies, shell banks and anonymous trusts were twenty-odd major banks involved in secret dealings with the Ambrosiano. They ranged from the Banco del Centro in Panama to the Banco de la Nacion in Lima, Chase Manhattan in Nassau, the Central Bank of Venezuela, the Bank of China, the USSR's Bank of Foreign Trade in Moscow and, inevitably, the Bank of Credit and Commerce International.[33]

Though the era of the single bent banker was over long before these facts emerged, the system perfected by Sindona and Calvi still works. The many legal impediments in place since their day are the merest beginning of an attempt to crack it.

Finding *and taking away* criminal money means making the act of laundering it a crime; catching the cash at its point of entry into the banking system; tracking it through the system if it gets in, and on to its re-investment in some legitimate enterprise; identifying the mover; identifying the owner behind the mover; identifying the source of the cash; providing the legal instruments to seize the money and arrest the owner as well as the mover; assuring investigations, seizures and arrests across national frontiers; and doing all this without violating the legitimate individual's right to privacy.

Every one of these requirements is immensely difficult. Reconciling the last with the rest may never be possible.

On paper, much of the world has been committed to fight money-laundering since 1988. The UN Vienna Convention, signed by sixty-seven nations that December, requires ratifying nations to make laundering a crime; identify bank clients; trace, freeze and seize the proceeds of drug trafficking; eliminate bank secrecy for such offences; extradite offenders and provide mutual assistance for investigations.

The Basel Declaration of Principles that same month committed the central banks of twelve leading nations to identify bank customers and the source of their funds, turn down dubious transactions, and collaborate with criminal investigations 'within the maximum limits permitted by domestic legislation'.

The G-7 and eight other key nations set up a Financial Action Task Force, GAFI, in 1989 with forty proposals to combat laundering.

The EC Directive of February 1990 compelled the twelve member-states to outlaw the laundering of proceeds from *any* serious crime, require identification of bank clients, 'carefully examine unusual transactions', and 'refrain from abetting' them.

The EC's Council of Europe Convention provided for 'Search, Seizure and Confiscation of the Proceeds from Crime'.[34]

These covenants are revolutionary compared to the inertia prevailing before. While they have undoubtedly made laundering harder in several major countries, however, they are only expressions of intent until the signatory states turn them into enforceable law.

The difference between the two may be judged from the fact that the Soviet Union was among the first countries to ratify the UN Vienna convention, in December 1990. Even unrepentant Austria has ratified the Council of Europe convention.

The United States is far out front among countries trying to do better. Having started earlier, ventured further and spent a great deal more than any other, it is actually getting somewhere. Only Australia, adopting the same bold measures, can say as much.

America's first move, the Bank Secrecy Act of 1970, required banks to report cash deposits above $10,000 – this on pain of confiscation and prison for failure to comply. Once the law got past eight years of challenge in the courts, the paperwork grew awesome. By 1989 it was up to seven million currency transaction reports (CTRs) a year, amounting to a quarter of a trillion dollars.[35]

A twenty-million-plus federal data bank and an artificial intelligence system called FINCEN (Financial Crimes Enforcement Network) made it possible by then to track unusual currency patterns even in this colossal mountain of paper.

Though the system costs a fortune, it has produced the biggest hits on record. Operation Polar Cap, the earliest, shut down a Medellín cartel laundry operating in six cities, washing over a billion dollars in cash. Seven hundred other successful court cases were made by 1989; 1,700 more were under way.[36]

Nevertheless, the Bank Secrecy Act has crippling limitations. It does not catch deposits of $9,999, for one thing. 'Smurfing', or spreading any number of such deposits around, is standard practice. The BCCI is famous for doing this to recycle General Noriega's money in Panama, and the proceeds of Adnan Khashoggi's arms sales to Iran.

The Act doesn't cover the trillion dollars a day in international wire-transfers either, or transactions with foreign banks or branches of US banks abroad. This huge loophole cannot be closed without international agreements, still decidedly rare.

A number of governments are willing to sit down and talk now, not just because America is leaning hard as always, but because they are genuinely alarmed by organized crime's advancing armies. Nevertheless, there are still profound differences between the policies of the United States and the rest of the world.

The US goes after every kind of criminal money, including undeclared taxes and flight capital, and this makes other countries extremely nervous. Several have 'blocking statutes' to forbid cooperation with American investigators who might like to hunt on their territory; France and Holland are among these.

Even US Senator John F. Kerry, a bulldog on such matters, understands the nearly universal reluctance abroad to bear down on truant taxpayers or any citizen's private stash. 'Countries like Italy have an enormous tradition of capacity for avoidance of taxation and hiding assets and so forth, and they are not alone. All kinds of countries have that,' he conceded at a Senate hearing on foreign cooperation, or the lack of it.

He admitted as well that 'there is an ingrained feeling in the minds, the psyches of many people, many countries, about the government reaching into bank accounts.'

While the feeling is undoubtedly shared by many Americans (though the Senator didn't say so), they have learned to put up with some loss of financial privacy in an inescapably necessary cause. They seem to be the only ones, or nearly.

For fear of reaching too far into bank accounts, or into hidden assets and so forth, most national laws on laundering are doomed to failure in advance. Criminal money goes where undeclared capital goes; not much can be expected of laws designed to search for the one while protecting the other.

Nearly all the legislation enacted in recent years is crafted with this end in mind. Laundering is outlawed only for drugs and extremely violent crimes – for drugs alone, in Britain and France. So many strings are attached as to render even such a modest law essentially useless.

Where American investigators can start with the launderer and track back to the drugs, the common pattern elsewhere is the other way round.

The launderer cannot be prosecuted in most countries – or even investigated in some – without proof that he *knows* he is laundering drug money, as well as proof that the money does come from drugs. It is nearly impossible to produce proof that will stand up in court on either count, let alone both.

In the improbable event of a big launderer coming forward of his own will to help out the police, he might well not know where a particular sum of money came from. Short of happening on the launderer, the trafficker and the drugs all at once, the police would not be likely to know either.

While drug traffickers and their drugs may be seized, therefore, their launderers almost without exception are not.

France, with a highly professional financial force called TRACFIN, had simply *detected* thirteen laundering cases from July 1990 to January 1993. French bankers, required to report 'suspicious transactions' only if they are drug-related, are understandably in a quandary.

Britain has been trying since 1986 to trace up to £2 billion a year laundered from the proceeds of its own drug traffic (not counting the proceeds flowing into the City from elsewhere). On average, however, it manages to confiscate only about £9 million a year (0.5%).[37]

The better part of its bank reports on suspicious transactions, now running to 4,000 a year, are discarded because the suspect money involves tax fraud or hidden assets, not drugs.[38] For all the reporting, Britain had only twenty-seven convictions in court from 1986 to the start of 1993.[39]

Italy, sinking under suspicious transactions, had only 122 such bank reports of any kind from 1991 to 1993.[40] It has made up for this in part with a murderous confiscation law, enabling Italian courts to seize three billion dollars' worth of assets directly from top Sicilian bosses in the space of a single year.[41] This is something the bosses really mind.

Nevertheless, 'confiscation' is still one of those buzz words that make governments nervous. Though several are beginning to show an interest in that direction, few have actually gone much further than suspicious transaction reports. A primary component of the international community's solemn covenants, these are no more disappointing than several others.

Banks are asked only to 'know their customers', for instance, not who is behind them. A bank's customer is frequently a lawyer or company officer in a country authorizing such front men to act for an unnamed party. Germany's law exempts lawyers, notaries, tax advisers and certified public accountants from the obligation to identify their clients.[42] Swiss lawyers are notoriously exempt as well.

Banks are also asked to keep records of cash deposits over a fixed amount. But the records generally stay in the bank, since there are no national centralized computers to screen them. Though the records can be consulted, they cannot produce the unusual currency pattern only detectible through a centralized data bank: the flash signal that would tell an inspector where to look.

Some national laws are stricter than others, but launderers are free to pick and choose. In the European Community, for instance, they can operate without hindrance in any of the twelve member-states, depending on which has the most lenient laws (or banks, or bankers).

'The Dutch have no bank secrets; Belgium does,' says Roelof Gerrand, police chief of Tilburg on the southern Dutch border. 'Just seven miles across our border is a Belgian town composed of seven banks, two bars and three houses. They guarantee bank secrecy there.'[43]

Should even Belgium fail to please – or Luxembourg, or Ireland, or free-entry islands like Aruba, or Belize, or Saint Martin – launderers in the EC can simply pack their cash into cargo containers and ship it anywhere outside EC territory. Agents guarding the European Community's external border only control goods crossing in to the single market, not goods going out.

Just beyond its external border is not just Vienna, but Budapest, Warsaw, Prague. 'Anybody can open a hard currency account in a Czech bank. You can bring in cash and deposit it in as many accounts as you like. You can buy kroner and get 14% interest, untaxed. You can put it in an investment fund and watch it grow. *Nobody* will inform on any foreigner doing this,' says a senior official monitoring investments in her country.[44]

The last word in comfort for the launderer is the portable washing-machine devised by Russian and American mafiosi. Instead of going to the trouble of buying rubles, the owner of dirty money can simply buy the Himbank's certificates of deposit, delivered to his door. This leaves no paper trail at all.

Whatever else the world may be doing to crack down on the big crime syndicates, therefore, it is failing abysmally to take away their money.

It is dangerously deceptive, then, to say that much if not most of the international community has made money-laundering a crime at last.

Though Senator Kerry's hammerhead assault has destroyed the composure of many diplomats, American and foreign, he is an expert at calling a spade a spade. In a thrusting exchange with the US Treasury's Assistant Secretary for Enforcement, Salvatore Martoche, he put this question:

As an ex-prosecutor, I sit here and I say to myself, 'Well, you know, it is terrific to call something a crime, but when a country comes along and says well, we are going to call it a crime, I find it hard to feel that that is sufficient . . .

What good does it do to make money-laundering a crime if there is no enforcement capacity to track who is laundering the money and where it is coming from? My question is really, Are we not at a point where we absolutely know we have got to take considerably greater steps more rapidly in order to buttress the naming of it as a crime?

To which Mr Martoche replied:

I think we have to face up to some realities here . . . In international relations, the sovereignty of other countries is one of those issues that leads them to resist some ideas simply because they have been proffered by the United States . . .

Still, he added: 'If you are asking me should we continue to do more, you bet.'[45]

13

Trust Thy Neighbour (If You Can)

America is decades ahead of any country in fighting organized crime, and it is failing. Western Europe, though straining to catch up, remains a great place to be a crook. Most other countries are as badly off or worse.

The enormity of the problem is just beginning to register, and with it a sense of doom. Modern criminal power has surpassed the ability of lawful governments to contain it. The phenomenon is too big; nobody knows how to deal with it.

Perhaps it cannot be dealt with, so long as the world is divided into nearly two hundred sovereign states. While the big crime syndicates simply go where the money is, sovereign states cannot do anything simply.

If they go down to dismal defeat, it will be largely because they are hampered by all the baggage of statehood – patriotism, politics, accountable governments, human rights, legal strictures, international conventions, bureaucracy, diplomacy – whereas the big syndicates have no national allegiances, no laws but their own, no frontiers.

Obviously the mafias of the world cannot be fought on these terms. The question is how far sovereign states can go towards a planet-wide defence, without falling into the mafias' own mould.

Presumably they are moving in that direction. A third of a billion

people in Western Europe became one community in 1993. More
than a third of a billion are entering into a free-trade zone embracing
the United States, Canada and Mexico, looking to include the whole
of the Western hemisphere eventually.

The six ASEAN nations of southeast Asia are creating a similar
area designed eventually to take in the entire Pacific Rim from South
Korea and Taiwan to Japan and China.[1]

These are the great trading blocs of the future, forming up because
single countries cannot compete in the global marketplace any more.
But the member-countries are still sovereign states, moving slowly
and laboriously towards a distant goal.

The most advanced model so far, the European Community, has
barely got to the point of opening enough space for economies in
scale: rationalized production, more consumers, easier communications, faster and cheaper transport.

The EC's open market should save a quarter of a trillion dollars a
year just by cutting the time a truck needs to cross its territory, and the
expense of checking cars, passengers and baggage at what used to be
twelve inner borders.

While these are necessary and commendable achievements, however, the EC states have taken a third of a century to get this far; and
what they have is no borderless union. Indeed, it is an epic joke where
fighting crime is concerned.

The baggage of statehood is perfectly illustrated by the fact that the
EC's inner borders have gone down for crooks, but not for cops. The
distinction seems inevitable, if perverse. Crooks are entitled to move
around freely in an open market like everyone else, a price to be paid
for the market's benefits. Cops are servants of the state – worse,
upholders of its fundamental law.

United in their pursuit of the market's benefits, the twelve EC
states are separate to the point of mutual aversion, even open hostil-
ity, where their fundamental laws are concerned.

The results are grotesque, not just for the twelve but for all countries exposed to the same international criminal forces, especially in
regard to drugs.

The drug traffic within the EC runs to $80 billion a year now. The
profits, a quarter of the French national budget, represent 'a grave
danger to democracy', says a special commission of the French Senate.
Half the arrests on EC territory are drug-related. Its addict population
is up to a million; little Luxembourg has the highest number of overdose deaths per head on the continent.[2]

Yet no two EC countries have matching laws on the sale, possession or use of drugs, or on distinctions between soft and hard varieties, or surveillance of suspected traffickers, exchange of police information, controlled deliveries, permissible courtroom evidence, prison terms. They cannot even agree on harmonizing police radio frequencies, still less on a common policy of extradition amongst themselves.

In an open space covering half the continent, therefore, drug traffickers play a running game of tag, jumping through the cracks in the law. Depending on their needs, they choose whichever of the twelve countries is most convenient for banking, laundering, shipping, storing, marketing, networking, hiding out and, if absolutely unavoidable, going to jail.

Holland, among the most civilized of sovereign states, is their favourite.

Holland sends nobody to jail for more than six years. Those who do go in are lodged one to a cell and – since there are only 5,000 cells nationwide – assured of early release to make room for others on the waiting list. Those who escape are not pursued, on the grounds that 'nothing is more natural for a human being than wanting to regain his liberty.'[3]

Not many traffickers are arrested anyway; none at all for soft drugs. While marijuana is outlawed in most EC states and much of the world, it is a commercial crop in Holland, worth $100 million a year and expanding. 'When the drug networks realize the possibilities of Dutch marijuana, they'll come running,' said a senior officer in Holland's Anti-Crime Information Service. They were doing so even as he spoke in 1992.[4]

Marijuana is bought and sold legally in some 300 licensed Dutch coffee-shops, known as hash cafés, frequented by customers from all over the world, known as drug tourists.

Up to a thousand drug tourists a day visit the town with a now famous name, Maastricht, near Holland's borders with Germany, Belgium and Luxembourg.[5] They come for cocaine and heroin as well as hash, to use on the spot or peddle at home. These hard drugs are illegal in Holland, but can easily fall off the back of a truck passing through.

Hard drugs passing through may head for any part of Western Europe without running into a roadblock. Mostly they head for Germany, Italy and France, all with large addict populations and tough drug laws – France with the toughest on the continent.

Holland's policy of dissuasion rather than prohibition is custom-built for its own population, and no other. It does not admit to having international responsibilities; its interest in traffic merely crossing its sovereign territory is slight.

Drugs in transit 'are not a priority for the Dutch police', observes the French Senate commission. 'Holland is essentially indifferent to the external drug traffic, since this does not affect its own citizens. That is undoubtedly why it has become a major staging-area for the international drug trade.'[6]

The staging-area works both ways: from the terminal of the Balkan route proceeding west to Canada and the United States, and from anywhere abroad going anywhere in Europe.

Such is Holland's indifference to this traffic that only five Dutch customs agents were allocated in 1992 to go systematically through the manifests of 32,000 ships docking in Rotterdam yearly. Of 6,000 containers offloaded every day, they were managing to check an average of six.[7]

Several countries try to limit the damage by keeping their own narcotics agents in Rotterdam: Britain, Germany, Sweden, Canada, Israel, Turkey, Spain and the United States.[8] Not only are they subject to Dutch law, however, but they are caught in a web of conflicting laws wherever they turn.

The most maddening tangle has to do with the exchange of police information, which is central to everything. If interlocking crime cartels are ever to be driven back, the war starts here. And it is here that the EC states, like all sovereign states, are tying their own hands.

Most police agencies dislike sharing information on principle, in or out of their own countries. Few have a compelling interest in crimes beyond their jurisdiction. Even within their jurisdiction, what generally matters most is not so much the nature of the crime as the score: numbers of arrests, convictions, citations, commendations, promotions.

When it comes to sharing information across borders, natural reluctance is often encouraged – imposed – by national policy.

Some EC states require disclosure in an ongoing investigation; others will not pass on information that will be disclosed to a suspect. Some permit relatively free exchange through authorized channels; others forbid it.

Belgium, for one, allows its police officers to talk only to other police officers, not to customs agents. This alone has been enough to hold up completion of a functioning European Drug Intelligence Unit, meant solely to be a 'relay station' for exchanging information within the EC.

The very idea shocked EC ministers when it was first proposed. 'The Germans are all for it. The Belgians say, "Let's research it to see if we really need it." The Greeks say, "We don't need it." The Portuguese say, "We can't afford it." The Dutch blow hot and cold because of their "normalization of the drug problem",' observed the head of Scotland Yard's Drugs Intelligence Unit in 1992.[9]

Resistance to this or any proposal for sharing information here or anywhere is often small-minded pigheadedness, but not always. One country's deeply felt moral and social values are not necessarily another's. Police agencies are not uniformly high-minded, meticulous or politically correct. Western and Eastern police cannot easily overcome the distrust accruing from having shared disinformation for half a century.

The most paralyzing issue, and the most sensitive, has to do with protecting personal privacy.

Nobody likes Big Brother. Anybody might reasonably want to know who is watching over his or her personal life, how much of it is recorded somewhere, what use can be made of the information, who can get at it.

Regulating such matters in a computerized age is increasingly urgent and unspeakably difficult. Nearly everybody winds up in some kind of data bank today, justly or otherwise. The right to know about a personal dossier cannot be denied.

Strictly speaking, the right applies to all, from upright citizens to criminals however villainous, and other assorted enemies of society. Some governments make no exceptions; some make a few; some make more.

Formally, the EC is for rectitude almost without reservations. Its entire programme for pooling information to fight organized crime is contingent on accepting this principle.

The EC Commission's 1990 directive provides that 'every person must be able to know the existence of a computerized file on personal data, its principle purpose, the identity of whoever is responsible for the file, and his habitual address.'[10]

A demand to see the file can be made 'at the moment the information is gathered', and must be met promptly; failure to comply carries criminal and civil penalties.

No computerized file can be started without the 'explicit consent' of the person involved, asked for and given in advance. Consent can be withdrawn at any time. Only secret service files are exempt from this rule.

Past criminal records cannot go into the file. Exceptions may be made for an inter-governmental data bank, but only regarding crimes subject to extradition. Most arrests made in the EC states are national, consequently not subject to extradition.

(Even the extraditable kind are extremely difficult to nail down. Holland will not extradite a Dutch national for a crime committed outside Dutch frontiers. Germany will not extradite a fugitive convicted of Mafia association in Italy. Britain is exceedingly starchy about extraditing anybody. 'You can't imagine how hard it is to get a person extradited from the UK to Germany,' says a senior BKA officer.)

The only grounds on which personal files may be withheld are national security and 'pre-eminent public interest', and this under strict judicial control.

Directives like these are referred to in Eurospeak as 'ministerially driven', meaning that they are thought up by politicians. Translated into plainspeak, this one means that no policeman with a grain of caution will put meaningful information into a data bank.

An Italian cop would crack up at the thought of asking the consent of a Mafia suspect before opening a file, providing his own name and address as he does so.

A German cop, on a tight rein already, would be driven to hide behind his desk. 'A mental barrier has developed in the minds of our policemen, who feel caught redhanded or think they've violated a law every time they exchange information with other authorities,' says BKA director Zachert.

Several EC states, notably Germany and France, have data protection laws as strict as the EC directive or stricter. Others tend toward America's early Freedom of Information Act, with a fairly wide margin of governmental discretion. Italy has no data protection law of any sort.

The standoff is complete, therefore. Without agreement on this issue among the twelve states, possibly years away, the European Community is incapable of a collective effort to pool police intelligence within its own confines.

The height of its aspirations is Europol, presented as the world's first international police force. But there is still no Europol behind the name and solemn declarations of intent. Nor is it meant to be anything like an operative international police force.

So far, Europol consists of twenty-two policemen encamped on a temporary construction-site near Strasbourg, whose mission has yet to be precisely defined. When and if the twelve can agree on what goes in to its future data bank, thus permitting it to come into existence, it will have at any rate no power to investigate, still less make arrests, inflict penalties, or operate in any way across borders.

There is no such machinery for law enforcement in the European Community: the Treaty of Rome, on which it was founded over three decades ago, gives it no jurisdiction over penal matters of any sort. Accordingly, Europol's sole function will be to coordinate the exchange of police data, essentially as a relay station from one national data bank to another.

Some EC states have excellent data banks: Germany's, Britain's and Italy's are outstanding. Others have none: Holland considers the very existence of one to be an intrusion on privacy. France has one but severely restricts the input; unless convicted in court, a suspected criminal cannot be listed, for instance.

At best, then, the information to relay will be spotty and inadequate. 'It will probably be good for catching a husband who isn't paying alimony, maybe finding a stolen car or lost child. The vital stuff will not go in,' says a ranking BKA officer.

Agreed upon at the Maastricht summit in December 1991, Europol was still the subject of truculent and inconclusive debate in the autumn of 1993.

Ministers spent hours at the London summit in 1992 'dancing round the edge of hair-splitting semantics,' said British Home Secretary Kenneth Clarke.[11]

Much time was lost debating the merits of Siemens (German) versus Bull (French) to furnish Europol's computerized data system. EC ministers could still not agree on where its headquarters should be, or which of the nine languages spoken in the Community should prevail in its communications, or which country's representative should head it.

In any case, the persistence of twelve disparate juridical systems promised a contentious future. 'Europol could not work because there does not yet exist a corpus of European criminal law permitting [it] to act across national frontiers,' said a special commission of the European Parliament.[12]

On the face of it, the United States resolved such internal problems two centuries ago when, after eleven years of debate, its independent colonies agreed on a federal constitution.

Actually, the US did not become a united nation until the end of the Civil War nearly a century later; nor did its internal frontiers fall after that. States' rights are still sacrosanct in America. A New York cop wouldn't dare chase a criminal across the Hudson River into New Jersey; many wouldn't believe how hard it is to get a wanted person extradited from Texas to Alabama.

But America has federal agencies empowered to cross state lines, and there lies its enormous advantage over the nascent union of Western Europe.

Authorized to act nationwide, the FBI has been running a Uniform Crime Reporting System since the 1930s, and a giant data base on organized crime since the early 1980s.

The data base includes names, numbers, profiles, electronic surveillance. Over a hundred intelligence research specialists review and analyze the material, all selected by competitive testing, proven ability and sensitive background checks. Controls over the material and access to it are nearly foolproof.

Several other US agencies have formidable data banks and operative powers across state lines: the DEA, Customs, Immigration, the Treasury, Internal Revenue.

Singly and jointly, they have mustered massive forces to combat the mafias invading America. For all that, they cannot contain the criminal power taking hold across the country.

Forever the prime target, America was the first to realize the futility of trying to cope on its own. It has been urging other nations for years to work together on drugs, money-washing, counterfeiting, fraud – to perceive modern organized crime as the planetary phenomenon it is.

For nearly a decade, the only serious response came from Italy. Relations between the two have been exceptionally close and productive since the early 1980s. No other country has gone as far, but a good number are trying today: with the US, with Italy, with each other.

Several in the West are starting to talk with their fellow-sufferers and the sources of their torment in the east, from Japan and China to Russia and the rest of the former Soviet empire. The DEA has training courses for narcotics agents in the ex-Soviet republics; the BKA and FBI both have men stationed in Moscow now.

Seminars, conferences, exploratory missions, academic studies, international resolutions, are a measure of the profound unease spreading across the world. Nobody in law enforcement imagines that any country, or continent, or hemisphere can defend itself on its own any more.

Condemned to work together, however, sovereign states still stand on their prerogatives.

Their sole international interlocutor continues to be Interpol, which goes back to the First World War. A private organization with no politics and no powers of its own, Interpol is a neutered body passing no information from one country to another without express permission and orders to that effect.

For nearly a century, it has served simply as a conduit for requests transmitted among member-states, mostly to execute international arrest warrants for trans-border fugitives.

Renovated and reinforced by sophisticated technology, however, Interpol has the capacity to do much more now. Apart from the most advanced and comprehensive international data bank in the world, it has 158 member-states – almost the entire roster of the United Nations. All the countries infested by the big crime syndicates belong to it, including post-communist Russia, the rest of the ex-Soviet Union and its former satellites in Eastern Europe.

Here is an organization already in place, expandable, open to improvement, where professionals in law enforcement from every continent might see the interlocking criminal circuit in its entirety, and explore every avenue pointing toward planet-wide defence.

But Interpol is an independent entity, not subject to political direction: 'not ministerially driven', observes its Secretary-General, Raymond Kendall. Few member-states are more than lukewarm to the idea of broadening its functions.

Rather than build on it, the EC's twelve have chosen to build an entity of their own, costing more, taking longer and reaching no further than their common outer frontier. The notion of a Europol operating across more than the western half of a single continent is not even spoken of – this as the eastern half is taken over by the biggest players in the international underworld.

Shouldn't it be the other way round? The great trading blocs in formation offer a chance the planet has never known. If ageless barriers can go down for trade, it should be possible to lower them for mutual protection.

A great many countries have done so already to face a lesser enemy. An impressive network of para-governmental and inter-governmental bodies, official and otherwise, has come into being to fight terrorism:

rising above national politics and frontiers, pooling resources, sharing deeply sensitive intelligence information.

Fear of terrorism can do that. We have only to realize that the Mafia and its confederates are the ultimate terrorists of our time.

Notes

Author's Note

1   The State Department's security official, Irving Soloway, cited in the *Washington Times* November 22, 1993 and *La Repubblica*, Rome, November 23, 1993.

Prologue

1   My interview with the FBI's Organized Crime Section, Washington DC, September 1993 (see Chapters 5 and 6 for clarification).

2   See Chapter 1.

3   Associated Press from Moscow, in the *Washington Times*, April 29, 1993.

4   My visit to the FBI, Washington, September 1993.

5   AP dispatch in the *Washington Times*.

6   Violante's statement on the Italian RAI news channel, GR 2, October 10, 1993.

Chapter One

1   Full-page story by Maria Antonietta Calabrò in *Corriere della Sera*, March 4, 1993.

Reportage by Emilio Piervincenzi in Venerdi of *La Repubblica*, April 2, 1993.

AP dispatch from Oranjestad Aruba, 'Under the Sun-and-Fun:

Mafia, Drugs and Money Laundering', 179229, May 1993.

2   The US threat to kidnap the Cuntreras was essentially confirmed by Undersecretary of State Melvyn Levitsky, who
confirmed that the 'United States had done its part to assure the
delivery of the Cuntreras to Italian justice.' ADN Kronos agency,
September 15, 1992.

The Supreme Court ruling was in the case of the US *v.*
Alvarez-Machain, decided June 15, 1992. The case involved the
DEA's forcible kidnapping of a Mexican citizen, Alvarez-
Machain, to be brought to Texas and arrested for the kidnapping
and murder of a DEA agent and his pilot in Mexico. The ruling
said that 'a court may properly exercise jurisdiction even though
the defendant's presence is procured by means of a forcible
abduction.' The US extradition treaty with Mexico did not
specifically prohibit abduction, the Court said. Its ruling was
based on a Supreme Court decision in 1906, in Ker *v.* Illinois.

Italian arrest warrants were first issued for Pasquale and Paolo
Cuntrera in 1984, following a lengthy investigation of the
Sicilian Mafia's activities abroad by the Criminalpol in Milan
and Rome. Formal requests for their extradition from Venezuela
followed, and were ignored.

3   Judge Falcone's statement to a seminar in Wiesbaden, Germany
sponsored by the Bundeskriminalamt, November 1990. Cited in
MicroMega, June 25, 1990. See also Judge Falcone's speech in
Rome a few days before his death, ADN Kronos, May 24, 1992.

4   Estimate in Stewart-Clark Report to Investigating Committee of
the European Parliament, 1986, cited in *La Mafia dell'Eroina*,
Luciano Violante, Editori Riuniti, Rome, 1988.

5   In his lecture to the Bundeskriminalamt (see note 3), Falcone
offered a broader definition of the word 'mafia' to include all
these big crime syndicates. He spoke of the 'operational welding'
taking place among them, and the 'non-aggression pact' already
stipulated by the fall of 1990.

In a speech a few days before his death in 1992, Falcone
underlined the danger of these syndicates joining forces, pointing
specifically to the Sicilian-Colombian partnership formed in
1987.

See note 18, Chapter 2.

6   *Ibid.*

7   Rogatory testimony of Joseph Cuffaro by Judge Falcone, in the
US Southern District, January 30, 1990.

8   The traffickers were John and Joe Gambino, Rosario Naimo, Paolo Loduca, Lorenzo Mannino and Domenico Mannino.

9   *Octopus*, Claire Sterling, Norton, New York, 1990.

10 *Ibid.*

11 The demand for an exclusive franchise, and the threat, were confirmed to me by Judge Giusto Sciacchitano, Palermo.

12 *Octopus, op. cit.*, Chapter 7.

13 My interview with Louis Freeh in New York, see *Octopus, op. cit.*

14 DEA on estimates starting 1985. Interpol figures in report to French Senate by a Gérard Larcher on behalf of a special commission studying the lowering of EC frontiers, January 15, 1992. See also *Independent*, London, March 31, 1992.

15 Summary of the Green Ice Operation in DEA press release September 28,1992.
    My interiews with Greg Passic, head of the DEA's money laundering section, December 1992 and September 1993.
    See also *La Repubblica* and *Corriere della Sera*, September 29, 1992, and the weekly *Panorama*, October 11, 1992.

16 The five Colombian cartels were Medellín, Cali, Pereira, Costa, Valle del Norte.

17 Duran represented the five Colombian cartels listed in note 16 above.

18 Report to French Chamber of Deputies by François D'Aubert, president of its Anti-Mafia Commission, February 28, 1993. Report to French Senate by Gérard Larcher, January 15, 1993. The 200-ton estimate by DEA Director Robert Bonner, in the *Independent*, London, March 31, 1992.

19 The description of the Italian part of this episode was given to me by Alessandro Pansa, Rome, October 1992.

20 *Ibid.*

21 Greg Passic, head of DEA's money-laundering section, in *The European*, October 1–4, 1992. He said, 'The Colombians have chosen Italy as their warehouse to store cocaine for distribution throughout Europe.'

22 Alessandro Pansa in *La Repubblica*, September 29, 1992. He said of Operation Green Ice: 'We've learned how the Corleonesi intend to monopolize the cocaine traffic in Europe, and how the Colombian cartels trust them.'

23 Judge Falcone cited in report by François D'Aubert, Anti-Mafia Commission of French Chamber of Deputies, January 3, 1993.

24 Alessandro Pansa, quoted in *La Repubblica*, September 30, 1992.

25 My interviews with Greg Passic, head of the DEA's money-laundering section, Washington, December 1992 and September 1993.

26 My interview with Luciano Violante, President of the Anti-Mafia Commission of the Italian parliament, April 1993.

27 See Chapter 12.

28 The Cuntreras' investment in Russia, *Corriere della Sera*, March 4, 1993. This was confirmed to the *Corriere's* reporter, Maria Antonietta Calabrò, by the Italian intelligence service SISDE.

29 See Chapters 8, 9, 10.

30 *La Repubblica*, February 13, 1993. See also *Herald Tribune*, same date.

Chapter Two

1 Testimony of Leonardo Messina before Italy's parliamentary Anti-Mafia Commission, December 11, 1992.

2 The boss in question was Giuseppe Madonia, boss of Gela in southern Sicily.

3 Judge Giuseppe Ayala, former chief prosecutor in Palermo s first maxi-trial, presently a member of Parliament for the Republican Party, cited in the *Washington Post*, October 5,1992.

I was told essentially the same thing by senior police officials in Moscow, Warsaw, Budapest, Prague, the BKA in Wiesbaden, the FBI and various Italian authorities in the police and judiciary. These will be cited in subsequent chapters.

4 Falone's lecture to the German Bundeskriminalamt in Wiesbaden, November 1990, cited just after his death in *MicroMega*, May 1992.

5 The drug traffic figure of $500 billion and comparison to the arms trade is the estimate of GAFI, the G-7's Groupe Anti-Fraude International.

6 Report to European Parliament, October 15, 1991, cited in report to French parliament by François D'Aubert for its Anti-Mafia Commission, February 1993.

7 *Guardian*, cited in *Corriere della Sera*, August 18, 1992.

8 Holland figure in a report to UN Rome conference, 'International Crime Survey', cited in *La Stampa*, January 5, 1993.

9 The EC Commission issued its White Paper on completion of the Single Market in June, 1985. The Single Market Act was approved in 1987.

10   My interview with Saphos, then tracking the global narcotics traffic, Washington DC, September 1990. Saphos was appointed subsequently to be general counsel for Interpol US.

11   Report by Pier van Reenan, European Affairs, summer 1989. The situation he described persisted practically without change until late in 1992. Even then, most of the problems he referred to remained.

12   The Schengen Agreement of June 14, 1985 originally covered five EC states, Germany, France, Belgium, Holland and Luxembourg, and was designed to prepare the way for the EC Single Market through the gradual abolition of internal borders amongst these five. Although all the other EC states save Great Britain, Ireland and Denmark adhered to the agreement later, they were unable to solve all the problems involved by the end of 1992, when the Single Market itself was to come into effect.

13   Council of Europe report by Co-operation Group to Combat Drug Abuse, the so-called Pompidou Group, Strasbourg, April 9, 1991,

14   Josef Jaffe in Munich's *Süddeutsche Zeitung*.

15   FBI, 'Attacking Organized Crime: 1991 National Strategy', 1990 Program Report.

16   Robert Friedman's excellent article in *Vanity Fair*, January 1993.

17   In his lecture to the BKA in Wiesbaden (see note 4 above), Falcone said: 'Organizations like the Triads, the Yakuza, the Russian clans growing exponentially, are all endowed, like the Mafia, with formal structures and great flexibility, capable of converting to every kind of illegal activity in an extraordinarily short time. All these organizations have a great deal of money, resort to violence, and try in every way to guarantee inaction by the police and judiciary as well as political connivance.' Cited in *MicroMega*, June 25, 1992.

In a speech a few days before his death, Falcone said: 'One asks if the Mafia model is exportable and susceptible not so much and not only of imitation in other countries, but of generating relationships, almost a sort of international illicit joint venture. In my opinion, the Mafia's criminal model with particularly specific environmental characteristics, would not be transformable to other realities. But . . . we must also judge whether Mafia criminality apart from [such] specifics . . . can be susceptible to imitation abroad. Put in these terms, the big organizations present characteristics not dissimilar to the Mafia's.' ADN Kronos, May 24,1992.

18   See *The Terror Network*, Claire Sterling, Holt, Rinehart & Winston, New York, 1981.

19   *Criminal Russia: Crime in the Soviet Union*, Valery Chalidze, Random House, New York, 1977.

20   *The Day is Born in Darkness*, Mikhail Dyomin, Alfred Knopf, New York, 1976.

21   Quoted in *Criminal Russia*, *op. cit.*

22   Description by Joe Serio. See Dyomin, p.46: 'Thieves have no dictators. They do, though, have their own form of ruling center, a kind of legislative committee composed of the worthy and the authoritative.'

23   *Criminal Russia*, *op. cit.*

24   *The Triads: The Chinese Criminal Fraternity*, Martin Booth, Grafton Books, London, 1990.

25   *The Chinese Mafia*, Fenton Bresler, Stein & Day, New York, 1984.

26   *The Triads*, *op. cit.*

27   *La Repubblica*, March 1, 1992.

28   Visit to Rome by Hidenori Yoshida, counsellor to the anti-mafia section of the Japanese police, quoted in the *Corriere della Sera*, March 1, 1992.

29   *Corriere della Sera* from Tokyo, February 27, 1992.

30   *Yakuza*, David Kaplan and Alec Dubro, Addison Wesley, Berkshire, 1986.

31   *Ibid.*

32   US President's Commission on Organized Crime, Hearings, October 23–25, 1984.

33   *San Francisco Chronicle*, July 10, 1991.

34   *La Repubblica* dispatch from Tokyo, March 14, 1992, concerning the members of parliament. The information had come to light the previous October. Two former Japanese premiers were linked to the Yakuza's largest family, the Yamaguchi-gumi, cited in a draft report to the European Parliament by Patrick Cooney, October 28, 1991. See also *Corriere della Sera*, February 18, 1992.

35   'Libro Bianco su Racket e Criminalità', FIPE (Federazione Italiana Pubblici Esercizi), 1992. See also *Herald Tribune*, June 28, 1991. 6,000 police were deployed when the 1,700 companies held their meetings.

36   Cited in *Los Angeles Times*, February 12, 1992.

Chapter Three

1 My dinner with Chancellor Kohl at his residence in Bonn, May 8, 1990.

2 My interviews with Gennady Chebotarev, head of the Russian Interior Ministry's Sixth Department on Organized Crime in 1992; with Alexander Gurov, his predecessor in that post and in the same post for the Soviet Union before its collapse; with the KGB officer watching the Russian mafia abroad; with Anatoly Volobuev, formerly of the Sixth Department's Research Division; Moscow, November, 1991 and July 1992.

See *The Soviet Mafia*, Arkady Vaksberg, St Martin's Press, New York, 1991: 'In the spring of 1990, the Soviet Interior Ministry got operational intelligence of a business meeting between Soviet and Western mafiosi for June in Warsaw, to discuss future cooperation during the Soviet switch to a market economy. One of the main items was a method for moving Soviet antiques to the West. The Ministry sent agents, and a journalist went along. They found nothing. The venue was changed after arrangements leaked. Later, a senior militia officer told me that the meeting was in East Berlin. Organizers had said Warsaw to throw authorities off the scent.'

3 My interview with the captain, Berlin, October 29, 1992.

4 My interview with the Deputy Police Chief, Warsaw, September 1991.

5 My interview with Andrzej Koweszko, head of Interpol Warsaw, October 1992.

6 My interview with Alexander Herzog, Warsaw, September 3, 1991.

7 My interview with Jurgen Maurer of the BKA Organized Crime Section. Wiesbaden, February 20, 1992.

8 Judge Pierluigi Vigna of Florence, investigating Eastern European arms traffic passing through Italy; *La Repubblica*, February 14, 1993.

9 BKA figures for 1990. BKA's 1992 figure cited in *Welt am Sonntag*, October 18, 1992.

10 My interview with captain of German border guards, Berlin, October 1992.

11 See *Octopus, op. cit.*, Chapter 9.

12 *Ibid.*, Chapter 9. The German OD deaths in 1990 were just over 2,000.

13 See *The Time of the Assassins*, Claire Sterling, Holt, Rinehart & Winston, New York, 1983.

14   He was a member of the Russo clan, reported the German daily
      Bild, August 15, 1992.

15 · *Octopus, op. cit.*, Chapter 10.

16   *Ibid.*, Prologue.

17   Palazzolo's laundering reported by *Corriere della Sera*, October
      17, 1988. This was when he escaped arrest in Lugano,
      Switzerland and took shelter in South Africa.

18   He was killed on December 20, 1984.

19   See *Octopus, op. cit.*

20   Tribunale Civile e Penale di Palermo, Ufficio Istruzione Processi
      Penali, Communication by Judge Gioacchino Natoli addressed
      to the Bundeskriminalamt in Wiesbaden, November 24, 1989.

21   BKA report to Interpol October 17, 1989.

22   Judge Gioacchino Natoli's query to German authorities.

23   Riina's one-time driver, the *pentito* Baldassare Di Maggio, told
      authorities of Riina's German visits in January 1993. Nuvoletta's
      and Alfieri's residences in Germany confirmed by Servizio
      Centrale Operativo (SCO) of Italy's Criminalpol.

24   My interview with Alessandro Pansa of the Italian Criminalpol's
      SCO, Rome, May 11, 1990.

25   My interview with Director Zachert, April 24, 1991.

26   *Der Spiegel*, August 4, 1992.

27   Falcone's statement to conference in Wiesbaden, November 7–8,
      1991.

28   My interview with Zachert. Several details confirmed in *Corriere
      della Sera*, April 11, 1991.

29   BKA in-house report on Italian organized crime, Wiesbaden,
      April 2, 1992.

30   My interview with Zachert.

31   My interview with Pansa.

32   BKA figures for 1990 and 1991, cited in *Berliner Zeitung*, January
      16–17, 1993, and *Die Welt*, January 25, 1993.

33   My briefing by BKA officers, Wiesbaden, April 1991.

34   BKA Director Zachert at conference of German, French,
      Spanish and Italian police chiefs, Rome, as reported in
      L'Indépendente, November 21, 1992.

35   Interpol General Secretariat, drugs sub-division: 'The Balkan
      Route: Increased shipment of Southwest Asian Heroin to Europe
      1986–1990', January 1991.

36   My BKA briefing, April 24, 1991.

37   'Contro e Dentro: Criminalità Istituzioni Società', Fondazione

Centro Studi Investimenti Sociali (CENSIS) report, January 7, 1992.

38   My BKA briefing. German press agency DPA, July 26, 1991. The traffickers were indicted in Mainz.

39   *Der Spiegel*, August 28, 1992.

40   BKA in-house study. *Süddeutsche Zeitung*, Munich, December 31, 1991. I was told of the BND study during my interviews with BKA officials in Wiesbaden, March 4, 1993.

41   *Corriere della Sera*, June 26,1990. The Holzmann case was among several brought to the attention of the Italian parliament's Anti-Mafia Commission.

42   Estimate of 80% by Frankfurt's State Counsel Wolfgang Schaupensteiner; *Corriere della Sera*, April 14, 1993.

43   Conference of Italian, French, Spanish and German police chiefs in Rome, reported in *L'Indépendente*, November 21, 1992.

44   'Contro e Dentro', CENSIS report, *op. cit.*

45   Report by Federazione Italiana Pubblici Esercizi (FIPE), 1992.

46   Reported by Zachert at the conference of police chiefs in Rome. The untranslatable word Buscetta used to describe German legislation was '*garantista*'.

47   My interview wih Jurgen Maurer of BKA's Organized Crime Section, Wiesbaden, February 20, 1992.

48   *Ibid.*

49   *Ibid.*

50   FIPE report, 1992.

51   Anti-Mafia Commission report to the UN assembly, extraordinary session on world drug problem. Communicated to the Prime Minister, March 20,1990.

Chapter Four

1   Messina's testimony before the Italian parliamentary Anti-Mafia Commission, December 11, 1992.

2   Judge Falcone was killed on May 23, 1992, Judge Borsellino the following July 19.

3   See *Octopus*, *op. cit.*, for a fuller description of the Great Mafia War.

4   Testimony of Gaspare Mutolo to parliamentary Anti-Mafia Commission, February 9, 1993. The mother, sister and aunt of Antonino Calderone, a major defector, were all shot dead on the same day in Palermo.

 5   He was Pietro Vernengo, a world-famous drug trafficker, recaptured some months after his escape.

 6   Messina's testimony before the parliamentary Anti-Mafia Commission December, 11, 1992. Another high-ranking *pentito*, Gaspare Mutolo, used the word 'combined' instead of 'adjusted' in his testimony before the Commission.

 7   Mutolo's testimony before the parliamentary Anti-Mafia Commission, February 10, 1993. A heavy drug trafficker working with Saro Riccobono's family, he turned over 1,000 names of mafiosi and their friends and helpers when he decided to collaborate in the spring of 1992.

 8   The Cassation verdict was announced on January 30,1992.

 9   Communication to the Italian Senate, requesting permission to investigate Andreotti, from the *Procura della Repubblica* of Palermo, March 27, 1993,

10   Testimony of half a dozen *pentiti*, including Messina and Mutolo. Testimony of major defector Francesco Mannino Mannoia on the fact that Salvo Lima was a sworn-in Man of Honour.

11   For Sicilian figures, see *Octopus, op. cit*. For these together with the southern mainland, see the weekly *Il Mondo*, cited in *La Repubblica*, March 1, 1992.

12   Text of Calderone's testimony under interrogation by judges in Palermo, *Corriere della Sera*, March 15, 1988.

13   Testimony of Leonardo Messina, Gaspare Mutolo, Antonino Calderone before the Anti-Mafia Commission. See also *Octopus, op. cit.*, on Stefano Bontate's preparations to join a covered lodge in 1977.

14   Combined testimony of Leonardo Messina, Gaspare Mutolo and Antonino Calderone to the parliamentary Anti-Mafia Commission. December 1992 to February 1993.

15   In June 1993, a court in Trapani convicted the head of a covered Masonic lodge called Iside 2, for the crime of 'secret association', the first such conviction ever in Italy. The lodge membership had included leading Christian Democrats, businessmen and Mafia bosses, among whom was the notorious boss of Mazara del Vallo, Mariano Agate, first on the list of defendants in Palermo's maxi-trial; *Corriere della Sera*, June 6, 1993.

16   *Octopus, op. cit.*, p.201.

17   Draft report to European Parliament by Patrick Cooney, for Committee of Enquiry into the Spread of Organized Crime

Linked to Drug Trafficking in Member States of European Community, October 28, 1991. See also *Il Giornale*, November 25, 1989.

18   See *Octopus*, *op. cit.*, for fuller account of Carnevale's record.

19   Testimony of Gaspare Mutolo, former lieutenant of Mafia boss Saro Riccobono, to the parliamentary Anti-Mafia Commission, February 9, 1993.

20   Leonardo Messina's testimony to the parliamentary Anti-Mafia Commission.

21   Report to parliament by Interior Minister Nicola Mancino, March 1993.

22   See Chapter 12.

23   My interview with head of financial police in Prague, October 1992, on Mafia buying banks in Slovakia. A new Sicilian-American Mafia bank in Sverdlovsk, in the Russian Urals, described in Chapter 6.

Roberto Palazzolo, the Mafia's big money-washer in the Pizza Case, went on to become Governor of the Bank of Sibekwe in Zimbabwe, near the South African border.

24   French parliament's Anti-Mafia Commission report, by its President François D'Aubert, citing Liliana Ferraro of Italy's Ministry of Justice. Speaking at a money-laundering conference sponsored by Italy's parliamentary Anti-Mafia commission, Colonel Cappelli of the Anti-Mafia police (DIA) estimated Mafia legitimate investments inside Italy as 60% in the financial sector, 17% in real estate, 11% in commerce, 5% in industry, agro-industry and gold mining; *La Stampa*, May 15, 1993.

25   'Contro e Dentro', CENSIS report, *op. cit.* Estimate of income for all organized crime inside Italy was 20 trillion lire. According to a study by the Confederazione di Esercizi Pubblici (bar and restaurant owners) its income from the *pizzo* alone was 30 trillion lire. The latter study, entitled 'Estorti e Riciclati', was released to press April 24, 1991.

26   The estimated EC swindles came to 345 billion lire, just for grain; *La Stampa*, June 6, 1993.

27   Messina's testimony before the Anti-Mafia Commission.

28   Buscetta's tesimony to the Anti-Mafia Commission, November 16, 1992.

29   Testimony to Anti-Mafia Commission by Domenico Sica, then High Commissioner to Combat the Mafia, *New York Times*, July 23, 1989. Sica spoke of 'total possession' of 'parts' of Sicily,

Calabria and Naples. Many police and government authorities
have enlarged the definition since then.

30   Draft of Commission's report to parliament on relations between
     the Mafia and politics, March 27, 1993.

31   Ruling by Judge Luigi Russo in Catania, *Corriere della Sera*, April
     5, 1991. Interview in *La Repubblica*, April 6, 1991. The Chamber
     of Commerce proposal was reported in the *New York Times*, July
     1, 1991.

32   Interview with Antonio Mauri, President of the Catania
     Industrialists' Association, *Corriere della Sera* and *La Repubblica*,
     November 2, 1992.

33   Salvo Lima's role in Sicily's so-called Tangentopoli was defined
     in a report to the judiciary by the special Carabiniere anti-Mafia
     unit, Ros (Riparto Operativo Speciale); *Corriere della Sera*, May
     28, 1993.

34   *La Repubblica*, March 11, 1992.

35   *La Repubblica*, March 4, 1992.

36   The car park in Via Salomone was in contact with various city
     officials, a high functionary of the Defence Ministry in Rome,
     and a big real estate operator heading a local Masonic lodge.
     Police phone intercepts revealed that the band running this cen-
     tre was planning to assassinate Judge Antonio Di Pietro, leading
     'Operation Clean Hands' in Milan; *Corriere della Sera*, September
     2, 1992. For summary of roundups, see *La Repubblica*, February 5,
     1993.

37   See *Octopus*, *op. cit.*, Chapter 16. Giuseppe Bono, a leader of the
     Pizza Connection ring, was a principal in the Milan CITAM
     case.

38   'Bono + 159', two-volume report by Gianni De Gennaro to the
     Rome Questura.

39   Interview with Sergio Pininfarina, President of Confindustria, *La
     Repubblica*, November 9, 1990.

40   Parliamentary Anti-Mafia Commission report on Milan and the
     province of Lombardy, July 1990.

41   Interior Minister Antonio Gava, interviewed by *La Repubblica*,
     July 6, 1989.

42   Borelli's address to a conference in Palermo, 'Mafia, che fare?',
     organized by Sicily's Regional Assembly; *L'Indépendente*,
     December 13, 1992.

43   'Libro Bianco su Racket e Criminalità', Federazione Italiana
     Pubblici Esercizi (FIPE), 1992. Guardia di Finanza report,

Corriere della Sera, May 6, 1989.

44   *Ibid.*

45   Piero Bassetti, President of Milan's Chamber of Commerce, in an interview with *La Repubblica,* November 9, 1990.

46   'Bozza di Relazione del Gruppo di Lavoro Incaricato di Svolgere Indagini Sulla Situazione di Milano'; Italian parliamentary Anti-Mafia Commission, July 13, 1990.

47   Operation Clean Hands began with the arrest of a Milanese Socialist functionary named Mario Chiesa, caught taking a 7-million-lire payoff in February,1992. The judges were Antonio Di Pietro, Gherardo Colombo and Pier Camillo Davigo, under the quietly firm command of Milan's Prosecutor-General Francesco Saverio Borelli.

48   Summary by Barry James. *International Herald Tribune,* July 29, 1993.

49   Li-Mo was the office in Chiasso used by Giuseppe Lottusi, in the Big John cocaine case cited in Chapter 1. The same agent, 'Enzo', provided washed dollars to the administrative secretaries of the Christian Democratic and Socialist Parties, Citaristi and Balzamo. See *L'Espresso,* May 2, 1993.

50   Piero Bassetti, President of Milan's Chamber of Commerce, at a press conference on May 17, 1992. *Il Giornale Nuovo,* Milan, May 18, 1992.

51   My interview with Domenico Sica, High Prefect to Combat the Mafia, Bologna, January 8, 1992. Sica estimated the Italian state tobacco monopoly turnover at around 11,000 billion lire a year, roughly $9 billion. The Camorra's contraband trade was equal or more, he told me.

52   The Vice-President of the EC Commission, Maretin Bangemann, said that 'restrictions on imports among member-states are forbidden' under Article 30 of the Treaty of Rome. He threatened an injunction against the Italian government unless the ban was lifted within twenty-four hours. *La Repubblica,* December 19, 1991.

53   My interview with Greg Passic, heading the DEA's department on money laundering, Washington, December 19, 1992. For tobacco profits and tax losses see Italian Interior Ministry's report to parliament, May 1993.

54   See *Octopus, op. cit.,* Chapter 9.

55   Interrogation of Michele Zaza by Judge Aurelio Galasso.

56   *Ibid.*

57 Report to the French Assembly by François D'Aubert, head of its special Anti-Mafia Commission, February 28, 1993.

58 *Ibid.*

59 *Ibid.*

60 *Corriere della Sera*, July 22,1992; September 9,1992,

61 Among Italian charges against him are the murders of Alfredo Taborra and Giuseppe Barbera on June 27, 1977, in complicity with Camorra boss Lorenzo Nuvoletta. Zaza's villa is located in Villeneuve Loubet, 20 kilometres from Nice.

62 D'Aubert report.

63 Zaza's latest arrest was part of a roundup including 35 others in Italy and France, in Operation Green Sea; *La Stampa*, May 13, 1993.

64 A map of Madonia's holdings was published in *La Repubblica*, November 21, 1992.

65 Semi-annual report by the DIA, Italy's super-police force *La Stampa*, July 3, 1993.

66 'Relazione sull'Attività delle Forze di Polizia e sullo Stato Dell' Ordine e della Sicurezza Pubblica Nei Territorio Nazionale'. (Report on the Activity of the Police Forces and state of Public Order and Security on the National Territory), Ministry of the Interior, Rome, March 1993. See also *Corriere della Sera*, May 21, 1993.

67 Judge PierLuigi Vigna of Florence, investigating the two-way arms traffic between Italy and Eastern Europe, *La Repubblica*, February 15, 1993.

Chapter Five

1 Official estimate of Russian Interior Ministry. My interview with I. Pavlovich, Deputy Chief of Ministry's Sixth Department on Organized Crime, July 1, 1992. See also report of Suzdal Conference on International Organized Crime, October 28–November 1, 1991.

2 *The Soviet Mafia, op. cit.*

3 'Moskovskiye Novosti', in the BBC's *Current Digest of the Soviet Press*, Vol. 40, No. 17. See also *The Soviet Mafia, op. cit.* p.158. The Mafia boss was Rashidin, who died during the investigation and was buried in a Lenin memorial boasting the tallest statue of Lenin in the world.

4 Geidar Aliev returned in triumph to become President of Azerbaijan in June 1993; *Corriere della Sera*, June 19, 1993.

5 'Moskovskiye Novosti', February 10, 1991.

6   *The Soviet Mafia, op. cit.*

7   Tass correspondent Larisa Kislinksaia in a speech to the Woodrow Wilson Center, Washington DC, November 14, 1989.

8   Yeltsin addressing emergency conference of 1,000 government officials, magistrates and policemen on the need to fight corruption; reported in *La Repubblica*, February 3, 1993. See also Reuters dispatch in *International Herald Tribune*, February 13, 1993. AP from Moscow same date.

9   My interview with Nina Piskaryova, economist of the All-Union Research Institute, Moscow, October 1991.

10 Prosecutor-General A.Y. Sukharev, reporting to the Second Congress of the USSR People's Deputies, December 1989, quoted in *Pravda* and *Izvestia*, in the BBC's *Current Digest of the Soviet Press*, Vol. 42.

11 Alexander Gurov, head of Soviet Interior Ministry's Sixth Department to Combat Organized Crime, cited in *La Nazione* of Florence, May 9, 1991. Confirmed to me by Gurov, Moscow, October 1991.

12 *Washington Post* quoting Moscow police chief Murashev, February 26, 1991.

13 My interview with Gurov, November 1991. The latter part of Gurov's statement is also quoted in *La Nazione*, May 9, 1991.

14 *Washington Post*, February 26, 1991.

15 My interview with Tatjana Korjagina, then the Soviet Interior Ministry's top social economist, Moscow, October 1991. The same estimates were given to me by Alexander Gurov, who headed the Ministry's Sixth Department at the time.

    Yeltsin's statement to a special conference on the problem of organized crime, attended by 1,000 government functionaries, judges and police officers, Associated Press dispatch, February 13, 1993.

16 Cited by Tass in Russian for abroad, July 9, 1991. Estimate confirmed to me by Tatjana Korjagina, July 1992.

17 On July 20, 1993, Russian Interior Minister Yerin gave the figure of 14,800 homicides in Russia in the first six months of 1993; *La Repubblica*, July 21, 1993.

    Russia's homicide rate was 18,000 in 1992, or around fifty a day, the official figure given by Attorney-General Valentino Stepankov at a press conference in Moscow; *Corriere della Sera*, February 12, 1993.

18 Stepankov announced that he would present a bill to parliament

to this effect; reported in *Corriere della Sera*, February 12, 1993.

19   *La Stampa* from Moscow, July 17, 1993.

20   Report by Interpol's Deputy Chief in Moscow, Anatoly Terechov, to the John Jay College International Conference on Organized Crime in St Petersburg, June 20–July 3, 1992.

21   *Argumenty i Fakty* No. 51–52, December 1992.

22   From a secretly filmed video in the possession of Captain Aleksandr Sirotkin of Russia's Sixth Department to Combat Organized Crime, cited in *La Stampa*, June 3,1993.

23   From a study by Joe Serio, presently a consultant on organized crime in Moscow. The Serio study is unpublished, but is quoted at length in the semi-annual report to Parliament by Italian Interior Minister Nicola Mancino, summer 1993. Joseph Serio is the President of Eurasian Business Services in Moscow.

24   *Ibid.*

25   My interviews with Alexander Gurov, November 1991 and July 1992, when he had become head of the Russian KGB's public relations office; with Gennady Chebotarev, Gurov's deputy in the Soviet Sixth Department, who became head of the Russian Republic's Sixth Department in 1992; with Anatoly Volobuev, formerly of the Sixth Department, later contributor to *Vizimayeva Novosti*; with Joe Serio of Chicago's Institute on International Organized Crime; with Tatjana Korjagina; with Evgen Mizlovsky, head of Russia's independent Anti-Mafia Commission, founded in 1992.

26   Estimate by Anatoly Volobuev, confirmed to me by Sixth Department.

27   My interview with Pavlovich in Moscow, July 1, 1992. The Sixth Department Captain is Captain Alexandr Sirotkin, cited in *La Stampa*, June 3, 1993.

28   Alexander Gurov on Soviet TV, January 24, 1991.

29   My interview with Tatjana Korjagina, November 1991.

30   *Ibid.* See also Tass section of 'Krim Press' as cited below; *Independent on Sunday*, London, February 9,1992; *Corriere della Sera*, January 31, 1992.

31   Tass section of 'Krim Press' January 31, 1992. The fact of the meeting was confirmed to me by Gennady Chebotarev, Chief of Russia's Sixth Department, in Moscow, July 1992.

32   My interview with Korjagina; 92 billion rubles was worth around $100 million in early 1992.

33   Cited in *Independent on Sunday*, London, February 9, 1992.

34   Tass section of 'Krim Press'.
35   Cited in *La Repubblica*, January 13, 1993.
36   *Moscow Business Week*, June 4, 1992.
37   Anatoly Verdenin, quoted in *The European*, January 1992.
38   The news story appeared in *La Repubblica*, November 27, 1991.
     It was confirmed in part, with blistering comments, by the
     Director of the Russian Commodities and Raw Materials
     Exchange, Konstantin Borovoi, in the *Moscow Times*, May
     19,1992.

     My interview with Tatjana Korjagina, Moscow, July 1992.
39   The charge was made by Konstantin Borovoi.
40   My interview with Boris Uvarov, Chief Investigator for Big
     Crimes in the Russian Prosecutor-General's office, Moscow, July
     1, 1992.
41   UPI dispatch from Moscow, October 14, 1990.
42   A 'galloping' crime rate is reported in the territories named, in
     Sovetskaya Rossiya, July 11, 1991.
43   Tass, January 16, 1991. The Italian documentary was shown on
     Speciale TG I, RAI TV, August 10, 1991.
44   Tass, December 26, 1990; *La Repubblica*, February 6, 1992; *ibid.*,
     February 11, 1992; *The European*, October 18,1991, *Corriere della
     Sera*, January 9, 1992; My interview with General Sotgiu, head of
     Italy's Anti-Narcotics Squad, after his visit to Moscow.
45   *Corriere della Sera* from Moscow, January 17, 1992.
46   See Chapter 3, my interview with Alexander Herzog, former
     Prosecutor General of Poland, October 1991.
47   The financial weekly *Commersant*, December 4, 1991, reported
     in the *New York Times*, December 6,1991. For more recent and
     fuller detail, Joe Serio's study of the Russian mafia, *op. cit.*
48   My interview with Boris Uvarov.
49   My interviews with Gennady Chebotarev and Anatoly
     Volobuev, Moscow, June 28 and July 2, 1992. My interviews with
     BKA in Wiesbaden, with police of Prague and Warsaw.
50   *Chicago Tribune*, October 14, 1991.
51   My briefing at BKA headquarters, Wiesbaden, April 1991.
52   'Moskovskiye Novosti', cited in *La Repubblica*, August 15,
     1991.
53   My interview with Colonel Alexander Sergeev, head of Anti-
     Narcotics unit, Soviet Interior Ministry, November 1991. See
     also UN International Narcotics Control Board, 1991 Report.
54   My interview with Sergeev.

55   *Chicago Tribune*, October 15, 1991.

56   Vladimir Burlaka, Anti-Narcotics Chief, St Petersburg, report to International Conference on Organized Crime, June 20–July 3, 1992. Latest 1992 estimates from anti-narcotics authorities, London, quoted in *Corriere della Sera*, September 6, 1992.

   On Chernobyl, *Commersant* of April 6, 1992 cites investigation of opium cultivation by International Association against Proliferation and Use of Drugs in Moscow; confirmed by Observatoire Géopolitique des Drogues.

57   Associated Press release 112109, May 1993.

58   Report on the Schengen Agreement to the French Senate, by Commission President Paul Masson, December 11, 1991.

59   Report by anti-narcotics authorities in London, cited in *Corriere della Sera*, September 6, 1992.

60   My interview with Colonel Sergeev; my interview with Vitaly Karpetz, Director Research Institute, Soviet Prosecutor-General's office, November 1991 and July 1992. See also International Narcotics Control Board, 1991 Report.

61   Gurov's TV interview, January 24, 1991.

62   My interview with Sergeev.

63   The 1.5 million figure from Sergeev cited by Associated Press, February 16, 1993. Sergeev had given me a similar figure in Moscow the previous July. For higher estimates, see interviews with I.A. Mamedov and Gela Georgiyeovich Lezhava, cited in Foreign Broadcast Information Service and Tass, as reported by Graham Turbiville, Jr. in 'Counter-Narcotics, International Dimensions of a Soviet Internal Security Problem', Soviet Army Studies Office, Fort Leavenworth, Kansas.

   St Petersburg's anti-narcotics chief, Vladimir Burlaka, reporting to the 1992 conference in St Petersburg.

64   My interview with Sergeev.

65   My interview with Interpol's deputy chief in Poland, Andrzej Koweszko, Warsaw, October 1992. See also ADN Kronos agency Rome, citing an interview with Koweszko in the *Guardian*, August 29, 1992.

66   *The European*, July 30, 1992. An Interpol flyer on the sandal shipment was sent to all member-countries.

67   My interviews with Karpetz, Moscow, November 1991 and July 1992 (when he held the same post in the Russian Republic as previously in the USSR). See also *Corriere della Sera*, April 25, 1991.

68   *Intersec*, Vol. 2, issue 4, September 1992.

69 The American was Ukrainian-born Alexander Dokijchuk, with a joint venture called D&K-Sov Group; my interview with Boris Uvarov, Moscow, July 1992. That summer, the black market ruble exchange rate was around 145 rubles to the dollar (see Chapter 10).

70 My interview with Gennady Chebotarev, Chief of Russia's Sixth Department, Moscow, July 1992.

71 The sum was specified by the Russian Interior Ministry on June 15, 1992, See *Commersant*, June 23, 1992. The whole story was confirmed to me in interviews with Boris Uvarov and Gennady Chebotarev, Moscow, July 1992.

The top black market exchange rate in July 1992 was 145 rubles to the dollar.

72 My interview with Chebotarev; see also *Commersant*, June 2, 1992.

73 At a press conference on July 7, 1992, V. Soltaganov, head of the Interior Ministry's Main Department to Combat Economic Crime, gave the figure of '150 billion to 200 billion' rubles for the first half of 1992. The full year's figure published in *Argumenty i Fakty*, No. 51–52, December 1992.

The figure of $1 billion foreign capital investment in *Izvestiya*, December 30, 1992.

74 Boris Yeltsin's address to a special conference on crime and corruption, Moscow, February 12, 1993; Reuters dispatch from Moscow, *International Herald Tribune*, February 13,1993; see also *La Repubblica*, February 13, 1993, AP, February 13, 1993.

75 *Ibid.*

76 My interview with Nina Piskaryova.

77 *Moscow Times*, May 19, 1992.

78 Cited in the *Los Angeles Times*, republished in the *Herald Tribune*, May 27, 1991.

79 Moscow Innovation Commercial Bank, Annual Report, January 1, 1990.

80 *Izvestiya*, June 5, 1992; July 8, 1992.

Komsomolskaya Pravda, February 1991; *Stern*, September 1991.

81 Tarasov's American associate was the billionaire oilman-swindler Marc David Rich (see Chapter 10).

82 Tarasov's account number at Paribas was 250924P Code 30026.

83 Tarasov's denial, and *Izvestiya*'s rebuttal in *Izvestiya*, July 9, 1992. The other officials not available for questioning are ex-Premier Silaev, ex-Minister of Soviet Foreign Economic Relations

Yaroshenko, two deputy chairmen of the Soviet Council of Ministers, and the head of the Soviet Main Administration Council for Customs Control, Boyarev.

84 My interview with Terechov, Moscow, July 1992. Terechov's report to St Petersburg International Conference on Organized Crime, June 20–July 3, 1992. See also interview with Constantin Rodionov, chief of Interpol Moscow until 1992, in *Corriere della Sera*, August 15, 1991.

85 Yeltsin's address to the conference on crime and corruption, February 13, 1993.

86 My interview with Boris Uvarov, Moscow, July 1992.

Chapter Six

1 My interview with BKA Organized Crime Section, Wiesbaden, February 1993.

2 Himbank's full name is Commercial Bank of Chemical Industry of Russia. Its address in Moscow is 28 Mjanickaja Street. Its address in Rochester is 111 Alexander Street. The American involved is Jack Tremonti (see Chapter 9).

3 Report on 'Operation Europa 1', a year-long investigation by Judges Nicola Gratteri and Andrea Canciani in Locri, Calabria. *La Repubblica*, November 5, 1993.

4 Two Chechen setting up the London base, the Utseyev brothers, were murdered in 1993. They had been sent to Britain by General Dzahkar Dudayev, President of the Chechen Republic, *Corriere della Sera*, March 8, 1993

5 ADN-Kronos report from Warsaw, August 29, 1992. The essentials of the report were confirmed to me in Warsaw the following October by Interpol chief Andrzej Koweszko.

6 *Le Monde*, January 27, 1993.

7 My interview with Jurgen Maurer and Gehm, head of Organized Crime for BKA, Wiesbaden, February 1993. According to BKA official figures, German authorities investigated 641 cases of organized crime in 1992, of which 1,268 (46.4%) had members of just one nationality. The rest were multinational, some with up to 100 members.

8 Sources in the Russian Interior Ministry to Joseph Serio, consultant on the Russian mafia and President of Eurasian Business Services in Moscow. Vladimir Lupskii and Boris Lysenko in *Izvestiya*, May 27, 1993.

9 Interview with Anatoly Oleynikov, head of the branch office of

Russia's Ministry of Security in Berlin-Karlshorst, *Der Spiegel*, June 21, 1993.

10 My interview with BKA, February 1993,

11 My interview with Wolfgang Bieling in BKA headquarters, Wiesbaden, March 1993.

12 The murdered pair were Ruslan and Nasabek Utseyev, who claimed to be semi-official representatives of General Dudayev's rump Chechen Republic. British police thought they controlled the London market in East European art objects stolen from museums. My interview with Scotland Yard organized crime section. See also *Corriere della Sera*, March 8, 1993.

13 Maurer, Gehm and Bieling, BKA Wiesbaden, February 1993.

14 ADN Berlin, August 11, 1991; *Der Spiegel*, August 17, 1992.

15 The border-crossing is 28 kilometres south of Kolbasowo, near Stettin. Confirmed by BKA.

16 When I checked my list of companies with Kroll Associates in London, investigating currency frauds for the Russian government in 1992, they got a couple of KGB hits.

17 Report to the Polish parliament, the Sejm, August 17, 1991 by two deputies from the Committee on Economic Relations with Foreign Countries.

18 The monetary union was agreed upon in July 1990.

19 United Press International dispatch, October 8, 1990.

20 My interview with Maurer and Gehm, Wiesbaden, February 1993. See also *Frankfurter Allgemeine*, February 6, 1993.

21 My interview with Maurer and Gehm, Wiesbaden, February 1993. They checked the figure with ZERV at my request. The *proven* figure came to 8 billion DM. The 20 billion DM figure was an informed estimate. The figure on all other damage by organized crime was 3.6 billion DM in 1991, according to the BKA.

22 BKA figures given to me in Wiesbaden, March 4, 1993. Of all organized crime cases in 1991, the criminals involved were 5,482. Of these, German nationals were 49.8%, Turks 16.6%, Yugoslavs 8.5%, Italians 7.5%, Polish 4.1%.

23 *La Stampa* of Turin, citing BKA President Hans-Ludwig Zachert and the head of Germany's police union Hermann Lutz, January 23, 1993. See also *Die Welt*, January 25, 1993; *Berliner Zeitung*, January 17, 1993; *Dusseldorf Handelsblatt*, March 29, 1993.

24 *Die Welt*, January 21, 1992, reported 655 arrests in a major Kurdish drug bust.

25   German Interior Minister Rudolf Seiters, in *Hamburg Bild*, February 12, 1993.

26   *L'Indépendente*, May 28, 1992; *Rheinische Post*, September 23, 1992.

27   Umberto Vecchione, Naples police chief and head of Italian Criminalpol for the south, provided the figure of Camorristi in eastern Germany; cited in *Bild am Sonntag*, August 2, 1992.

28   ZFD television programme *Frontal*, June 8, 1993,

29   Half-yearly report to the Italian parliament by Interior Minister Nicola Mancino, May 1993.

30   My interview with Maurer and Gehm, Wiesbaden, March 3, 1993. The estimate of $120 billion in drug money alone circulating worldwide yearly was made by the G-7's Groupe d'Action Financière Internationale (GAFI) in April 1990.

31   *Le Monde*, January 27, 1993. The Japanese police commissioner was Akinori Tsuruya.

32   *Yakuza*, Kaplan and Dubro, *op. cit.*

33   *The European*, April 9, 1993.

34   President's Commission on Organized Crime Hearings on Asian Organized Crime, October 23–25, 1984 (see Chapter 7).

35   *Ibid.*

36   See Chapter 7.

37   Patrick Cooney report for 'Committee of Enquiry into the Spread of Organized Crime Linked to Drugs Trafficking in the Member States of the European Community', October 28, 1991.

38   The two Japanese police officers were Hidenori Yoshida, ministerial counsellor for the anti-Mafia department, and Uchida Yunichi, deputy director of the criminal police; *Corriere della Sera*, March 1992.

39   My interview with an intelligence source, Australian embassy, Rome, February 6, 1992.

40   *La Stampa*, March 17, 1993; *La Repubblica*, same date.

41   Investigation by Roberto Cavaciocchi, deputy police chief of Milan, reported at length in *Il Mondo*, March 1–8,1993.

42   Criminalpol report on Triad penetration of Italy, March 1993.

43   My interview with Alessandro Pansa of Servizio Centrale Operativo (SCO), Rome, March 25, 1993.

44   My interview with François D'Aubert, head of the French parliamentary Anti-Mafia Commission, Paris, February 8, 1993.

45   The sum was 1.5 billion francs, roughly $300 million, washed by various sources including the Chinese community and the

Colombian Medellín cartel. A wave of arrests ended this operation in May 1991; see D'Aubert Commission report, also report
to French Interior Ministry's Institut des Hautes Etudes, April 8,
1993.

46   See Chapter 7.

47   My interview with Nesbitt. UN conference on organized crime
in Suzdal, Russia, October 1991.

48   *Corriere della Sera* from Hong Kong, March 18, 1992.

49   *The Chinese Mafia*, Bresler, *op. cit.*, p. 207.

50   See *Octopus*, *op. cit.*, p.289, citing the proceedings of Palermo's
maxi-trial.

51   Interpol report to Dutch authorities. My interview with Roelof
Gerrard, senior Dutch police officer, St Petersburg, June 1992.

52   Speech by Mayor Gabor Demszky in Budapest, reported in *The
Uncaptive Mind*, April 1992. My interview with head of Polish
Interpol Andrzej Koweszko, Warsaw, October 1992.

53   This information from Russian intelligence was confirmed to
me by the BKA and FBI, March 1993.

54   Kenneth R. Timmerman, editor of the confidential newsletter
Mednews, in the *Wall Street Journal*, June 14, 1992 (see Chapter
12).

55   See Chapter 8.

56   Report to parliament on public security for the year 1992, by
Italian Interior Ministry ('Relazione sull'Attività delle Forze di
Polizia e sullo stato dell'Ordine e della Sicurezza Pubblica nel
Territorio Nazionale'), March 1993.

57   See Chapter 10.

58   My interview with Alessandro Pansa of SCO, Rome, March 24,
1993. SCO's findings in Russia and Eastern Europe covered
1991–92.

59   My interview with Koweszko, Warsaw, October 29, 1992.

60   My interview with Oprovil, October 29, 1992.

61   *The European*, December 20, 1992.

62   *Corriere della Sera*, August 7, 1991.

63   The Charleroi ring was briefly described in a BKA report to
Italian Interpol in 1989. The castle's owner was Salvatore Di
Luciano.

64   *L'Evénément du Jeudi*, August 20–26, 1992. See also *L'Europe des
Parrains*, Fabrizio Calvi, Bernard Grasset, Paris, 1993. The young
reporter was Stéphane Steigner.

65   *Corriere della Sera*, September 9, 1992.

66   D'Aubert report, *op. cit.*
67   The joint company was Semacor.
68   The figure in the commission report is 80% to 85%.
69   D'Aubert report. The incinerator is in Saint-Aulbas (Ain).

Chapter Seven
  1   Phone intercept, quoted in Pennsylvania Crime Commission report: 'Organized Crime in Pennsylvania: A Decade of Change', 1990.
  2   The FBI's National Strategy Report of 1991 lists the LCN strongholds as the east coast from Philadelphia to Boston; west to Buffalo and other Great Lakes cities; Miami, Tampa and Atlanta in the Southeast; New Orleans and Houston in the south and southwest; Kansas City, Denver, Phoenix and Las Vegas in the midwest; and on to California on the west coast.
  3   FBI National Strategy Report 1991. Jim Moody, chief of the Bureau's organized crime section, confirmed to me that the situation described was substantially unchanged in December 1992. See also Pennsylvania Crime Commission, 1990 Report, *op. cit.*
  4   *Ibid.*
  5   My interview with Jim Moody, Washington DC, December 1992.
  6   The reporter was Daniel Klaidman, the date September 8, 1992.
  7   1991 estimate in FBI's '1991 National Strategy'. 1992 estimate, FBI Packet on Organized Crime 1992, which indicates Camorra presence at 200 to 300, and 'Ndrangheta's at over 100. Latest estimate in my interview with Jim Moody, December, 1992.
  8   FBI phone intercept, see *Octopus, op. cit.*, p.309.
  9   Gravano's testimony at Gotti trial, February 1993.
 10   *Octopus, op. cit.*
 11   *Ibid.*, Chapter 12. John Gambino also organized the fake kidnapping of Sindona in 1979, bringing him to Palermo for an accounting with top Mafia bosses.
 12   *Octopus, op. cit.*, Chapter 4.
 13   'Overview of Patriarca La Cosa Nostra Induction Ceremony, Boston, Massachusetts, October 29, 1989', FBI, Washington.
 14   *Crime, Inc: The Story of Organized Crime*, Martin Short, Thames Methuen, London, 1984.
 15   These charges came under two crucial American laws: the 'drug kingpin' RICO statute, acronym for Racketeer Influenced and

Corrupt Organizations; and the Continuing Criminal Enterprise Act of 1970, directed against organized drug trafficking. Scarfo was convicted in November 1988.

16   Pennsylvania Crime Commission, 1991 Report .

17   *Octopus, op. cit.*

18   *Donnie Brasco*, Joseph D. Pistone with Richard Woodley, New American Library, New York, 1987.

19   Pennsylvania Crime Commission, 1991 Report.

20   Mueller's testimony to the Committee on Governmental Affairs, November 6, 1991.

21   *Octopus, op. cit.*, p.310.

22   FBI 1991 Strategy Report.

23   President's Commission on Organized Crime, Hearings on Organized Crime of Asian Origin, October 23–25, 1984.

24   *Ibid.*

25   *Ibid.* See also Pennsylvania Crime Commission, 1991 Report.

26   *Yakuza*, Kaplan and Dubro, *op. cit.*

27   The Sun Yee On dominates the Chinatowns of San Francisco, Los Angeles, Portland, Boston, Philadelphia and New York. The 14K works the same cities. The Wo Hop To controls Asian organized crime in the San Francisco Bay area. The United Bamboo Gang does Denver, Phoenix, Chicago and Atlantic City as well as New York and the West Coast; Report by US Senate Permanent Sub-Committee on Investigations, December 1992.

28   US Senate Permanent Sub-Committee on Investigations, hearings, October 3, 1992; testimony of Michael T. Lempres, Immigration and Naturalization Service.

29   Testimony of Assistant Attorney General Robert Mueller to Senate Permanent Sub-Committee on Investigations.

30   Senate Sub-Committee on Investigations Report on Asian Organized Crime.

31   The 1993 figure cited in *Time*, February 1, 1993. In his testimony before the Senate Sub-Committee on Investigations, INS Commissioner Michael T. Lempres said that 57,000 Chinese nationals, 'the vast majority smuggled', were issued employment authorization documents in the 16 months ending in January 1991. An additional 13,000 overstayed their visas in that period.

32   *Time*, February 1, 1993.

33   *Ibid.*

34   Senate Permanent Sub-Committee on Investigations.

35   *La Stampa*, March 17, 1991.

36   President's Commission on Organized Crime, Asian Organized Crime Hearings

37   *Los Angeles Times*, February 12, 1992. Also Senate Sub-Commission on Investigation Report.

38   The front company, Cosmo World, sold out in 1992, when its request to sell club memberships in lieu of payment was turned down; Senate Sub-Committee on Investigations.

39   Report of Senate Sub-Committee. One Japanese national named Ken Mizuno owned an estimated $400 million worth of hotels and golf courses, recently seized by the courts.

40   According to the Kyoto News Service, Ishii set up a company called Hokusho Sangyo in 1985 to handle his speculative stock dealings, and West Tsusho as its 'overseas investment arm'. *Washington Post*, June 11, 1991; *San Francisco Chronicle*, July 10, 1991; *Los Angeles Times*, February 12, 1992.

41   President's Commission on Organized Crime, Asian Hearings; Senate Sub-Committee on Investigations. See also *Yakuza, op.cit.*

42   *Yakuza, op. cit.*

43   *Ibid.*

44   *Ibid.*

45   Robert Friedman in *Vanity Fair*, January 1993.

46   The 500 figure was an FBI estimate in 1986; article by Daniel Burstein in *New York Magazine*, November 24,1986.

47   Article by Nathan Adams in *Readers' Digest*, August 1992; 'Russian Mafia in Brighton Beach', *New York Times*, February 14, 1983; cited in *The Soviet Way of Crime* by Lydia S. Rosner, Bergin & Garvey Publishers, Massachusetts, 1986.

48   *New York Times*, June 4, 1989.

49   My interview with Grant, December 1992.

50   *New York Times*, June 4, 1989.

51   Robert Friedman in *Vanity Fair*, January 1993.

52   *Newsday*, February 19, 1992.

53   *Washington Times*, September 29, 1991; *USA Today*, July 10, 1991.

54   *Vanity Fair*, New York, January 1993.

Chapter Eight

1   *Philadelphia Inquirer*, February 16, 1991.

2   My interview with Alexandra Zawlocka, financial correspondent of *Tygodnik Solidarnosc* in Warsaw.

3   *Sunday Times*, London, February 19, 1991.

My interview with Russian investigator Vladimir Kalinichenko, who told me that Belgian police had come to Moscow looking for more information about the ruble traffic passing through their country; Moscow, November 1991. See Chapter 9.

4   An agent involved in the tracking for Italy's secret service, Servizio Italiano di Operazioni Speciali (SIOS), who does not want to be identified.

5   An agent for the guardia's Nucleo Centrale, who does not want to be identified; Rome, April 1993.

6   Recorded by the guardia di finanza at the Banco Lariano, May 29, 1990.

7   My interview with Sica, presently Prefect of Bologna, January 13, 1992.

8   Order of arrest for twenty-four Sicilian, German, Austrian and Turkish defendants, signed by Judge Agostino Gristina, March 16, 1992.

9   *L'Europe des Parrains*, Fabrizio Calvi. See also *La Repubblica*, October 10, 1990.

10   My interview with undercover agent Fausto Cattaneo, who bought the rubles; Bellinzona, September 23–24, 1991.

11   *Journal de Genève*, January 13,1991; January 17, 1991; February 28, 1991.

Interview with Judge Trembley by that newspaper's Silvie Arsever.

12   *Sunday Times*, London, February 17, 1991.

13   My interview with Judge Carrara, April 21, 1992. The purchase was confirmed in the Italian Interior Ministry's annual report for 1992, published May 1993.

14   My interview with Judge Roberto Sapio, Rimini, June 1993.

15   My interview with Dr Alessandro Pansa, Rome, September 1991.

16   All details of the case as written above are from the arrest order (Ordinanza di custodia cautelare) by Judge Agostino Gristina, March 16, 1992.

17   The black market rate was 120 lire or ten cents per ruble, in the description of the Bahl case provided by Achille Serra, head of Criminalpol's Nucleo Centrale Anticrimine (Central Anticrime Nucleus), cited in *La Repubblica*, March 19, 1992. By December 1990, however, the sliding ruble was down to six or seven cents. See Chapter 9.

19   My interview with Judge Sapio on Coppola's interrogation,
      Rimini, June 1993.
          My interview with Judge Carrara in Palermo, April 1992. The
      Marsala-Jumblatt transaction passed through the Union des
      Banques Suisses in Lugano and another bank in Lichtenstein,
      Judge Carrara told me.
19   Phone intercept, November 29, 1990.
20   Copies of all credentials listed are in my possession. Yeltsin and
      Kozyrov signed theirs on October 16, 1990. According to
      Komsomolskaya Pravda, the government had given the appoint-
      ment in error before his background was checked and in January
      1991 Russia informed Italy the appointment had been revoked.
21   *Guardian* report from Moscow correspondents Dan Atkinson
      and Mark Milner, cited in *Pravda*, September 24, 1991.
      Geraschenko was quoted in *Izvestiya* and *Trud*, cited by *Corriere
      della Sera* and *La Repubblica*, November 7, 1991. His statement
      was confirmed in full by Aleksandr Orlov, head of the Control
      Commission of the Supreme Soviet, in the same day's Moscow
      press.
          The estimated reserves of 2,000 to 3,000 tons cited by
      Lawrence Malkin in the *International Herald Tribune*, October 17,
      1991; also by the *Washington Post* in the *International Herald
      Tribune*, September 30, 1991.
          The remaining 240 tons in the Central Bank reported by
      Grigori Yavlinsky to G-7, *Herald Tribune*, September 30, 1991.
      Izvestiya of November 5, 1991 reports five tons of gold and plat-
      inum exported illegally from the USSR in the previous six
      weeks.

Chapter Nine
1   Holman Jenkins Jr. in the *Washington Times* Insight, June 17,
      1991.
2   Pochinok's statement, read into the parliamentary record, pro-
      posed that 'the legislature should not cast doubt on the motives
      which guided the government members nor on their probity,'
      Izvestiya, February 8, 1991.
3   Chief Investigator Kalinichenko still knew nothing of this ruble
      traffic when I first met him in October 1991, nor did I.
4   All the documented material cited in this book is stored in a
      bank vault, and will be made available for any legitimate inspec-
      tion.

5   The parliamentary commission issued a preliminary report on February 15, 1991 and a final one on the following March 1st.

6   Preliminary commission report, February 15, 1991.

7   The protocol was signed August 31, 1990. The black market ruble stood at around ten to the dollar at the time.

8   My interview with Chief Investigator Kalinichenko in the Soviet Prosecutor-General's office. Moscow, November 1991.

9   The parliamentary commission quotes only part of this letter. The full text, read in closed session, was reported by Yuri Nikolayev in *Sovetskaya Rossiya*, February 21, 1991. Nikolayev's reporting on this case was consistently accurate, I was told by Chief Investigator Kalinichenko.

10   Russian Parliamentary Report.

11   My interview with Kalinichenko, Moscow, July 1992.

12   Article 154 of the Russian Republic's Criminal Code states: 'Speculation in currency or securities on a large scale is punishable by deprivation of freedom for 5–15 years with confiscation of property, with or without additional exile for a term of 2 to 5 years, or *by death with* confiscation of property.' The abolition of the death sentence was reported by Reuters, December 5, 1991.

13   Filshin's letter of guarantee was sent to Gibbins on January 11, 1991.

14   Filshin quoted in *Izvestiya*, January 26, 1991.

15   Cited in *The Times*, London, February 15, 1991.

16   My interview with an agent who cannot be identified, pursuing the case for British customs, London, January 1992. The British warrant for Gibbin's arrest was issued in July 1984.

17   My interview with Gurov, Moscow, July 1992.

18   My telephone interview with Frye in Johannesburg.

19   My interview with the same British customs agent.

20   *Independent on Sunday*, July 1991.

21   Final report of the commission of inquiry, March 15, 1991.

22   Preliminary report of the parliamentary commission, February 15, 1991.

23   Parliamentary commission's final report, March 1, 1991.

24   Filshin's interview in *Izvestiya*, January 26, 1991.

25   *Independent*, November 6, 1991.

26   Yeltsin statement on Filshin cited in *Izvestiya*, February 22, 1991. Filshin is presently the Russian government's trade representative in Vienna. Former Prime Minister Silaev is the Russian government's representative to the EC in Brussels.

27   Tass, February 22, 1991.

28   *Sunday Times*, London, February 17, 1991.

29   *Corriere della Sera*, January 20, 1992.

30   As no judicial case has yet been opened against Wanta in the US, the FBI spokesman prefers not to be named.

31   The US Secret Service confirms Wanta's arrest in Switzerland on July 7, 1993, his subsequent conviction and imprisonment in Switzerland, his deportation to the US on November 17, 1993, to face tax fraud charges, and the Austrian arrest warrant issued through Interpol, resulting from an investigation dating back to September 24, 1990.

32   The gas masks were offered on February 7, 1991. The same gas masks were on offer at the time by KGB Colonel Aleksandr Kuzin, running a huge arms traffic out of Vienna (see Chapter 12).

33   My phone interview with US Attorney Keith Corbett of Detroit, December 1992.

34   *Ibid.*

35   Preisfreund's account number in Vaduz was 775.260. 7–10. 333.01.

36   My interview with Uvarov, July 1992.

37   Moscow Radio World Service reported on November 5, 1991 that Russia's Prosecutor-General and forty investigators had begun to look into a sum of 5.5 billion rubles exported by old guard communist leaders the previous year. This was just one case.

38   Wanta's fax to Preisfreund's Consulting Liberty Group, July 2, 1990.

39   A heavily documented report on the KGB's project was published by *Literaturnaya Gazeta* on June 24, 1992. It provides the dates and numbers of coded cables, the names of top KGB officials involved, and the name of a French national, Jean-Pierre Tercu, allegedly recruited to help in the undertaking. Known as 'Jacques', Tercu is said in the article to have used the same Knights of Malta ploy as 'Monsignore' Roberto Coppola to work a $5 billion scam on the Ukrainian government.

In 1993, scandalous revelations about old communist party money going abroad from 1990 on revolved around the ambiguous figure of Bershteyn and his Seabeco Group, accused of arranging ruble-dollar transfers amounting to billions of dollars, and of bribing many top Russian government officials, including Vice-Premier Rutskoi.

40 Mr X's faxed letter to me, April 12, 1993.

41 Wanta's account number at the Avenue Banque was 416050091.

42 Tremonti's letter is dated July 9, 1990 (see photo section). The other transactions dated as follows: Hutschenraiter, June 27–28, 1990; Impex Vienna, July 4, 1990, confirmed by buyer, July 3; Unitrade, July 9, 1990; Budapest Bank, July 13, 1990; Van Moerre, Santerre, July 25, 1990; Faisal Finance, October 7, 1990; Volksbank, Wachtberg-Villip confirming letter, October 8, 1990; Sofidad, September 26, October 5, October 26, December 8, 1990; Wanta's Metishe Bank offer, September 16, 1990; Noweka through Regio Bank, October 8, 1990; AB Invest for client Gamma Kelberg, November 28, 1990, for Kerakos of Le Laren, the Netherlands, November 28, 1990; Corep-Gestion, October 25, 1990; Starl, September 24, 25, 1990.

43 Central Bank estimate reported by Reuters from Moscow, December 24, 1990. Leonid L. Fituni, President of the Russian Academy of Sciences' Centre for Strategic and Global Studies, made this report to a conference in Germany in 1993.

44 My interview with Gennady Chebotarev, Moscow, July 1992.

45 Holman Jenkins Jr. in the *Washington Times* Insight, June 17, 1991.

46 Wanta memo to Mr X, February 19, 1991.

47 My telephone interview with David Frye in Johannesburg.

48 Commission report.

49 Jenkins, *Washington Times*, *op. cit.* For a fuller account of such food-for-petroleum deals see Chapter 10.

50 Wanta opened his Russian bank account for the joint venture on December 20, 1991 (see Chapter 10).

51 My interview with Vladimir Kalinichenko, July 1992.

52 The Geneva arrests were made July 20, 1993; the Vicenza arrests were made August 25, 1993. Cesium-133 is stable, but highly explosive when treated (see Chapter 11).

53 The FBI discovered that the Himbank's Rochester branch was an empty room in September 1993. The Italian secret agent tracking Wanta and Tremonti, who cannot be named, was the first to discover Tremonti's connection to the Himbank.

54 The Italian investigators looking at Wanta and Tremonti are agents of the Servizio Italiano Operazioni Speciali (SIOS), who do not want to be named. Seizure of the $25 million in Himbank's CDs was confirmed to me by the carabinieri of

Vicenza, and by Judge Pecori, in charge of the case. August 25, 1993. Upon learning of this seizure, the FBI got into the act.

55   Leonid Fituni's report in 1993.

56   Wanta's fax of January 16, 1991: 'We, New Republic/USA Financial Group Ltd, GmbH, with full legal and corporate responsibility, offer the following under the terms and conditions set forth, as AU Bullion 999.5/1000 fineness or better with accepted international hallmarks.' His banking coordinates listed are: Algemene Spaar-En Lufrentekas, Brussels, account number 005 438963-26, Bank Manager Farouk Khan.

57   Wanta's fax on 'availability, closing location and discount offering' of gold, January 16, 1991. A thick wad of similar faxes followed.

58   The query from Moscow was on June 11, 1991. My interview with Interpol, Washington, December 1992.

59   *Kuranty*, cited in *Corriere della Sera*, September 15, 1992.

60   Fituni report.

61   See note 31.

62   *Kuranty, op. cit.* Judge Crochet's opinion is cited by Leonid Fituni in his German report.

Chapter Ten

1   Grishin's statement in *Corriere della Sera* from Moscow, November 16, 1991. Similar statement by Yeltsin's economic adviser Yegor Gaidar, *Los Angeles Times*, November 16, 1991. See also *Washington Post*, November 16, 1991.

The licensed export figures by V. Isayev, section manager of the Oriental Studies Institute, Russian Academy of Sciences, in *Argumenty I Fakty*, No. 29–30, August 1992.

2   Moscow financial daily, *Commersant*, March 16, 1992 lists domestic market price at $26 a ton at the going exchange rate for rubles.

3   *Financial Times*, May 13, 1992. The deputy minister was Leonid Zapalsky. He was within a month of leaving the ministry when he issued the licences.

4   Presentation of the USSR delegation, written by Chebotarev, to 20th European Regional Conference of Interpol, London, April 3–5, 1991.

5   My interview with Chebotarev, Moscow, July 1992.

6   VEK reports from Russia's Sixth Department, December 18–25,1992.

7   Article by Vladimir Kuznetsov in *Rossiyskaya Gazeta*, July 2, 1992.

8   Associated Press dispatch from Moscow citing Russia's top defence daily, *Krasnaya Zvezda*, October 24, 1992.

9   Gurtivoy's interview in *Trud*, October 2, 1992.

10 *Izvestiya* in *Current Digest of the Soviet Press*, Vol. 43, No. 22; up to 16/10/91.

11 Moscow VEK, November 27–December 4, 1992. The Department chief was Alexander Gurov, transferred from the Interior Ministry's Sixth Department to this new post in the Security Ministry.

12 *Moscow Times*, May 19, 1992.

13 My interview with I. Pavlovich in Russia's Sixth Department, Moscow, July 1992.

14 'Draft Decree of the Russian President on the Liberalization of Foreign Economic Activity in the Russian Federation', *Commersant*, November 16, 1991.

15 *Il Sole-24 Ore*, Milanese financial daily , May 3, 1991; also the head of St Petersburg customs in St Petersburg, Andrei Belonaiov, at John Jay College international conference on organized crime. 'Foreign investors with over 15% holdings in a plant need not be licensed for export: so exporters name these plants in customs declarations,' he said.

16 My interview with Kalinichenko, July 1992.

17 Mr X told me that Wanta and Dokiychuk often worked together.

18 My interview with Kalinichenko, Moscow, July 1992. See also *Moscow Times*, April 20, 1992.

19 My interview with the Sixth Department's Deputy Chief Pavlovich, Moscow, July 1, 1992.

20 *Ibid.*

21 Nineteenth report by the House of Representatives' Committee on Government Operations, May 27, 1992.

22 *Izvestiya*, August 15, 1992: 'TV Star Marc Rich and his "Producers" '.

23 *Izvestiya*, June 5,1992; also my interview with Kalinichenko, Moscow, July 1992.

24 *Commersant*, March 16, 1993.

25 *Rossiyskaya Gazeta*, August 21, 1992; article by Prof. Igro Kaszakov of Marketing Department, Foreign Trade Academy. *Wall Street Journal*, Europe, May 13, 1993.

26 Ignatov is quoted at length in *Izvestiya*, August 15, 1992, in a long article on Marc Rich. The TV film commissioned and paid

for by Rich was done in a programme called 'Reporter' (same *Izvestiya* article). See also 'Bilan', September 1992.

27 *Forbes*, quoted in *Izvestiya*, July 31, 1991.

28 *Wall Street Journal*, Europe, May 13, 1993.

29 *Ibid.*

30 *Ibid.*

31 *Izvestiya*, June 5, 1992. The permits were allotted in part to Marc Rich & Co, and in part to his joint venture, Rosrich, as follows: 230,000 tons of diesel fuel to Marc Rich and 1,300,000 tons to Rosrich; 716,000 tons of heating oil to Mark Rich and 1,900,000 tons of heating oil to Rosrich. Total: 4,146,000 tons.

     A continuing exemption on export duties for food suppliers is confirmed by Dr Igor Kazakov, of Russia's Marketing Department of the Foreign Trade Academy in 'We Say Homeland, Meaning Raw Materials', *Rossiyskaya Gazeta*, August 21, 1992.

32 Rutskoi's address to the emergency conference on crime and corruption attended by a thousand judges, police officers and government officials, also addressed by President Yeltsin in tones of great alarm; Moscow, February 2, 1993, AP from Moscow, February 13, 1993, also reported in *La Repubblica*, same date.

33 My interview with Judge Romano Dolce of Como, coordinating this investigation with Russian authorities. See also *Corriere della Sera* and *La Repubblica*, December 17, 1992 and *Corriere della Sera*, January 23, 1993. For more details on the arms traffic see Chapter 12.

34 My interview with Judge Toro, investigating magistrate for the theft of CDs amounting to a quarter of a billion dollars (294 billion lire), from Rome's Banco di Santo Spirito in November 1990; Rome, July 2, 1993.

35 *The European*, March 18–21, 1993.

36 *Ibid.*

37 Despatch from Moscow by Fiammetta Cucurnia, *La Repubblica*, July 2, 1993. Prosecutor Makarov made the announcement to the Russian parliament in the last week of June. On July 23, Russian Prosecutor-General Valentin Stepankov formally asked parliament to lift the immunity of Vice-Premier Shumeiko and Information Chief Poltoranin. The Russian parliament, loathing both, was happy to oblige.

38 *La Repubblica*, February 13, 1993. See also *International Herald Tribune*, same date.

Chapter Eleven

1   *Corriere della Sera*, February 2, 1993; 55 million Kalashnikovs had been sold by 1993.

2   The Middle East estimate was made by Safeword Foundation, present at the fair.

3   *Corriere della Sera*, July 25, 1993.

4   Kenneth R. Timmerman, editor of the confidential newsletter Mednews, in the *Wall Street Journal*, June 14, 1992.

5   The Pentagon official was Michael Sparrow, *Commersant*, November 18, 1991.

6   *Ibid.*

7   *La Stampa* from London, May 29, 1993.

8   *Commersant*, October 21, 1991.

9   This last was the most credited version offered to investigating magistrate Romano Dolce in Como, he told me.

10 My interview with Czech Deputy Interior Minister, Petrushka Sostrova, September 1991.

11 Rutskoi's address to the Russian parliament, April 16, 1993; in *La Stampa* of the following day.

12 'Red Mercury' by A. Craig Copetas, in *Moscow Times*, January 16–17, 1993.

13 *Ibid.*

14 The expert did not want to be named. The Institute, ENEA, is among the most authoritative in Europe.

15 The analyst in Washington is Richard Levine. The British customs agent, who does not want to be named, had several good laughs whenever I called to report yet another red mercury sighting.

16 My interview with Judge Dolce. See also *Corriere della Sera*, November 13, 1991.

17 Text of Nielsen's interrogation by Judge Dolce, October 30, 1991.

18 My two day-long interviews with Judge Dolce and his prize investigator Antonio Erdas in Como.

19 Texts of Ostrogonac's interrogation by Judge Dolce, January 21, 29 and February 14, 1992. Others named were General Abramov and KGB officers Kudeziev and Ilurin.

20 Judicial Police of Como Report to the police command in Lugano, Switzerland, April 24, 1992. My interview with Judge Dolce. 'Boris' is named by several Kuzin intermediaries now known to Italian undercover agents. Who 'the friends' are is not specified.

21 Prospectus dated August 7, 1991. No substantial change has been noted since.
22 Extract of the register in Udine's Chamber of Commerce, June 10, 1992.
23 My interviews with Judge Dolce and Antonio Erdas.
24 I have photocopies of Affatigato's transactions in rubles and red mercury.
25 See Chapter 9.
26 My interview with Judge Dolce and Antonio Erdas. Ostrogonac's testimony and other interrogations in the Como documents.
27 Judicial Police of Como report to police command in Lugano, Switzerland, April 24, 1992.
28 Ostrogonac interrogation by Judge Dolce.
29 My interviews with Jan Dubrowski of Lidove Noviny; Deputy Interior Minister Petrushka Suslova, US Public Affairs Officer Tom Hull, September 2–9, 1991.
30 My interview with an agent of Italy's SIOS, who cannot be named.
31 *Commersant*, March 23, 1992.
32 Vienna TV documentary, January 23, 1992. The trafficker was Yugoslav-born Marian Sokolovic.
33 Associated Press dispatch from Berlin, October 13, 1992; *Bild Am Sonntag*, October 11, 1992; *The European*, October 22, 1992.
34 Three grams of cesium were impounded in Geneva on July 16, 1993. Ten grams were impounded in Vicenza on August 25, 1993.
35 Hamburg DPA, October 16, 1992. See also *Corriere della Sera*, October 17, 1992.
36 *Corriere della Sera*, April 5, 1993.
37 Judge Vigna in an address to a national arms exhibition, 'Exa '93', in Brescia; *La Repubblica*, February 5, 1993.

Chapter Twelve

1 Gaspare Mutolo's testimony, February 9, 1993.
2 Italy seized 3,500 billion lire, roughly $3 billion, in money and assets from Italian organized crime between August 1992 and August 1993; Italian Interior Minister Nicola Mancino, cited in all Italian papers, August 17, 1993.
3 'Global Drug Trafficking', Alison Jamieson, Research Institute for the Study of Conflict and Terrorism, London, September 1990.

4   Report to the French Senate by Gérard Larcher, for the Senate's Commission of Information on the Schengen Accord, January 15, 1993.

5   UN Crime Congress 1990: US Senate Subcommittee on Terrorism, Narcotics and International Operations hearings, September 27 and October 4,1989.

6   My interview with Alessandro Pansa, Rome, September 1992.

7   *The European*, January 7–10, 1993.

8   My interview with experts of BKA's Organized Crime section, February 1993.

9   International Narcotics Control Board strategy report, US State Department, March 1990.

10 The Swiss law, passed in November 1989, does not make all laundering a crime, but does 'establish liability for money laundering where it impedes investigation into some other act that is a crime under Swiss law'.

11 *Corriere della Sera* report on Italian Interior Minister Nicola Mancino's visit to Vienna to discuss the problem, February 11, 1993.

12 *Corriere della Sera*, September 27, 1992.

13 *Le Figaro*, January 16–17, 1993.

14 Larcher report to French Senate, *op. cit.*

15 *International Herald Tribune*, January 23–4, 1993.

16 Paris daily *Libération*, June 7,1991. For confirmation of Monaco's continuing role as a fiscal paradise see Report to the French Assembly by François D'Aubert's Anti-Mafia Commission, February 1993.

17 Hungary was the first ex-communist state actually to copy Austria's inflexible bank secrecy laws.

18 Larcher Report to the French Senate, *op. cit.*

19 *Business Week*, September 23, 1991.

20 Belize ad in *Commersant*, inserted by a newly born joint venture called Miros, whose founders and charter capital were unknown, March 16, 1992.

21 'Drug Trafficking After 1992', Alison Jamieson, Research Institute for the Study of Conflict and Terrorism, 1992. See also International Narcotics Control Board strategy report, 1990.

22 See *Octopus*, *op. cit.*, for a lengthy documented account of the Sindona fake kidnapping.

23 The reigning prince was Stefano Bontate, murdered by the

Corleonesi in 1981; the confidant was future defector Francesco Mannino Mannoia.

24   *Le Mani della Mafia*, Maria Antonietta Calabrò, an outstanding book for a comprehensive and documented report on the Calvi affair.

25   Sindona's life sentence in Italy was for commissioning the murder of Giorgio Ambrosoli, who had been appointed to investigate his fraudulent operations in the Banco Ambrosiano before turning it over to Calvi and skipping the country. He died in March 1986.

26   Calvi died June 17, 1982.

27   *La Repubblica*, July 28–29, 1991.

28   Francesco Di Carlo, ranking member of the Altofonte clan actually created by the Corleonesi, was working directly with the Cuntrera brothers in London. He was arrested there in June 1985 in the act of shipping 59 kilos of heroin to the US via Canada. A British court sentenced him to 25 years in prison.

29   Revelation by Umberto Ortolani, Gelli's financial right arm, who said that he and Gelli were approached directly by Calvi for the Mafia contact; *L'Indépendente*, February 5, 1993.

30   Francesco Mannino Mannoia's testimony is summed up in the Italian parliamentary Anti-Mafia Commission report, 'Relations between the Mafia and Politics', March 12, 1992. See also *La Repubblica*, July 29, 1991 and April 28, 1992.

31   *Le Mani della Mafia, op. cit.*

32   *Ibid.*

33   *Ibid.*

34   'Drug Trafficking After 1992', *op. cit.*

35   The exact figure is $249 billion; hearings by US Senate Subcommittee on Terrorism, Narcotics and International Operations, September 27–October 4, 1989.

36   Hearings of Subcommittee on Terrorism, Narcotics and International Operations: Senate Committee on Foreign Relations, September 2 and October 4, 1989.

37   'Drug Trafficking After 1992: A Special Report', by Alison Jamieson, published by the Research Institute for the Study of Conflict and Terrorism, London, 1992.

38   'Drug Trafficking After 1992', *op. cit.* Here she cites a Report on Confiscation Law and Asset Tracing in the United Kingdom by Tom Wren, National Criminal Intelligence Service, London, May 1992.

39 Wren report, *op. cit.*, quoted in *Valeurs Actuelles*, December 7, 1992.
40 The British case in 'Drug Trafficking After 1992', *op. cit.* The Italian figure released by Consiglio Nazionale dell'Economia e Lavoro (CNEL), cited in *Corriere della Sera*, March 2, 1993.
41 Interior minister Nicola Mancino's report to the Italian parliament.
42 *Welt am Sonntag*, Hamburg, May 2, 1993.
43 My interview with Gerrand at the John Jay College International Conference on Organized Crime, St Petersburg, June 28–July 3, 1992.
44 My interview with Eva Klovacova, consultant for the Czech Ministry of Privatization, Prague, September 8, 1991.
45 Senate Subcommittee hearings, September 27–October 4, 1989.

Chapter Thirteen

1 The ASEAN states are Indonesia, Philippines, Malaysia, Thailand, Singapore and Brunei.
2 Final report to the French Senate by Paul Masson, on behalf of the Commission to Study the Schengen Agreement, June 23, 1993.
3 *Ibid.*
4 ANP news bulletin from Amsterdam, August 20, 1992.
5 *Agence France-Presse*, August 6, 1992.
6 Report to the French Senate by the Commission's President, Paul Masson, Tome III, November 27, 1991.
7 8th Annual Policing Executive Conference, Madrid, April 1991.
8 *Ibid.*
9 My interview with Barry Price at Scotland Yard. The European Drugs Intelligence Unit was approved by EC ministers at the Lisbon summit in 1992. It still cannot get off the ground, largely because of arguments over what information should go into its data bank.
10 Declaration of the EC Commission on the proposed directive of the EC Council of Ministers 'concerning the protection of persons relative to the handling of personal data', September 24, 1990.
    Exceptions to the right of access are specified 'in certain cases, counterbalanced then by an indirect right of access'; Report to French Senate by the Masson Commission, December 11, 1991.
11 *International Herald Tribune*, December 2, 1992.

12   The Cooney Report, a report to the European Parliament by
     Patrick Cooney, on behalf of the Committee of Enquiry into the
     Spread of Organized Crime Linked to Drug Trafficking in the
     Member States of the European Community, Strasbourg,
     October 28, 1991.

Bibliography

Anderson, Malcolm: *Policing the World*; Clarendon Press, Oxford, 1989
Andrew, Christopher and Gordievsky, Andrew: *KGB*; Hodder & Stoughton, London, 1990
Arlacchi, Pino: *Gli Uomini del Disonore*; Arnoldo Mondadori Editore, Milano, 1992
Auchlin, Pascal and Garbely, Frank: *Contre-Enquete*; Editions Favre, Lausanne, 1990
Booth, Martin: *The Triads*; Grafton Books, London, 1990
Bresler, Fenton: *The Chinese Mafia*; Stein & Day, New York, 1981
Calabrò, Maria Antonietta: *Le Mani della Mafia*; Edizioni Associate, Roma, 1991
Calvi, Fabrizio: *L'Europe des Parrains*; Bernard Grasset, Paris, 1993
Chalidze, Valery: *Criminal Russia*; Random House, New York, 1977
Clutterbuck, Richard: *Terrorism, Drugs & Crime in Europe After 1992*; Routledge, Chapman & Hall, New York, 1990
Copetas, A. Craig: *Bear Hunting with the Politburo*; Simon & Schuster, 1991
di Gennaro, Giuseppe: *La Guerra della Droga*; Arnoldo Mondadori Editore, Milano, 1991
Ehrenfeld, Rachel: *NarcoTerrorism*; Basic Books, New York, 1990
Francis, Diane: *Contrepreneuers*; Scorpio Publishing Ltd, Cincinati, 1988
Gurwin, Larry: *The Calvi Affair*; Macmillan, London, 1983

Kaplan, David E. and Dubro, Alex: *Yakuza*; Addison-Wesley Publishing Co, Inc, UK 1986 (Copyright, Centre for Investigative Reporting)

Labrousse, Alain: *La Drogue, l'Argent et les Armes*; Arthème Fayard, Paris, 1991

Ministero dell'Interno: *L'Attività Antidroga Della Polizia Guidiziaria*; Utet, Rome, 1991

Naylor, Robin T.: *Denaro che Scotta*; Edizioni di Communità, Milano, 1987

O'Brien, Joseph F. and Kurins, Andris: *Boss of Bosses*; Simon & Schuster, New York, 1991

Orlando, Leoluca: *Palermo*; Arnoldo Mondadori Editore, Milano, 1990

Palermo, Carlo: *Armi e Droga*; Editori Riuniti, Rome, 1988

———: *L'Attentato*; Editrice Publiprint, Trento, 1993

Rosner, Lydia S.: *The Soviet Way of Crime*; Bergin & Garvey, Westport, CT, 1986

Russo, Enzo: *Il Quattordicesimo Zero*; Arnaldo Mondadori Editore, Milano, 1990

Short, Martin: *Crime Inc: The Story of Organized Crime*; Methuen, London, 1984

———: *Inside the Brotherhood*; Grafton Books, London, 1989

Sobchiak, Anatoli: *Leningrado San Pietroburgo*; Arnoldo Mondadori Editore, Milano, 1991

Sterling, Claire: *Octopus*; Norton, New York, 1990

———: *The Time of the Assassins*; Holt Rinehart, New York, 1983

Terrill, Richard J.: *World Criminal Justice Systems, A Survey*; Anderson Publishing Co, Cincinnati, Ohio, 1992

Tosches, Nick: *Power on Earth*; Arbor House, New York, 1986

Vaksberg, Arkady: *The Soviet Mafia*; St Martin's Press, New York, 1992

Violante, Luciano: *La Mafia Dell' Eroina*; Editori Riuniti, Rome, 1987

Wistrich, Ernest: *After 1992: The United States of Europe*; Routledge, London, 1989

Ziegler, Jean: *La Suisse Lave Plus Blanc*; Seuil, Paris, 1990

Index